The Scripture
Principle

Selected Previous Works

Clark H. Pinnock

Biblical Revelation: Foundation of Christian Theology (1982)

Tracking the Maze: Modern Theology from an Evangelical Perspective (1990)

The Openness of God, by Pinnock and others (1994)

Flame of Love: A Theology of the Holy Spirit (1996)

Most Moved Mover: A Theology of God's Openness (2001)

Barry L. Callen

Clark H. Pinnock: Journey toward Renewal (2000)

Authentic Spirituality: Moving beyond Mere Religion (2001, 2006)

Discerning the Divine: God in Christian Theology (2004)

Reading the Bible in Wesleyan Ways, edited with Richard P. Thompson (2004)

Caught between Truths (2006)

The Scripture Principle

Reclaiming the Full Authority of the Bible

2nd edition

Clark H. Pinnock
with Barry L. Callen

Baker Academic

Grand Rapids, Michigan

Published by Baker Academic
a division of Baker Publishing Group
P.O. Box 6287, Grand Rapids, MI 49516-6287
www.bakeracademic.com

Printed in the United States of America

First edition published by Harper & Row, 1984

Library of Congress Cataloging-in-Publication Data
Pinnock, Clark H., 1937–
    The Scripture principle : reclaiming the full authority of the Bible / Clark H. Pinnock with Barry L. Callen. — 2nd ed.
        p.   cm.
    Includes bibliographical references and index.
    ISBN 10: 0-8010-3155-9 (pbk.)
    ISBN 978-0-8010-3155-7 (pbk.)
    1. Bible—Evidences, authority, etc. I. Callen, Barry L. II. Title.
BS480.P63 2006
220.601—dc22   2006021178

Contents

Preface

We have three aims in mind in writing this book. The primary aim is to present an understanding of the Scripture principle and the authority of the Bible in a positive, systematic, and relevant way. Our purpose is not negative, as if to answer errors on the theological left or right; nor is it parochial, as if to speak only to the conservative Protestant community, of which we both are members. We write first of all for the person who asks, "How should I regard the Bible and respond to it?" Our emphasis is on that vital, practical certainty one can have in the Bible we now possess, the Bible that is the transforming medium of the saving message of God.

The reader may have an advantage in that the excessively academic study of theology has distorted some of the most basic issues in connection with the Bible. It has given people the impression that what is crucially important is the ability to rationally comprehend these matters rather than to come to know, love, and obey the God who speaks in the Scriptures. We recognize that Bible study today proceeds "as the 'assured results' of modern scholarship have become *less assured* in the rubble of the Enlightenment experiment."[1] There is, in fact, a spiritual dimension to the recognition, interpretation, and application of the biblical text as the Word of God, a dimension that does not easily fit into scholarly technique and comes more naturally to those "uncorrupted" by excessive rationalism. For this reason, in our own approach we consider it essential to listen to the Spirit of God, not only in scholarly circles, but in the community of faith, which tends to keep a healthier balance in the dialectic of mind and spirit.

1. Barry L. Callen and Richard P. Thompson, eds., *Reading the Bible in Wesleyan Ways*, 12.

Writing for the general, unspecialized reader, we also bear in mind the vulnerable inquirer who may be disturbed by the quantity and depth of the problems that must be discussed in a book that strives to be responsible to the state of the discussion as it exists today. Some of us must face up to these problems, for the good of the church and the defense of the gospel. Even so, the reader may well ask if he or she is one who ought to do so. There is a spiritual danger involved in exposing ourselves, as we intend to do, to the starkest and most vehement objections to faith in the God of the Bible. In doing so, we pit ourselves against the most seasoned critics of the Christian gospel and may even expose ourselves to some of the most penetrating of the "flaming arrows of the evil one" (Eph. 6:16). We need to be clad in God's armor and in prayer, for in seeking to guard the gospel, one becomes exposed to increased assaults. Let the reader take care, then, in approaching this subject and this book and look to divine strength for sustenance in testing basic truths of the Christian faith. God's promises are, of course, sufficient even for this.

Our second aim in the book is to speak out, in the context of the crisis of the Scripture principle, in defense of the full authority and trustworthiness of the Bible. Unfortunately, this is necessary because of a major and widespread shift in contemporary theology toward seeing the Bible as a fallible testament of human opinion and religious experience, not as the reliable deposit and canon of normative instruction. Although the number of those involved in such a depreciation is relatively small in relation to the many comprising the faithful church as a whole, they are often influential scholars and teachers whose opinions sway the unwary and subvert the faith of those who are weak and ill-informed.

The seriousness of the present crisis is plain once we consider that a decline in respect for the Bible results in the church not hearing clearly the saving message of the Scriptures, thus becoming liable to being overtaken by the religious philosophies of the moment. This crisis of the Scripture principle is one of the greatest crises of all. Polemical theology is sadly unavoidable in the age of theological decline in which we live. We can only promise that we will not permit unavoidable controversy to steal the limelight from our basically positive and joyful presentation. Unsound theology must not succeed in making orthodoxy ill-tempered and unloving.

Our third aim is to assist Christians who hold to the full authority of the Bible to move ahead in the understanding of their conviction. It is sad when critics are able to nail us on one point or another simply because we have not done our work very well. Too often we have been smug in our belief and have not faced important issues squarely and honestly. We have made cheap shots and taken shortcuts, deserving some of the ridicule we have received. Some of the skirmishes in the evangelical community could be avoided with more clarity of thought and charity of spirit. We hope to provide the reader with a systematic proposal about biblical authority that will cover all the bases tolerably well.

Our sense is that large numbers of Christians are yearning to move ahead in their understanding and get beyond futile arguments about imponderables. They do not like to run scared before the religious liberals and have their beliefs defended in neurotic and unconvincing ways that glorify neither God nor God's cause. We think we can move ahead, and this is the time to do it. On so many points of the theological spectrum today, believers are longing for an evangelical confidence in the Bible, and many minds are open as never before to a serious consideration of the classic Scripture principle presented in a viable and convincing way. We only hope that this book offers the kind of presentation that is needed.

We admit that we have not found this an easy book to write. We agree with James Orr, who said: "There is perhaps no subject at the present moment more difficult to write upon, and above all to write upon wisely, than this of revelation and inspiration."[2] As in trying to smooth down a large rug, one gets rid of a wrinkle here only to find it reappearing somewhere else. We undertake here a task that brings out the finite nature of human resources. Our aim is not so much to uncover new data as to produce a better understanding of what we know already. We seek to offer wisdom rather than mere expertise, and the measure of our success will be the fruitfulness people find in looking at the subject this way.

Why have we undertaken a revised edition of this book? Since the original work, published in 1984, has stood well the test of time, we have felt no need to alter its basic organization or point of view. Our concern in revising the text now has been to simplify language and format for the sake of the contemporary reader, update a range of illustrations and source references in light of some excellent scholarship that has occurred in the last two decades, and add a new appendix on our own recent and current thinking. Our intent is to give new life to an older treatment of crucial issues that we judge is still needed urgently in today's Christian community.

2. James Orr, *Revelation and Inspiration*, 1. Our struggle over the decades with this important subject is summarized fairly by Gary Dorrien, *The Remaking of Evangelical Theology*, 129–38; Stanley J. Grenz, *Renewing the Center*, 141–44; Barry L. Callen, *Clark H. Pinnock: Journey toward Renewal*, chaps. 3 and 4; and idem, "The Struggle of Evangelicalism," in *Reading the Bible in Wesleyan Ways*, ed. Callen and Thompson, chap. 7.

....

Maintaining the Scripture Principle Today

The "Scripture principle" is the assertion that the Bible is the primary and fully trustworthy canon of Christian revelation, the reliable medium for encountering and understanding the God who seeks to transform all persons who read the sacred text into the image of Jesus Christ. In this regard, when we affirm the term "inerrancy," we basically mean the belief that Scripture never leads one astray in regard to what it intentionally teaches.[1]

The adoption of the Bible, Old and New Testaments, as the authoritative Scripture of the church was probably the most momentous choice ever made in the history of doctrine. By doing so, the church provided itself with a standard of identity by which to evaluate and shape its theology, life, and mission. Therefore, the place to begin a discussion of biblical authority is with the simple fact that entrenched in Christian thinking is a central and persistent belief in the Bible as the written and trustworthy Word of God. Even if we are not impressed with or persuaded by this belief, we should acknowledge it and appreciate why it has been held so stoutly by the historic community of Christian faith.

For better or worse, belief in the Scriptures as the canon and yardstick of Christian truth, the unique locus of the Word of God, is part of an almost universal Christian consensus going back at least to the

---

1. For an extended statement of what we mean by "the Scripture principle," see the first few pages of chapter 3.

second century. Until the recent rise of what we judge to be revisionist theology, Christian thinking was done in the house of biblical authority, a fact that is not doubted even by a writer eager to overturn such belief, Edward Farley.[2] Theology in the premodern period was always done on the assumption that the Bible was the written Word of God.

Although this classic belief in the Scripture principle can be documented from numerous other authors and documents, we wish to quote one sample, an eloquent paragraph from the New Hampshire Baptist Confession of 1833:

> We believe that the Bible was written by men divinely inspired, and is a perfect treasure of heavenly instruction; that it has God for its author, salvation for its end, and truth without any mixture of error for its matter; that it reveals the principles by which God will judge us; and therefore is, and shall remain to the end of the world, the true center of Christian union and the supreme standard by which all human conduct, creeds, and opinions shall be tried.[3]

The Roman Catholic scholar Bruce Vawter and the Anglican evangelical Geoffrey Bromiley have both observed that the early fathers of the church everywhere and always presuppose the divine dimension of the Bible.[4] This is even more true of the Protestant Reformers and their successors to this day, since their entire ecclesial project in the sixteenth century was founded on the assumption of the infallible teaching of the Scriptures—as opposed to numerous supposed errors that had crept into the church's traditions. Hence, it is from this period that we receive the most explicit and tightly drawn statements about the authority of the Bible. Martin Luther and John Calvin expressed themselves in the strongest terms on this matter. They regarded Scripture as the divine teacher that reliably delivers to us essential understanding of the ways and will of God. If there is a "Protestant principle," this is it.[5]

More than an isolated belief, this conviction about the authority of the Bible was an integral part of a larger package of classical convictions and cannot be discarded without tearing apart the fabric of the whole garment of traditional Christian beliefs. Without much exaggeration,

2. Edward Farley, *Ecclesial Reflection: An Anatomy of Theological Method*.

3. Along with other confessional statements of its kind, the *New Hampshire Baptist Confession* can be found in Philip Schaff, *The Creeds of Christendom*, 3:742.

4. Bruce Vawter, *Biblical Inspiration*, 20–43; and Geoffrey Bromiley in his chapter "The Church Fathers and Holy Scripture," in *Scripture and Truth*, ed. D. A. Carson and John D. Woodbridge, 199–220.

5. Although a polemical book directed at refuting another, *Biblical Authority*, by John D. Woodbridge is an excellent source of information about the classical belief in full biblical infallibility.

one could say that the history of Christian theology is a history of the interpretation of the Bible, so basic to the faith has been this medium of divine communication. The way Christians have thought about God, Christ, humanity, salvation, and the church is indebted heavily to the teachings of the Bible. This is not to deny that cultural factors have entered into the various belief formulations at different periods, but to point out that the creed is utterly tied up with its scriptural foundations, making the authority of the Bible, if not a soteriologically indispensable belief, at least an epistemologically crucial one.

Without belief in the authority of the Bible, there would not have been any creedal backbone to the Christian movement, and certainly not the sturdy structures of Nicea and Chalcedon. Beliefs like the atonement and the resurrection unquestionably stand or fall with belief in biblical authority, and that is the measure of the seriousness of the modern debate about such authority. We are not arguing over some minor detail in Christian belief, like the rapture or the classes of angels, but over the basis of religious knowledge and how we know what God has promised and commanded.

How can we worship God if we do not know who God is? How can we trust God's promises if we do not know what they are? How can we obey God if we have no sure knowledge of God's will? Historically, Christians have felt that the authority of the Bible is a crucial conviction because the Bible is needed to give us reliable knowledge of the truth, without which we cannot exist long as Christians. Calvin spoke of this practically when he referred to the Bible as the spectacles our dim eyes require to make out the will of our Creator (*Institutes* 1.6).

The facts that belief in biblical authority has been the majority opinion traditionally and that the orthodox creed depends upon it do not necessarily prove that this belief is right. But these facts do prevent us from foolishly saying that the Scripture principle can be jettisoned without affecting anything else. This also explains why conservative Christians get so upset when their belief in biblical authority comes under attack, or even seems to. The Scripture principle is a very fundamental one epistemologically, with far-reaching consequences in every area of doctrine and practice. Thus, this belief will not be overturned without a momentous struggle in the churches. It is our present intent to help ensure that it is not overturned.

Thus far, only a few critics of orthodoxy seem to be aware of what they are up against. Even James Barr, who has given it much thought and hopes to lure Christians away from what he calls "fundamentalism," has not taken proper account of the conviction he dislikes so much. Large numbers of us are not easily going to abandon our belief in the Bible as the written Word of God in favor of some view of it as mere human tradition. We know, as our opponents ought to know, that any

Christianity deserving of the name stands or falls on belief in the Scripture principle.[6]

We will be using the term "evangelical" to refer to those believers who, like ourselves, are committed to the Christian gospel as it is biblically defined. Our basic concern is with the good news in Jesus Christ, not with the Bible per se, but we are convinced nonetheless that the one will not remain pure very long without the other. A few decades ago, the fortunes of evangelical theology appeared unpromising, but now there is a strong recovery under way, a real renaissance in such convictions.[7] To be candid, however, the classical conviction about Holy Scripture has not always been developed in sound and healthy ways, even among evangelicals, and some of our difficulties today are due in part to such past inadequacies. Given the polemical atmosphere between evangelicals and more liberal Christians, it is uncommon for conservatives to admit any less-than-ideal elements in the orthodox view of the Bible, but we must admit them if we hope to gain a fair hearing and to advance in our own understanding.

There has been, for example, a tendency among conservatives to exaggerate the absolute perfection of the biblical text and minimize the true humanity of it. One of the weaknesses of the church fathers, as Geoffrey Bromiley notes, was their failure to give full weight to the human and historical aspects of the text. The truth is that "the fathers seem not to have appreciated the real significance of the human dimension nor to have grasped the possibilities of a better exegesis that lexical, literary, and historical inquiry would present."[8] This docetic tendency, as Cornelius Berkouwer later would call it, has meant that many features of the biblical text were left unobserved, leaving us badly prepared for advances in literary criticism that the modern age would produce.[9] Karl Barth also has taken note of the mechanical view of the Bible that many of the fathers held.[10] In addition, there was a strong "catholic" tendency to link the authoritative Scriptures to an infallible ecclesiastical institution, thus providing even more security for the believer—more, in fact, than the Lord had planned for us.

It must be obvious to any reader of classical theology that the people who spoke so highly of the infallibility of the Bible very often spoke just

6. Occasionally Barr seems to be aware of how ancient is the belief in the Scripture principle, but for the most part he vigorously critiques conservative believers, from whose company he himself had moved away. See his book *Fundamentalism*.

7. Donald G. Bloesch is one of our favorite observers of theological trends. We recommend his *Future of Evangelical Christianity* (1983) and his more recent *Holy Scripture* (1994).

8. Bromiley, "Church Fathers and Holy Scripture," 217.

9. G. C. Berkouwer, *Holy Scripture*, 9–38.

10. Karl Barth, *Church Dogmatics*, 1/2:517–19.

as highly of the church's creeds and hierarchy, and they did not witness to what we today would regard as an evangelical position, though they are repeatedly cited by evangelicals today for that purpose.[11] Evangelicals who hold to the sole authority of the Bible do not do justice to themselves when they appear to be uncritical of church tradition, even when it happens to be tradition about the Bible. Rather than try to argue unconvincingly, as Jack Rogers and Donald McKim did in their 1979 book *The Authority and Interpretation of the Bible*, that the traditional view of authority was less rigorous than we have thought (John Woodbridge has shown it was very rigorous indeed), we should admit honestly that the old view of the Bible that we treasure is not biblical and serviceable in every detail today.

Like every other theological topic, the old view can use some improvement and development by the thinkers and scholars of our generation.[12] We simply must transcend the neglect of the humanity of the Bible, so familiar in orthodoxy, and liberate the Bible from too close an association with mother church, an association that can easily smother its independent voice. The teaching legacy we honor is noble and true, but it is not infallible or perfect, and we must be free to improve it if we can.

The Crisis of the Scripture Principle

Despite the ecumenical range and great antiquity of the classical conviction about the Bible as the written Word of God, we face a "crisis of the Scripture principle" today, and with it the unraveling of traditional Christian doctrine.[13] Peter Hodgson and Robert King put it succinctly and accurately in 1985: "Until recently, almost the entire spectrum of theological opinion would have agreed that the scriptures of the Old and New Testaments, together with their doctrinal interpretations, occupy a unique and indispensable place of authority for Christian faith, practice, and reflection. But this consensus now seems to be falling apart."[14] Out of the liberal theological revision has come a flat denial of

11. Virtually all "evangelicals" have done this in times past, so eager have they been to enlist such great worthies as Augustine on their side in the battle with liberalism. Farley exposes this practice very effectively in *Ecclesial Reflection*, 83–105.

12. Woodbridge's book effectively refutes the view that classical theologians limited the inerrancy of the Bible to matters of faith and practice.

13. Wolfhart Pannenberg, "The Crisis of the Scripture Principle," in *Basic Questions in Theology*, 1:1–14. We appreciate the candid humor of Maurice Wiles near the end of his book *The Remaking of Christian Doctrine* when he asked himself, in view of the radical nature of the changes he was proposing, whether the title of the book ought not to be "The Unmaking of Christian Doctrine."

14. Peter C. Hodgson and Robert H. King, eds., *Christian Theology: An Introduction to Its Traditions and Tasks*, 35.

the Scripture principle in the classical sense, the virtual collapse of the house of authority based upon it, and the subsequent disintegration of the orthodox creed. Whether the denial comes in a direct[15] or indirect form[16] does not matter much. The point is that the normative authority of the Bible has been called into question deliberately and repeatedly by adherents of the new theology ever since Schleiermacher (d. 1834).

What can possibly explain why Christian theologians would deny the Scripture principle when the Christian message has historically depended on it? It seems on the surface to be a suicidal act. How could such denial bring anything but harm to Christianity, and who could it possibly please except the enemies of Jesus Christ? As we see it, there are three basic reasons for this far-reaching change of theological opinion.

The first and most important reason for this change is the cultural shift to secular modernity beginning in the Renaissance and moving to a rationalist modernity brought on by the Enlightenment and the liberal response by some Christian scholars to this major shift. The modern mind dislikes traditional authorities such as the Bible and insists on subjecting them to rational scrutiny. Alongside this fiercely independent spirit of inquiry, in itself not a bad thing, goes a deeper antipathy to a book that speaks about God and humanity in premodern categories. Speaking as it does of a sovereign God and subject humanity, of resurrection and atonement, of grace and wrath, of incarnation and cognitive revelation, the Bible lacks credibility in the eyes of those taught to prize human autonomy and self-sufficiency.

Lack of belief in the authoritative message of Scripture lies behind denial of the Scripture principle. The final authority of the Bible can hardly stand if the message it conveys provokes not belief but unbelief. Edward Farley makes it plain that this is a fundamental reason for his own rejection of biblical authority.[17] We face a rebelliousness in the

15. For direct denials, in addition to the work of Farley and Pannenberg (see above), consult C. F. Evans, *Is "Holy Scripture" Christian?*; James Barr, *The Bible in the Modern World*; idem, *Holy Scripture: Canon, Authority, Criticism*; and Gordon D. Kaufman, *Theological Imagination: Constructing the Concept of God.*

16. For indirect denials, note the shift of the "functional" authority of the Bible in a wide range of modern writers who take the Bible to be authoritative, not in its teachings or history but in its power to occasion new experiences of revelation in us. See David H. Kelsey, *The Uses of Scripture in Recent Theology.* For Langdon Gilkey, the Bible is a fallible human witness reflecting all the biases and fears of its age and is subject to our correcting its errors. What he holds to be true is the symbolic structure and its power to illuminate our existence. See Gilkey, *Message and Existence: An Introduction to Christian Theology,* 52–53. Many prominent theologians make the shift to the functional while continuing to pretend that they are operating within the classical picture. Hodgson and King (*Christian Theology,* 53) name Bultmann, Tillich, and Barth in this category.

17. Farley, *Ecclesial Reflection,* 153–65.

modern period that seeks to edge God out of the world and leave humanity autonomous in it. To achieve this, the Bible that challenges this insurrection must be silenced as divinely authoritative.

The second reason for change is the rise of biblical criticism that tends to treat Scripture as a merely human document and frequently debunks its claims on various levels. At first this criticism consisted in a discrediting of traditional views as to the literary nature of the books of the Bible; then it questioned the historical details of the biblical narrative; and then it exposed supposed difficulties with the truth claims themselves. Pretending to be a key to the proper elucidation of the text, criticism had the effect of situating the Bible so thoroughly in the human context as to make it nearly impossible to consider its authority as anything more than human. It became less and less natural to regard the text as divine communication and more and more plausible to regard it as fallible human utterance.[18]

What made it even more difficult for the conservative believers who wanted to be honest in their study of the Bible was the burden of their own heritage, which had erred both by exaggerating the absolute perfection of the biblical text and obscuring its genuine, humble humanity. They were thus not in a strong position to distinguish between the positive and the negative proposals that the new criticism advanced. To this day, this is the conservative burden. It makes it difficult for those who keenly desire to respect the Bible highly but are put off by the form of belief that the conservative tradition often still takes.

The third reason for change is theological in character. Orthodoxy, it often is claimed, silences God from speaking today—locking the divine in a book—and creates a petrified and rigid style of faith that is false to the dynamic transcendence of the Bible. It closes us off from appropriating fresh truth and creates a whole set of oppressive attitudes and dogmas. Surely, religious experience is the heart of Christianity, and although this gives rise to dogmas in time, such are the work of human beings, not the declarations of God.[19]

Why should a religion that celebrates an inner spiritual guide be so concerned with written rules and doctrines? Christianity is a religion of the Spirit, not of a book.[20] A Scripture principle that is too rigid tends both to inhibit each new generation from seeking the will of God afresh and to lose touch with the glorious fact that God is at work in us. Of course, we will need the New Testament, but we do not need an infallible testa-

---

18. Ibid., 135–40.

19. Auguste Sabatier, *Religions of Authority and Religions of the Spirit*.

20. This is a favorite theme of liberal Christianity. See Edgar J. Goodspeed, "The Canon of the New Testament," in *The Interpreter's Bible*, ed. George A. Buttrick et al. (New York: Abingdon, 1952), 1:63.

ment incapable of any error, only a kerygma collection to bear witness to the originating experiences of revelation through Jesus Christ.[21]

Leaving aside for now how the conservative theologian might counter these three contentions, claimed reasons for abandoning true biblical authority, it is obvious that we are facing a confrontation between classical Christianity based on the Scripture principle and a neo-Christianity largely without a Scripture principle. This is a collision that, in the realm of theological ideas, makes the differences between Roman Catholicism and Protestantism seem trivial by comparison. Theology without the controlling influence of the Scripture principle can only degenerate into open-ended pluralism of belief that none can adjudicate, and its classical concepts could only suffer unlimited revision in the process. The crisis of the Scriptures is the crisis of Christian theology itself and the cause of the deepest polarization of all in the churches. The gap is wide between those who stand by the historic confidence in the infallible truth of the Bible and those who adopt the pan-critical view that relativizes the entire theological enterprise. When the full measure of the difference of perspectives is taken, we doubt that reconciliation is possible without serious compromise of one perspective or the other.[22]

At stake here is the well-being of the church and the effective proclamation of its saving message to the world. The church depends upon a sure word of instruction in regard to its gospel foundations. We need to possess a trustworthy knowledge of God and his salvation, and this is what the inspired Scriptures provide. Should they be discredited, we would lack the requisite knowledge of God's Word and the necessary foundations for the life of faith. It is as if a person were to place a great charge of dynamite at the base of orthodox Christianity that would cause the structure to crumble to the ground, collapsing under its own weight.

Assuming that confidence in the Bible is basic to the memory, theology, and liturgy of the church universal, it is most unlikely that the crisis of the Scripture principle will last or have the effect of carrying more than a small percentage of Christian people with it. Like the false teachers Paul faced, these unreliable guides are not likely to get very far (2 Tim. 3:9). Nevertheless, a definite threat is posed to the solidity and soundness of the teaching office in the church today, a threat that can harm believers who come under its influence.

James Barr rightly protests when conservatives link salvation and belief in the Scriptures so closely as to suggest that those who hold a non-conservative view of the Bible have no right to the hope of salvation.

21. Farley, *Ecclesial Reflection*, 272–81.
22. Compare Richard J. Coleman, *Issues of Theological Conflict*.

He correctly points out that the judgment of God turns upon a person's response to Jesus Christ, not to the Bible, and that this decision and no other matters ultimately.[23] B. B. Warfield granted Barr's point when he said that Christianity does not depend upon the Scriptures for its truth or saving power.[24] Even so, there is something very important at stake here: the well-being of the church, which draws its sustenance and instruction from the Bible. The necessity of the Scripture principle is, we admit, practical rather than absolute, but it is a practical necessity of the greatest importance.[25]

Of scarcely less importance is the necessity of presenting to a lost world the sure Word of salvation. Now that the entire world is being sucked into the vortex of atheism and self-absorption, it is more important than ever to be able to declare God's reliable Word of good news, which comes to us with clarity and forthrightness from outside the human situation. How will people of the modern world recognize truth of eternal validity and saving power unless it originates outside the flux of the human situation? How else will they come into contact with the basis of meaning and hope that they need? And how will the church be able to communicate effectively its confidence in such a saving gospel without confidence in the sources of the knowledge of God? Not only does the church need the Bible for its own renewal and health; the fortunes of the nations depend as well on the validity of the good news and the integrity of its scriptural vehicle.[26]

The Struggle to Maintain the Scripture Principle

Seeing a real threat to the authority of the Bible and thus to the well-being of the churches, classical Christians today respond by wanting to defend vigorously and explicate freshly the Scripture principle in this newly critical context. In one sense, they are in a strong position to do so. The conservative position is deeply rooted not only in the most ancient of the church's traditions, but also in the Bible itself, as we shall see. The task is made easier by the fact that the liberals are scrambling to find a viable alternative to the Scripture principle—not an easy thing to do. The church as a whole is not likely to respond well to a denial

---

23. Barr, *Holy Scripture*, 19.

24. Benjamin B. Warfield, *The Inspiration and Authority of the Bible*, 210–14.

25. See J. I. Packer, "The Necessity of the Revealed Word," in *The Bible: The Living Word of Revelation*, ed. Merrill C. Tenney, 31–49.

26. John W. Montgomery enters an eloquent plea along these lines in "The Relevance of Scripture Today," in *The Bible*, ed. Tenney, 201–18. This is also the motivating factor behind Carl F. H. Henry's magnum opus, *God, Revelation, and Authority*.

of the real basis of its apostolicity when nothing solid and satisfying is being proposed in its place.

In another sense, however, a fresh explication is not so easy because, in the course of the criticism of the Scripture principle, some very tough questions have been raised and placed on the agendas of all serious students of the matter. How shall we use as an authority a text that was written when people thought in very different ways than we do? How shall we respond to critical "discoveries" on a host of issues pertaining to biblical literature and history? What about the diversity of biblical teaching? How should we think about the currently available and to some degree defective copies and translations of the Bible? Which books properly belong to the sacred canon? How is the Old Testament authoritative when the New Testament appears to supersede it? What is the nature of the claim that the Bible makes for itself?

Those who are honest in pursuing these issues (not all Christians are) know that there are some hard questions for the conservative scholar to answer. They also know that there is little agreement among such scholars about how to answer some of them. Even though there is agreement on the basic approach to the Bible as God's written Word, and a widely felt desire to preserve unity among Bible-believing Christians in the face of the present crisis, there is a disturbing lack of consensus on some rather important questions and on what to do about them. From a distance it seems that everyone dwells in the same house of biblical authority; but, closer in, it becomes quite apparent that the house contains various rooms and closets in which one or another of this mixed multitude of conservatives resides. Thus, there are serious debates among evangelicals, despite the need for a united front.[27]

Some evangelicals take their stand with the inerrancy of the King James Version, seeing the need to locate an absolute truth in an accessible text, not in lost autographs. Some posit the perfect errorlessness of the original Hebrew, Aramaic, and Greek biblical texts and try to make that meaningful despite their not being completely available now. Some work with terms like "infallible" and "inerrant," although these terms sometimes are used more flexibly than their simple definitions would indicate. Some suggest a lesser claim of inerrancy, one that would apply to the purpose of a biblical writer rather than to everything that was written. Some speak of a set radius of biblical authority that encompasses a plurality of theological styles not to be forced into systematic unity. Some refer to the time-conditioned and culture-bound character of the Bible at certain

---

27. No conservative book we know of responds to the full range of hard critical questions, although most questions are treated helpfully by someone. We hope that this book will fill this important gap satisfactorily.

key points that obviates the need to bring those elements forward into the church of the twenty-first century. And there are still others who fancy themselves catholic evangelicals, who appeal to ecclesiastical authority in order to buttress biblical authority. Although "evangelical" may be a good umbrella term to describe this large company of conservative believers, there is an obvious lack of theological unity among them regarding how we ought to maintain the Scripture principle today. These differences are not trivial, but well worth careful attention and, hopefully, resolution.

It is easy to become impatient with evangelicals who attack other evangelicals for holding what they consider unsound positions, but one must recognize that the differences can be quite important, and positions can be taken for well-considered although differing reasons. Often there is logic at work that is easier to deplore than to answer, and rhetorical shortcuts will not get us anywhere. The problem is aggravated by the success of the evangelical movement. In the past few decades, evangelicals have moved out of a religious subculture, where their disagreements went largely unnoticed, to a position in the public limelight, where their differences are given attention and subjected to considerable analysis. The opportunity is now available for evangelicals to set forth their understanding of the Bible before a listening world, yet they are caught without a united opinion on a host of detailed questions.[28]

Obviously, a systematic treatment of the Scripture principle is needed to face all the questions squarely and supply a model for understanding that will help transcend the current impasse. Although one has the impression that evangelicals are always writing such tomes, in reality there are almost no full-scale expositions that cover the ground adequately and set forth the evangelical conviction in a balanced and sensible way. Much of the work operates within a circle of limited public visibility, presupposing mostly evangelical readers, and never raises its eyes to the larger perimeter of the theological mainstream where such issues are discussed professionally and in depth.[29]

28. People are just beginning to take account of the amazing diversity in evangelical theology and to classify the various genres by approach. The best taxonomy we have seen is Robert M. Price, "The Crisis of Biblical Authority: The Setting and Range of the Current Evangelical Crisis."

29. Barth and Berkouwer see themselves in line with the historic doctrine of biblical authority and address themselves to the contemporary discussion, but, partly because of the European context and partly because of their emphasis on event rather than content, neither one really speaks for or to the evangelicals in the English-speaking world. Carl Henry is the one thus far to fulfill the prescription (*God, Revelation, and Authority*). There are signs that better work will come forth from the diverse circle that groups itself around the *Chicago Statement on Biblical Inerrancy*. The appearance of Millard J. Erickson's multi-volume *Christian Theology* is an extensive treatment of the subject in a full-scale systematic theology.

In broad outline, as a glance at the table of contents will reveal, we suggest in the following pages a paradigm that we hope is a model of the Scripture principle that can transcend the current evangelical impasse. It utilizes three dimensions: first, the divine inspiration of Holy Scripture that arises organically out of the Christian pattern of revelation; second, the human character of the biblical text as the form in which the Word of God has been communicated to us; and third, the ministry of the Spirit in relation to the Bible and the dynamic interaction between the two. Such a paradigm is sufficiently broad to capture the major themes and specific enough, when opened up, to introduce the reader to a large number of the related issues.

More specifically, our treatment of the Scripture principle will focus on and orient itself to the kind of practical, evangelical emphasis found in 2 Timothy 3:15–17: "From childhood you have known the sacred writings that are able to instruct you for salvation through faith in Christ Jesus. All scripture is inspired by God and is useful for teaching, for reproof, for correction, and for training in righteousness, so that everyone who belongs to God may be proficient, equipped for every good work." In this wonderful text Paul places his emphasis on the plenary profitability of the Scriptures in conveying a saving and equipping knowledge of God. He does not present a theory about a perfect Bible given long ago but now lost (autographs), but declares the Scriptures actually in Timothy's possession to be alive with the breath of God and full of the transforming information the young disciple would need in his life of faith and obedience. We can all learn from this kind of concentration and orientation.[30] It is important for us to stress the practical effectiveness of the accessible Bible in facilitating a saving and transforming knowledge of God in Jesus Christ. We must not shift the emphasis to the unavailable Bible of the past, about which one can only speculate, or to the inaccessible Bible of the future, after the experts will (supposedly) have cleared away every perplexing feature of the text. God has provided what we now have in hand—and it is quite adequate in relation to God's purposes for us.

It is this present Bible that we need to be able to trust, whether the New International Version or King James Version or New Revised Standard Version. We need to focus on the practical purpose of God communicating the saving and equipping knowledge of God. Furthermore, across the centuries it is this Bible that most Christians have come to trust through the grace of God, and this purpose that has proven valid in their experience. Given originally by God's breath, the Bible still proves

---

30. Paul's text is discussed helpfully in Edward W. Goodrick, "Let's Put 2 Timothy 3:16 Back in the Bible," and Howard J. Loewen, "Karl Barth and the Church Doctrine of Inspiration," chap. 2.

to be quick and powerful and sharper than any two-edged sword and gives life and truth to the one who trusts in Jesus. This is the doctrine of Scripture we are concerned to discuss and defend, not the Bible of academic debate, but the Bible given and handed down as the medium of the gospel message and the primary sacrament of the knowledge of God. The Bible is not a book wholly free of perplexing features, but one that bears effective witness to the Savior of all.

Why, in the last analysis, do Christians believe the Bible to be God's Word? It is not because they have studied Christian evidences and apologetics, however useful these may prove to some. Christians believe the Bible because it has been able to do for them exactly what Paul promised it would—introduce them to a saving and transforming knowledge of God in Jesus Christ. Reasons for faith and answers to perplexing difficulties in the text are supportive but not constitutive of faith in God and his Word. Faith rests ultimately not in human wisdom but in a demonstration of the Spirit and power. Therefore, let us not quench the Spirit in our theology of biblical inspiration, whether by rationalist liberal doubts or by rationalist conservative proofs. Both rationalisms shift the focus away from the power of God in the Scriptures and onto our human ability to rationally comprehend and control these matters.

There is, of course, a place for ordinary understanding with the mind and a place for scholarly discussion and vindication. But the significance of the latter is greatly overdone if we leave the slightest impression that we are able to ground faith in God's Word by rational arguments alone or that God's working in the human heart in response to faith is not the main cause of faith. The Bible is not so interested in our academically proving as in our holistically seeing the truth, in our believing the gospel and actually obeying God. This is something we have had to learn ourselves, and it is a liberating truth.[31]

We conservatives should ask ourselves why it is that ordinary believers can go on trusting the Bible, even though it appears to have literary or historical defects due to transmission discrepancies and other causes.

---

31. While still wary of fideism, we understand better what scholars like Daane, Berkouwer, Rogers, Bloesch, Barth, Wink, and Grounds have been trying to tell conservatives who have an overly rationalist bent. Ray Roennfeldt insightfully observes this about the changing perspective of Clark Pinnock: "In the formulation of his early view of Scripture, Pinnock used the presuppositions of Reformed theism, whereas the later Pinnock consciously works from a more Arminian model without rejecting all aspects of Calvinism. He now considers that Scripture should be understood as the result of both divine initiative and human response. It is his contention that a strict belief in biblical inerrancy is incompatible with anything less than belief in Calvinistic determinism. The Arminian paradigm, which took about ten years to affect Pinnock's doctrine of Scripture, has been gradually filtering down into all of his theological reflections" (Roennfeldt, *Clark H. Pinnock on Biblical Authority* [Berrien Springs, MI: Andrews University Press, 1993], 364).

How do they go on believing the Bible when so many technical details remain unresolved? The answer is obvious and important. For their certainty, believers depend not on the interpretive "experts" but on God, who really speaks to them in the Scriptures. They can tolerate some textual uncertainties and perplexities because their confidence rests not on human expertise, liberal or conservative, but on God himself. They are not tied to human authorities but are free in the liberty of the children of God. They know that what is primary is the saving and transforming truth of the Bible, and what is secondary are those curious numbers, those details that will not line up, those obscure allusions that, however questionable, do not begin to upset the truly fundamental point of biblical teaching. It has always been a marvel to us how ordinary believers show themselves wiser in these matters than those who would be their teachers and who often introduce them to arcane discussions that never end and never deliver the kind of certainty these ordinary believers already possess.

We are not saying that Christians need to believe the Bible with only their hearts and not their minds, or believe only when the Bible seems to be speaking about saving matters as opposed to other things. This would be to introduce a distinction of true and false into our attitude to the text that would be unfruitful and even dangerous. On the contrary, our experience of the truth and power of God's Word predisposes us to be open in an unlimited way to all of its assertions, even when they are perplexing. The smallest detail can prove to be important and not incidental at all. An emphasis on an evangelical certainty implies that we will be open to the sort of text that God actually has given us and not tend to predetermine according to rationalistic criteria the form it ought to take and then twist it into that form by clever scholarly devices.

Concentration on the saving truth of the Bible does not mean that we ought to make a distinction between value judgments and speculative judgments, as Albrecht Ritschl and later Rudolf Bultmann did. It does not mean that we ought to depreciate in the slightest the cognitive substance of what the Bible teaches. Rather, it means that we should focus our attention on the transforming message of the Bible, which comes across with tremendous power from the texts we now possess, and place the great bulk of our concern on heeding, digesting, and being changed by that glorious and liberating Word.

PART I

The Word of God

The Pattern of Revelation

The goal of this first major section of the book is to determine the pattern of divine revelation as it is laid down in the biblical witness, and then to locate the place of the Bible itself in this pattern. The provision of inspired Scriptures was integral to the divine self-disclosure and cannot be put aside. In this first chapter we present the general picture, painting with a broad brush. We will look in greater detail at the crucial biblical testimony to inspiration in chapter 2 and go on, in chapter 3, to consider the Bible's normative authority as the school of the Holy Spirit.

In the context of religion, revelation refers to the vision people have of what is ultimate and sacred to them; it gives them an orientation for life and a criterion of what is true and valuable. In theistic religions, like Judaism, Islam, and Christianity, revelation refers to the self-disclosure of God, the only way for us to know God. How could we know the One whose ways and thoughts are higher than our ways and thoughts unless God has given us his Word? (Isa. 55:6–11). Without revelation we would be left groping in darkness. Thus, we cannot take too seriously those who suggest that Christianity has no revelation when it is so apparent that it rests on a definite vision of what is ultimate and true based on the revelation of God.[1] Says the New Testament: "He has made known to us the mystery of his will, according to his good pleasure that he set forth in Christ" (Eph. 1:9).

1. F. Gerald Downing, *Has Christianity a Revelation?* A more convincing account can be found in Avery Dulles, *Revelation Theology: A History*; and Gordon D. Kaufman, *Systematic Theology: A Historicist Perspective* (New York: Scribner, 1978), chaps. 2–3.

What sort of revelation does Christianity claim to possess, and what is its pattern? A great deal hangs on getting the answers to these questions right because the essence of Christianity is bound up in it. What one decides revelation to be will be reflected in how one defines Christianity. If revelation is primarily a matter of personal encounter with the divine, as it is in the work of Rudolf Bultmann, then the real historicity of the salvation narrative in Scripture and the trustworthiness of apostolic teachings will seem relatively unimportant. If revelation is a universal intuition that takes differing forms in the world religions, then the Christian revelation will be handled as a human construct and assimilated with insights from other quarters. If revelation consists primarily of historical acts of God, not verbal communication, Christianity must be divined from the meanings inherent in those events in the context of universal history. Or, if revelation comes with cognitive substance intrinsic to it, the shape of Christianity will be determined by the information revelation delivers.

There are few questions more important to theology and the essence of Christian faith than the nature of revelation, and no better way to answer this question than to interrogate the revelation itself. As Avery Dulles says, "To construct a sound and credible notion of revelation is an urgent task in our day, both for the church's dialogue with the surrounding world, and for her own internal development."[2] We heartily agree.

Revelation according to the Bible

The first point to make about revelation, as the Bible presents it, is that it is complex. It is not a single activity or a simple entity, but a complexity designed to disclose the divine message of salvation. As Hebrews puts it, "Long ago God spoke to our ancestors in many and various ways by the prophets, but in these last days he has spoken to us by a Son, whom he appointed heir of all things" (Heb. 1:1–2). Revelation appears to be multifaceted, and we need to try to avoid losing any of its richness. Its unity consists in its overall function of communicating the gracious truth and actions of God; and its diversity arises from the various forms and features of this communication. God's Word has a prism-like effect when it breaks into the world, and we have to speak of a pattern of revelation to do it justice.[3]

We find as we look into God's Word that God acts in human history, gives some understanding of his will to prophets and apostles, becomes

2. Avery Dulles, *Revelation and the Quest for Unity*, 48.
3. Bernard Ramm, *The Pattern of Authority*.

flesh in the person of Jesus, moves in power in the Spirit of Pentecost, and provides written Scriptures for the church. Each facet contributes something vital to the disclosure, and we ought to view each in complementary relationship with the others. The temptation to select one aspect, such as experience or event or oracle, and make it the whole—with revelation being nothing but that—is a serious mistake. Such restriction can only distort the total picture. The only valid model of revelation will be one that welcomes each of the original elements in the ancient pattern and does not pick and choose among them arbitrarily. Among modern theologians, some see revelation chiefly in terms of content, some in terms of historical events, and others as inner experience or transforming encounter. Much of the disagreement could be removed if arbitrary selectivity were avoided.[4]

A second point to notice from the outset, because of its contemporary relevance, is the bipolar structure of revelation, *objective* and *subjective*. We always ought to be concerned about both the content of what has been revealed and the ways it is being received and appropriated. We also should be careful not to suppress either aspect. Orthodoxy often tends to highlight the propositional nature of revelation at the expense of the existential, whereas contemporary liberal thought certainly stresses to a fault the inner, subjective dimension. One jeopardizes the vitality of revelation, the other, the noetic content. We are concerned to correct both errors and, in this chapter, particularly the precarious shift to the subjective in the contemporary theologies of revelation.

As we begin to distinguish the various facets of God's multifaceted revelation, the first thing we notice is a distinction between what have been called "general" and "special" revelation. On the one hand, the whole of nature declares the glory of God and, in a limited but very true sense, reveals God. On the other hand, a more focused and specific revelation of the will of God to Israel and then to the church is the main emphasis in the Bible. There is a cosmic revelation accessible to all peoples as well as a special initiative in history to reveal the heart of God and make his saving plan effective. Scripture declares:

> For ask now about former ages, long before your own, ever since the day that God created human beings on the earth; ask from one end of heaven to the other: has anything so great as this ever happened or has its like even been heard of? Has any people ever heard the voice of a god speaking out of a fire, as you have heard, and lived? Or has any god ever attempted to go and take a nation for himself from the midst of another nation, by trials, by signs and wonders, by war, by a mighty hand and an

4. Avery Dulles, *Models of Revelation*.

outstretched arm, and by terrifying displays of power, as the LORD your
God did for you in Egypt before your very eyes? To you it was shown so
that you would acknowledge that the LORD is God; there is no other besides
him (Deut. 4:32–35).[5]

Although the Bible does not dwell upon it, it does present a form
of revelation that is universal in scope and accessible to all peoples.
God is, after all, the creator of the world and is revealed as its Maker
in all things. God's power and divinity are plainly evident before our
very eyes (Rom. 1:19). Human beings exist necessarily and inescapably
in the presence of God, being created for God and by God. Though
we certainly can rebel and even curse God, we cannot escape him altogether, at least not in this life, but must encounter him everywhere
and always. For those who come to know God, God is the meaning
and truth of their being.[6] Just as individuals reveal themselves in their
general conduct and also, more self-consciously, by means of specific
acts, so God reveals himself in both these ways and never leaves himself without a witness (Acts 14:17). General revelation in the creation
provides valuable common ground between the Christian and all others
and can open the door to an encounter with special revelation through
Jesus Christ.[7]

Among recent theologians, Karl Barth was particularly reluctant to
speak positively about general revelation because of the danger of it
eclipsing and even distorting the specific revelation of the Bible. Just
because it is so minimal and inarticulate, general revelation lends itself
to human rebelliousness and to being twisted in support of some favorite
project. Barth saw this happening in the Nazi ideology as the propaganda
machine appealed to general revelation in support of its perverted notions of race and national calling. Furthermore, an overemphasis on it
can easily lead to the arrogance of humans thinking that they can ap-
prehend truth about God by their own powers of reason and experience
and not rely upon the saving revelation of the gospel.

Liberal theology is largely a theology built upon supposed general
revelation coming through human consciousness, and it distorts the
biblical revelation by relying on insights drawn independently of it.
Knowledge of God is sought by delving into the depths of experience
and finding revelation there. When God has been found in the depths
of everyday experience, there is no great need to seek him elsewhere,

5. William Temple seems to keep a balance between these two kinds of revelation. See
his *Nature, Man and God*.

6. See Karl Rahner's challenging treatment in *Foundations of Christian Faith*, chaps.
1–4.

7. The best treatment of this whole subject is Bruce A. Demarest, *General Revelation*.

either in heaven or in the pages of the Bible.[8] Thus, the danger Barth feared is not an imaginary one.

Nevertheless, the Bible itself speaks of a general revelation. The creation bears the mark of the handiwork of its maker and proclaims the glory of God (Ps. 19:1). No one is far from God's presence, because we all live, move, and have our being in him (Acts 17:28). The light of creation falls upon the heart of everyone coming into the world (John 1:9). Far from negating special revelation, general revelation opens the door through which God can then approach his creatures, not as an alien and stranger, but as the One who has a proper claim on us, a claim of which we are already aware. Just as salvation is the restoration of creation, so Christian revelation is the representation and amplification of the offer of salvation already present in general revelation.

It is true that many evangelical theologians are nervous about recognizing any saving significance in general revelation. Like Barth, they are jealous for the utter uniqueness of Christian salvation based on the special revelation in Jesus Christ. They allow themselves to see general revelation only in terms of a restraining influence on sinners that keeps them from degenerating into utter bestiality. In general revelation God presents himself only as a power to be encountered, whereas in the gospel he comes as a person to be known in faith and trust.

For our part, we cannot see how any revelation from the God of the gospel can be other than saving in its basic significance if it is truly a revelation of God. If we grant the availability of such a revelation to all peoples, as Scripture appears to report, then it must be the disclosure of the gracious God from whom our creaturely existence flows. God is the mystery of created life and lovingly offers himself to everyone. We meet God in a thousand ways, such as when we ask if there is anything to trust in, or any justice to be had, or any basis of final meaning. God is present even when not named. Now, this is not to say that people always respond favorably to this availability of revelation—they do not. God is near and they ought to seek after him, but often they do not (Acts 17:27). If they do respond, God "rewards those who seek him" (Heb. 11:6).

In relating general revelation to special revelation, we ought to see the first as leading into the second. In general revelation, God offers himself to everyone in the whole of creation, doing so through the creation itself and in the secret of each person's heart. We believe that God, by his grace, makes an offer of salvation to all people, in keeping with his stated desire (1 Tim. 2:4). This offer can be accepted or refused. Even so, general revelation remains rather hidden, is relatively unclear, and

8. Kenneth Hamilton writes against earthbound theology in *Revolt against Heaven*.

calls for further revelation that is more definitive and out in the open. This is exactly what we have in special revelation.

In the biblical history of salvation, we have a segment of world history in which God has made good on the divine offer of salvation. Indeed, the whole world was created for the salvation brought by the Word made flesh in Jesus. What all humanity has hoped and longed for, the dwelling of the gracious God with them, has come to pass. The God who "has not left himself without a witness" (Acts 14:17) has surpassed the mute witness of general revelation by granting the supreme miracle of reconciliation by the divine Son of God. The world and its history were made by and for the Son and fitted to become the stage of his incarnation. The God who loves the world and presents himself to every soul has communicated himself without reservation for the salvation of all believers.

The Pattern of Special Revelation

The glory of revelation in the Bible is that it presents an infinite, personal God making himself known as the saving Lord who desires a covenant relationship with all human creatures (unlike various mythic gods who never spoke to humankind and never revealed themselves in historical deeds). Our interest is not so much in revelation as an abstraction or as the linchpin in a philosophical theology but in revelation as the unveiling of the grace and mercy of God that calls for trust and commitment. This, in the last analysis, is what makes the Christian revelation so convincing. It is not the objective proofs extrinsic to its substance (although proofs there are), but the intrinsic appeal of the pearl of great price that is made available in it.

Revelation by itself might have no appeal if, for example, it portrayed a remote and austere deity. However convincing its external credentials might be, we would turn away from it in disappointment and even disgust. The Qur'an makes the highest claims for itself (even higher than does the Bible) and, in a tight apologetic case for Islam as God's truth, offers to supply the revelational axiom. Yet it has little good news to offer, only law and submission. What makes Christian revelation, and the Bible as its primary medium, different is the message of grace and forgiveness it enshrines, which draws sinners almost irresistibly to the mercy seat of God. It drew them before there even was a Bible, and it draws them still.[9]

---

9. James Barr (*Holy Scripture*, chap. 1) rightly speaks of the time before there was any canonical Scripture as such, although he depreciates somewhat the fact that Scripture was present even then and was in the making.

In the Old Testament, revelation occurs in the context of establishing a covenant with Israel and calling forth trust in the divine promise.[10] In a variety of ways, God made himself known to the people as the true and living God. God gave his word of promise to their forefather Abraham that he would bless the whole world through Abraham's descendants and, in dealing with the other patriarchs, God continued to show his fidelity to that pledge. Later on, God made himself known to Moses and called him to be the leader of the people and to liberate them from bondage in Egypt. At Sinai, God gave his ten words of holy law and opened up deeper dimensions of his contract with Israel. History became the theater in which God showed himself to be the redeemer and savior of humankind. God wants to be known, not so much from nature, but from the acts he performs before human eyes, as Pannenberg emphasizes. If sin has twisted and corrupted history, grace will come and begin to put it right.[11]

The events of divine action are not left uninterpreted, according to the biblical record. The Old Testament does not downplay the importance of the Word of God that comes to bring out the redemptive significance of God's acts of salvation. Just as the words of a person have as much importance as deeds in conveying character and intention, so God acts in order to achieve redemption and speaks in order to communicate the meaning of his plan. It is fruitless to ask which is more important for revelation, history or language; the Scriptures give them equal emphasis and refuse to choose between them. Facts without words are blind, and words without facts are empty.

The Old Testament presents revelation as the story of what God has done and the witness to what God has spoken—content and confirmation.[12] The pattern is abundantly plain in the case of Moses himself. He was both the agent of a great deliverance and the prophet par excellence who spoke to God "face to face" (Num. 12:8). Deuteronomy also makes clear that the Word of God thus communicated embraces the whole corpus of legislation and not simply the original ten words of Sinai. There is revelation also in the messianic and eschatological prophecy scattered throughout the Old Testament in which the coming king is described and the kingdom that shall not be overthrown is promised. A

10. Walter C. Kaiser (*Toward an Old Testament Theology*) portrays the entire Old Testament as the developing story of the unfolding promise of God, given first to Eve and then to Abraham, Moses, Isaiah, and the others, leading up to the coming of Jesus, the messianic seed of Abraham and of Eve.

11. On the revelational modality of the historical event, see Bernard Ramm, *Special Revelation and the Word of God*, chap. 4.

12. John Goldingay, *Approaches to Old Testament Interpretation*, 74–77.

blessed era is foretold in which there will be a new David, a new Moses, a new covenant, and a new exodus.

The books of wisdom also contain revelation that, although it sounds like ordinary human insight, is understood to be the product of divine illumination. For instance, "God gave Solomon very great wisdom, discernment, and breadth of understanding as vast as the sand on the seashore" (1 Kings 4:29). Wisdom comes from God, and the Old Testament wisdom literature reveals a divine pattern of behavior disclosing the will of the Lord. Even the psalms are more than merely human responses to God. They are linked to inspiration and prophecy, as when Miriam, the prophet of God, sang her canticle (Exod. 15:20–21). Even the narratives in the historical books are not just interesting tales but a form of instruction for our sakes to spell out the shape and directions of the life of faith. In many and various ways, Yahweh, God of Israel, was self-revealing as the holy, loving, and saving God.[13] God manifests himself as the Lord of history, performing acts of deliverance and giving messages for the people. Although the initial focus is on a single nation, the horizon of God's salvation reaches out to include all peoples.[14]

In the New Testament, revelation builds on the modalities of the Old and focuses on a new covenant, made effective in Jesus Christ and open to all who believe from every tribe and nation. In Christ, the promises formerly directed toward Israel are made universally available, extended, and transformed. The witness is now anchored in a new set of realities brought about by the coming of Jesus in the fullness of time, the Word made flesh, and the sending of the Spirit to empower the church to proclaim the gospel to the whole world. Not simply the fulfillment of discrete prophecies concerning the coming of a great king, the advent of Christ is the fulfillment of the great promise to save the world through Abraham's seed. Yahweh is once again actively bringing salvation to earth.

Jesus Christ is and must be the centerpiece of the Christian revelation because, in Jesus, God entered our world within the parameters of a human life. Quite properly, Luther pointed to Jesus as the material center of the Christian message and inquired of every book of the Bible how it preached Christ, the incarnate Word of God. The Scriptures exist to bear witness to Jesus (John 5:39), and he is the sum and substance of their message. No mere emissary of the prophetic sort, the Son is God incarnate, dwelling among us, the revelation of God without peer. Of all the forms of revelation, this is the best. We are not able to come to God on the basis of our own wisdom or righteousness, but a way has been

13. Christopher B. Kaiser (*The Doctrine of God*, chap. 1) devotes a fine chapter to God's self-revelation in the Old Testament period.

14. Dulles (*Revelation Theology*, chap. 1) provides a good summary of the pattern of revelation in the Old and New Testaments.

opened for us to come, and the way has been made manifest—visibly, audibly, and tangibly. Small wonder that Christian orthodoxy has made response to Jesus the touchstone of a sound confession. In Jesus Christ, the divine nature is mirrored and there appears the fulfillment of the divine plan to restore fallen humanity to a true and saving knowledge of God.

The moral miracle of the incarnation is as great as the metaphysical. God came into the world, not as might be expected, in the form of a powerful king, but in the form of a lowly servant. Shattering the almost universal stereotype of God as one who is too high a being to be much concerned with human affairs, one who keeps his distance and protects his honor, God does the utterly unexpected thing and humbles himself in the service of humanity, even unto death on a cross. The pagan philosopher Celsus was right to feel that this claim is something incredible, judged by the standards of religious opinion he was familiar with. But nothing other than this could have revealed more effectively the heart of God as the loving shepherd of humankind.

In the incarnation, God makes use of human culture and interacts with people in human terms. Although by no means devoid of content, revelation in this mode is much more than a set of lifeless propositions; the information conveyed through it is personal and inexhaustible. For this reason, John said that he did not think all the books in the world could tell the story exhaustively (John 21:25). God does not keep a divine distance, as in Islam, but crosses the great divide between heaven and earth and communicates with us personally and in human terms.[15]

Such a declaration is wonderful, but is it true? From the standpoint of ordinary people in history, it certainly rings true. This story has to be the greatest ever told, the fulfillment of the boldest human dreams. No other story can give such a basis to the dignity and worth of human life and at the same time promise us healing and deliverance from the forces that enslave us. The incarnation of God in Jesus is less the projection of a mere human wish and more the promised fulfillment of the deepest needs of the human heart. From the point of view of Judaism and Islam, such a divine incarnation is certainly possible. The God of Abraham, Isaac, and Jacob came near to redeem his people and cares passionately for them. He is the kind of God who could (because of his power) and would (because of his love) make such a gesture of saving concern as the incarnation. God is free and merciful, and therefore believers must be open to the unexpected and not shut themselves against

15. As a cultural anthropologist, Charles H. Kraft has unusual insight into cross-cultural communication and into the incarnation as "a case study in receptor-oriented revelation" (*Christianity in Culture*, chap. 9).

this revelation. One can only respect Rabbi Pinchas Lapide for admitting that, if it turns out that Jesus is the messiah of Jewish hope, he would have no objection: "Who am I as a devout Jew to define *a priori* God's saving activity?"[16]

The question of truth, so deceptively simple, can be asked on so many levels at once that the answers must tumble over one another. Did Jesus himself claim to be the ultimate revelation of God? It would seem that he did when he set himself apart from all others in the authority of his word and the uniqueness of his relation of sonship with God his Father.[17] Was this claim in any way vindicated? It seems that it was when the mighty power of God raised him up and left the tomb empty as a wondrous testimony.[18] Did the apostles claim incarnation or something less? John affirms the incarnation quite literally, but other writers say as much in other terms.[19] Does incarnation make theological sense—Godhead united to humanity? This is a mystery, without doubt, but one in keeping with humans being made in the image of God and God limiting himself to the lowly conditions of earthly life.[20] How reasonable is the idea of incarnation? As reasonable as need be, if we grant the reality of a living Lord and Creator, within whose possibilities even incarnation must surely lie.[21] But these issues, important as they are, cannot be explored in this chapter. The more modest purpose here is to call attention to Jesus Christ as the center of the claim to revelation in the New Testament.

The coming of the Spirit on the day of Pentecost is, after the incarnation, the second crucial feature of the New Testament's revelation claim. It fills in the subjective side of revelation in the Christian understanding and balances the objective pole. It answers the human need for subjective immediacy in religion and forces us to the dynamic and contemporary dimensions of revelation. The Spirit makes it impossible to construe revelation in a static way and removes the need to defend the authority of revelation in ways wholly objective. Since the Spirit is required to make revelation real in our lives, then the Spirit cannot easily be squeezed out of the picture when it comes to questions like the ones we are facing in this book. The neglect of this crucial Spirit factor may be what has led to some of the difficulties that seem not to go away.

16. Lapide engaged in a dialogue with Hans Küng. See Küng, *Signposts for the Future*, 85.

17. Royce G. Gruenler (*New Approaches to Jesus and the Gospels*) sees Jesus as the source of the high Christology that characterizes both the New Testament and the orthodox faith of the church.

18. Wolfhart Pannenberg, *Jesus—God and Man* (Philadelphia: Westminster, 1968), chap. 3; and Gary R. Habermas, *The Resurrection of Jesus: An Apologetic*.

19. John 1:1–18; 20:28; but also 2 Cor. 8:9; Phil. 2:6; Col. 2:9; Titus 2:13; Heb. 10:5–7.

20. Stephen T. Davis, *Logic and the Nature of God*, chap. 8.

21. Karl Barth, *Church Dogmatics*, 4/2:85.

Jews in the first century believed that the Spirit had been withdrawn because of human disobedience, but the Christians claimed that the Spirit was restored in connection with the messianic work of Jesus.[22] Each of the main New Testament writers is very conscious that the Spirit was poured out afresh and in power and was rendering the lordship of Christ effective in the world.[23] The Gospel of Luke and the book of Acts are full of the conviction that the Spirit has come to empower believers to proclaim the gospel effectively to the whole world. John's Gospel presents the Paraclete Spirit, who bears witness to the truth in Jesus, and 1 John refers to the anointing of the believer for the knowledge of God. Paul gives us an extensive doctrine of the Spirit. Preaching, in order to be effective, has to be done in the power of the Spirit. The experience of salvation and the assurance of adoption are made possible by the Spirit's witness in us.

Believers can expect the Spirit to lead and guide them and give them gifts to equip them in the work of building up the community of faith and ministering in love. The Spirit searches the deep things of God and reveals them to the apostles, inspiring their teaching and, in turn, enlightening their hearers (1 Cor. 2:10–16). Paul says that "we speak of these things in words not taught by human wisdom but taught by the Spirit" (1 Cor. 2:13). The Spirit gives an ability to receive and understand spiritual things that the unbeliever lacks; things will remain enigmatic until the Spirit opens the believer's eyes to them. Of course, the words can be comprehended and the sentences understood before the Spirit works, but they do not register in their full significance and do not carry conviction until that time.

The overall picture the New Testament gives us of the coming of the Spirit is that the Spirit desires to make the Word of the gospel in all its forms existentially real to people, so that they awaken to the reality of God's grace and love and receive what Christ has done for them personally. Mere information about these topics will not be effective until the Spirit renders the information dynamically effective in a human heart.

The coming of the Spirit does not mean that the norms of the gospel established by Jesus and the apostles have lost their authority and can be transcended at any time by persons claiming the Spirit. There are some today who want to construe their spiritual liberty in this way and launch out in altogether new directions of belief and praxis for which there is no scriptural support—or even where there is scriptural opposition. If unbridled liberty in the Spirit were the case, Christianity would

22. Joachim Jeremias, *New Testament Theology*, 76–96.
23. George T. Montague, *The Holy Spirit*; and James D. G. Dunn, *Jesus and the Spirit*.

be an open question, not decided on the basis of past norms but pliable to creative change as the Spirit leads.[24] Thus, we could appeal to the Spirit in order to break out of the restrictions of orthodoxy, leaving us free to shape religion for ourselves.

Tempting though this perspective is, it is not true to the New Testament witness about the Spirit. In John's Gospel, for example, there is no idea of the Spirit canceling the truth given through Jesus. Rather, the Spirit is presented as freshly focusing the truth in Jesus for the current situation. The Spirit works to bring each generation of believers as close to the Lord as the first apostles were and enables them to penetrate the same truth in relation to their different contexts. It is not that a new message will be given but that the old message will continue to be made effective by the Spirit as the Spirit helps us in new circumstances to properly reinterpret and apply the truth once delivered. Even these fresh interpretations depend for their validity on the original truth and are limited in their authority to the special circumstances they address.[25]

What the coming of the Spirit does mean for the Christian doctrine of revelation is that we understand the norms given in the original disclosure to be dynamic in the sense that they can be interpreted and freshly applied in ever-changing situations. It means that revelation is not locked in the past as a collection of inflexible rules, but is a disclosure that comes alive today, opening up a relationship with God and transforming human life. The Bible cannot be seen as simply a set of ancient religious propositions; it is a means of grace by which God is able to speak to us in new ways. For this reason, Paul prays that believers will be given "a spirit of wisdom and revelation" so that the truth of what he is teaching them will come alive in their experience and they will begin to understand its significance for their own circumstances (Eph. 1:17). Obviously, then, the issues surrounding revelation and inspiration cannot be handled simply from the outside in an academic way, but will have to be considered from the inside in relation to commitment.

A further dimension of revelation in the New Testament is brought out by the phrase so often used in it: "the word of God." In our day it is common to hear this phrase used to refer to the Christian Bible, which is quite an extension of its original meaning. The New Testament, apart from the special instance where it mentions the incarnate Word (John 1:14), refers to the message about Jesus that the apostles proclaimed. For instance, "they were all filled with the Holy Spirit and spoke the

24. Sallie McFague seems to be pointing in this direction in *Christian Theology*, ed. Hodgson and King, 334–35.

25. Dunn, *Jesus and the Spirit*, 356.

word of God with boldness" (Acts 4:31). It is sometimes called the "word of the Lord" (Acts 8:25), the "word of Christ" (Col. 3:16), the "word of the cross" (1 Cor. 1:18), the "word of truth" (Eph. 1:13), or the "word of reconciliation" (2 Cor. 5:19). Hebrews calls it a living and powerful sword (Heb. 4:12), whereas Peter credits it with the ability to create life in us (1 Pet. 1:23).

The word of God in the New Testament refers primarily to the proclamation of the gospel at work in the lives of people when received by faith. It is a message that "cannot be bound," because of the power of the Spirit. When we today use the phrase "Word of God" to refer to the Bible as a whole, we should realize that we are using it in a more developed and different sense than the New Testament itself does. The positive side of our usage is to secure for the Bible a place under the category "word of God" that it deserves, as we will show. The negative side is that it can hamper and inhibit our use of the phrase "word of God" for the activities of proclaiming the gospel today in our own words. When, for example, a person testifies to the saving grace of God, he or she is indeed speaking the word of God.

Content is an important facet of this phrase. The word of God is not a bare existential address, but includes objective truths about the gospel and ourselves. Paul made it clear that the gospel he preached was a communication full of content, centering on the vicarious death of Christ for sinners and on his bodily resurrection from the dead (1 Cor. 15:1–19). This goes directly against a strong tendency in modern theology to affirm revelation as a transforming experience but not to affirm a message full of content and truth given in intelligible speech and language—as if there were some kind of opposition between personal revelation and verbal communication. The New Testament knows of no such dichotomy, which stems from modern philosophical objections to cognitive revelation and an objective knowledge of God. Revelation according to the New Testament is content-full, intelligible, and speaks to human beings about subjects we are able to understand. The loss of confidence in revelation as cognitive has led to a great crisis in theology, and it is important to recover this confidence if we hope to make an effective proclamation of the gospel in our generation.[26]

In brief, the Old Testament gives us a richly variegated pattern of revelation that sets forth Israel's covenant with God and anticipates further developments to come. The New Testament focuses all its emphasis on the fulfillment of that hope in Jesus Christ. At last the promise to Abra-

---

26. Carl F. H. Henry (*God, Revelation, and Authority*, vol. 3, thesis 10) and Ronald H. Nash (*The Word of God and the Mind of Man*) hammer this point home. They may overdo it, but something had to be said.

ham, which was meant to encompass all nations on earth, has reached out to include them in Jesus Christ, the incarnate Word.

Revelation and the Scripture Principle

Where does Scripture fit into this pattern of revelation? Obviously, it has a place as documentation, as a collection of ancient texts mediating to us the formative insights that were reached or received long ago. But why consider the Bible anything more than a human text or consider it to have been miraculously produced? B. B. Warfield admitted that Christianity could be completely true without having any such thing as biblical inspiration.[27] Perhaps Scripture is just part of the tradition and not intended as revelation in the proper sense. Of course, we know that both Judaism and Christianity developed a Scripture principle early on. After the exile, the Jews needed a Torah to preserve their ethnic identity, and in the second century after Jesus, Christians, feeling pressure from the likes of Marcion, followed the Judaic pattern and settled on a New Testament canon of divinely inspired texts. But this development did not have to happen, and some would say should not have happened, at least in the case of Christianity.

After all, a religion oriented to the living Christ and universal in scope does not want to be tied to a sacred text that would hamper its life in the Spirit.[28] As James Barr says, "It is not at all clear from the New Testament itself that Jesus or the earliest Christians intended Christianity to be a scriptural religion, a faith bound and controlled by its own scriptures and one in which such scriptures would have ultimate authoritative status; indeed, the New Testament seems to make it clear that they did not so intend."[29] What problems we could avoid if this appealing line of thought were true! The Bible could still be prized as the unique medium of revelation, but we would not have to be worried by the presence of a few textual irregularities and imponderables.

Whether we would have fewer problems were we to believe in a Christianity without the Scripture principle is certainly debatable, given the rather chaotic state of liberal theology, which does for the most part operate without it. The fact is that the notion of inspired Scripture accompanying and affirming God's covenant with humanity is present in revelation reality as far back as we can go (Moses is depicted as the writer of Scripture as well as the great prophet) and, most importantly, is integral to the thinking

---

27. Warfield, *The Inspiration and Authority of the Bible*, 210.
28. Edward Farley, *Ecclesial Reflection*, 140–52.
29. Barr, *Holy Scripture*, 13.

of Jesus and the apostles. On the basis of the evidence that we will present fully in the next chapter, there is a kind of symbiosis between revelation and its scriptural objectification that makes it impossible to separate them except as a thought experiment. "Then what advantage has the Jew? Or what is the value of circumcision? Much, in every way. For in the first place the Jews were entrusted with the oracles of God" (Rom. 3:1–2). Not merely did these writings bridge the generations from the time of past revelation to the present, but God intended writings that would do so in a way that would carry his own authority and fidelity.

There is too much testimony about the character of these biblical documents for us to set them aside and pretend to examine revelation apart from them. It would seem that God gave us Holy Scripture along with other products of his disclosure and intended for us to receive them as his written Word. Said otherwise, Scripture was not added on to biblical faith, but is intrinsic to it. Salvation, as far as one can trace it, is supported by documentation in which the covenantal obligations are spelled out and sustained. From the way in which Christ and the apostles received the Scripture principle from Judaism and regarded it as a product generated by divine revelation itself, the issue is settled for Christianity in principle. It could no more get rid of that Jewish legacy than get rid of Jesus himself.[30] God had spoken to his people Israel in the past, and the Scriptures were seen to be an extension of this modality of divine speech, revelation cast into written form for the direction of the church.[31] Living in such a universe, it was natural for the early Christians to receive new covenant scriptures in much the same way and move in the direction of a full Christian Bible.

Inspired Scripture constitutes the central place in the rich pattern of revelation given to humanity in Jesus Christ. It is a capstone and completion of it in the sense that it conveys in a reliable manner the burden of revelation secured in an appropriate form by God's own action. We view this development not as merely fortuitous and contingent, but as an essential component of the revelational activity God was intending and performing. In no way does this fact affect the sheer centrality of Jesus Christ in revelation or hinder the ministry of the Spirit. The Bible is a witness, although the primary one, to the revelation of God in the face of Jesus Christ. Christology, not Bibliology, occupies center stage in Christianity.

Holy Scripture is an important part of the revelational picture, but not the whole. It is a central form of the Word of God through which the

---

30. John W. Wenham (*Christ and the Bible*) supplies the abundant data on which this judgment rests.

31. On Scripture as a product of special revelation, see Ramm, *Special Revelation and the Word of God*, 161–87.

light reaches us. What a wonderful gift it is! The Bible is a durable and objective record of the burden of divine revelation, engendered by the Spirit, and given to bring us to the saving knowledge of God. It would have been possible, of course, for God to have the message passed under ordinary conditions, much the way our knowledge of Plato's thought depends on human authorship and transmission of texts. In that case, there is no inspired vehicle required. But such a course of action opens the door to an undetermined amount of dilution, distortion, corruption, and decay. It pleased God to add to his gifts the benefit of Holy Scripture, the literary objectification of his Word and revelation, so that we might have a light and a guide in matters of faith. Thus, we can say with the psalmist: "More to be desired are they than gold, even much fine gold; sweeter also than honey, and drippings of the honeycomb" (Ps. 19:10).

The Functions of Scripture

Just as revelation itself has many sides, so the Bible has a number of functions in the lives of believers. Most important of all, it is the medium of the Christian message. Like a telescope, it summons us to look through it more than at it and thus see the starry heavens. The most crucial question to ask is, Have you seen the stars? rather than, What do you think of the lens? Like a loudspeaker, the Bible invites us to hear the Word of God. What is urgent is to receive the Word that was given, not to focus on background noise. Like a lamp, the Scriptures make it possible for us to see; like bread, they satisfy our appetite and nourish us.

When we are discussing the topic of biblical authority academically, it is very important not to forget that the Bible is a means to an end, not an end in itself. It is a God-given vehicle that puts us in touch with the Light of the world and the Bread that came down from heaven. It is proper to think of the Bible in sacramental terms—as Rupert of Deutz did in the eleventh century: "As often as the Holy Spirit opens the mouths of apostles and prophets and even doctors, to preach the word of salvation, to unveil the mysteries of the Scriptures, the Lord opens the gates of heaven to rain down manna for us to eat. We are fed in our minds by reading and hearing the Word of God; we are fed in our mouths by eating the bread of eternal life from the table of the Lord, and drinking the chalice of eternal salvation."[32]

How barren it is to regard the Bible only as a study document when from the divine storehouse it nourishes believers in every aspect of their

32. Geoffrey Wainwright, *Doxology: The Praise of God in Worship, Doctrine, and Life*, 180.

being. The paper and the ink act as the outward and visible signs of an inward and invisible grace as faith toward God is invited and extended. It is wrong not only to treat the Bible as a merely human text, but also to treat it as a merely natural object that will yield its treasures to the scholar and learned exegete. It is more appropriate to think of it as the context in which to stand when you want to encounter God and have God address you. As Vatican II expressed it, "God is present in his Word, since it is he himself who speaks when the Holy Scriptures are read in church" (*Constitution on the Sacred Liturgy*, 7). We wait patiently and prayerfully in the midst of the biblical witnesses, expecting God to teach and lead us.[33] The problem is deeper than one that can be addressed with apologetic arguments about the text. How God speaks to us and leads us through Scripture is a mystery wrapped in the hidden operations of the Spirit in our hearts. The medium has to be empowered by the Spirit to deliver the message effectively.

The Bible performs a number of functions in addition to the basically religious function of leading us to the saving knowledge of God in Jesus Christ. We need all of them to be performed. Here are three of them. First, the Bible functions as a witness to the saving deeds of God and their significance for us. Having this witness in the durable form of writing ensures that the impact of the divine deeds continues to be felt. We recall Job's ironic words: "O that my words were written down! O that they were inscribed in a book!" (Job 19:23). Like John the Baptist, the Scriptures bear witness to Christ and keep the subject of God's gracious redemption ever before us. The Bible announces that light has come into the world, and human beings can walk in that light. When we say that the Bible is a witness, we do not deny that it is part of the revelation to which it witnesses; we simply make it clear what the burden of the Bible as witness is.[34]

Second, as a deposit of revealed truth, the Bible provides the church with a kind of charter or constitution by which to measure doctrine and practice. By setting forth central symbols, doctrinal commentary, and ethical instruction, the Scriptures reliably inform us of the basic issues that confront the church. They serve as a memory bank, reminding us continually of what God has said and done. As the psalmist said, "Let this be recorded for a generation to come, so that a people yet unborn may praise the LORD" (Ps. 102:18).

Because it is so easy to forget even basic principles that lead to salvation, the Bible exists to remind us of them. The Scriptures, in effect,

33. Brevard S. Childs (*Biblical Theology in Crisis*, chap. 7) has a good feeling for how this works.

34. Klaas Runia (*Karl Barth's Doctrine of Holy Scripture*, 17–56) critiques and corrects Barth's tendency to exclude the scriptural text from the revelation it attests.

draw a circle around us, indicating the ground where it is spiritually and theologically safe to walk and the field where it is nourishing to feed. They do not answer every question we may wish to put to them, but they do establish a fundamental orientation and direction for the community. They indicate the basic symbolic structure and norms by which we ought to be living. God has willed the Bible to be a charter document that will help to prevent the church from being swept away into human philosophy and vain deceit (Col. 2:8). By being faithful to the Scriptures, the church declares its desire to be rooted in the original and decisive revelation through Jesus Christ and the apostles that has been objectified in Holy Writ.[35]

Third, the Bible is the religious classic of Christianity. It uniquely embodies the style of faith and experience that characterizes Christians. Without in any way detracting from its other functions, the Bible enjoys pride of place in witnessing to the experience of the risen Lord. As such, it illumines and transforms the lives of those who place themselves under its authority. Experiential theologians are not wrong when they appeal to the Bible for inspiration and direction, for it does speak often of encounter with God and communion with God. But they are wrong insofar as they do not equally intend to receive the other aspects of biblical authority, such as its teaching, and when they construe "religious classic" to mean a merely human text with power to illumine experience.[36] The Bible is our religious classic, to be sure, and Christianity is inconceivable apart from it. It is preposterous to suppose that at this late date Christianity will be anything other than a scriptural religion.

The overall picture of revelation according to the Bible is quite clear. God is engaged in effecting the salvation of sinners and, in pursuance of this goal, has revealed himself and his plan. Revelational activity includes a great variety of products, including historical events, verbal communication, the astounding event of incarnation, and the outpouring of the Spirit; it has generated a scriptural witness to render effective in an ongoing way the revelation itself.[37] Rather than turning the gospel truth over to fallible human beings in its entirety, as he might have done, God has given the church the canonical Scriptures to help ensure the integrity of our knowledge of God and to prevent the proclamation from being lost or twisted beyond recognition. It is not that Christianity rests

35. Rahner (*Foundations of Christian Faith*, 369–78) develops the idea of Scripture as charter and constitution.

36. David Tracy (*Analogical Imagination*, chaps. 3–5) celebrates the Bible as the Christian classic, but we judge him not to mean more than that it is a human document lacking in reliable truth in all its parts.

37. Carl Henry (*God, Revelation, and Authority*, vols. 2–4) develops fifteen magnificent theses on revelation.

upon the foundation of the Bible (its foundation is Jesus Christ) as much as that Christian truth comes in and through the medium of Scripture and brings a doctrine of inspiration with it. As Athanasius said, the Bible is "a holy school of the knowledge of God and the conduct of the soul" (*Incarnation of the Word*, 12). In this manner, the objective side of revelation is secured by means of scriptural symbols and doctrines that set forth the shape of saving truth.

Is revelation only in the past, in the witness of the Bible, and in the present, in the leading of the Spirit? Is it altogether signed, sealed, and delivered? No, the New Testament indicates a mighty revelation that is to come ("the revealing of our Lord Jesus Christ") and a time when we shall know not only in part but fully (1 Cor. 1:7; 13:12). The Bible itself points forward to the full revelation when all flesh shall see the glory of the Lord (Isa. 40:5). At present, there are many questions that have to go unanswered, even though we have the norms of Scripture. We operate with a provisional revelation, a form of God's Word that, although valid and true, conceals as well as reveals and is destined to be replaced and supplanted by the fuller revelation that is coming. Although we look back for the gospel norms that bring us salvation, we also look forward to greater light and direction, both in this present age and in the age to come. Although loyal to the scriptural words from the past, we live and walk in the Spirit of God and anticipate being led into the fuller truth of Christ and to the coming of his kingdom.

If revelation has not been exhausted, even though normatively outlined in the Scriptures, then it is possible to hope that our understanding of the truth will grow and mature over the years. Now that we are in closer touch with the world religions, for example, and in a position to learn what is true in their experience of the God who addresses everyone, it may be possible to sharpen our understanding of what God is intending in the Bible. In the mutual struggle and competition of religions we can all be stimulated and challenged to learn more of the divine mystery. This need not relativize the absolute truth given in Jesus Christ that is, we firmly believe, the definitive revelation of God.

The Shift from Objective Content

The most pronounced feature of contemporary theology is the way in which it has moved away from the biblical and orthodox belief that revelation involves content (among other things). While the older view did not fail to recognize the subjective side of revelation, it did so in a balanced way, together with confidence in the message God gave through revelation. As is so clear in Augustine, Aquinas, Calvin, and Luther, God

communicated truth about himself and his plan in the course of revealing himself. Admittedly, in scholastic theology, revelation was too closely
identified with supernaturally given information and not sufficiently in-
clusive of symbolic and existential aspects, and it became too narrow. But
the conviction that God spoke to human beings as well as encountered
them in revelation was almost universal in Christian theology before the
Enlightenment. John Baillie has taken note of the shift from revelation
as information to revelation as inner experience or encounter, a much
vaguer concept and one more difficult to grasp.[38]

There are many modern views of revelation, but many of these tend
to share a reaction against content and opt for a more ethereal concept
that leaves people free to develop their own content. Piously declaring
that revelation is not something human beings can possess or control,
this view has delivered revelation over to autonomous human beings to
do precisely that. Instead of revelation coming from God in deed and
word, yielding norms and doctrines to guide the church, the emphasis
in many modern views is on the human contribution and construction.
Revelation wells up from human subjectivity, affecting the human spirit
in some fashion, but not issuing controls over what people think and
what they ought to do.[39]

The deists were among the first to attack the historic view of revelation. They maintained that reason alone was competent in the realm
of truth, and thus revelation ought to concern itself with questions of
piety and obedience. Revelation can add nothing to what we can know
by reason and does not offer valid information about the nature and
purposes of God. As Gotthold Lessing said, the truth of revelation is
intended for the heart and not the mind. Religion must be kept within
the limits of reason. Kant was prepared to say that practical reason can
supply certain convictions about God, the soul, and immortality, but
agreed that we cannot claim to know anything about the noumenal, and
therefore about God himself and God's Word. All human beings can do
is respond to the ethical side of revelation as if it came from God, even
though, strictly speaking, they cannot be sure that it did.

Friedrich Schleiermacher, the father of modern theology who was
reared as a pietist, connected revelation to the experiences of the heart.
We experience the feeling of absolute dependence, and this gives rise to
the idea of God, on whom we depend. Revelation does not break upon us
from without, but occurs as a transformation of human consciousness.
All religions, not only Christianity, rest on the same experiential base and

38. John Baillie, *Idea of Revelation in Recent Thought*, chap. 1.
39. Richard J. Coleman (*Issues of Theological Conflict*, chap. 3) compares and contrasts
the approaches made to revelation by liberals and conservatives.

can claim revelation in the same sense (although Schleiermacher would say that Christianity rests on a unique God-consciousness possessed by Jesus). The main point is that revelation does not involve content given by God, even though it leads to doctrinal formulations out of religious communion. These formulations are human in nature and authority; thus, revelation really has no infallible substance of truth content to offer. This is a radical departure from historic Christianity and a shift to revelation as inner experience.

For Albrecht Ritschl, too, although the emphasis is upon morality rather than experience, revelation involves no communication of information to be believed, but only the manifestation of an ethical ideal to lure us on to moral maturity. With Georg Hegel, the stress is upon philosophical theology, but the bottom line is the same: revelation bubbles up from below, offers only obscure symbolism, and needs to be supplemented by clear philosophical thought. The French liberal Auguste Sabatier identifies revelation with religious experience and finds it in all religions and particularly in Jesus. For him, it is a revelatory experience that is important and by which one knows oneself to be a child of God; it is an inner, subjective experience and develops with the evolution of the race. Although a subjective element is part of the biblical and historic pattern of revelation, this kind of modern position is totally opposed to a balanced picture and distorts it beyond recognition.[40]

Following World War I, a number of theologians, often called neo-orthodox or dialectical thinkers, made a similar shift from the objective in revelation, but in a new way that one might call neo-liberal. It consisted in thinking of revelation, not as a universal human capacity of mystical experience, but as an encounter with God and God's Word. Revelation can be captured neither in propositions, as in orthodoxy, nor in experience or rationality, as in liberalism. Utterly transcendent, God encounters the human subject by means of an experience of the Word, which faith recognizes to be present. Kierkegaard initiated this way of thinking about revelation in reaction to Hegel's rational approach and maintained that the truths of revelation are existential and paradoxical and could by no means be made to seem plausible. Like the mature Barth, Kierkegaard did not intend his emphasis to work any substantial change in orthodox beliefs. In Bultmann, however, it is plain that the emphasis had very radical implications indeed.

Believing that liberalism had neglected the otherness of God and revelation, Bultmann conceived of revelation as an eschatological event that encounters an individual in decision. In a famous paragraph in an essay

---

40. Dulles (*Revelation Theology*, chap. 3) sketches the history of the doctrine of revelation in the nineteenth century.

on the concept of revelation, he says: "What then has been revealed? Nothing at all, as far as the question concerning revelation asks for doctrines. . . . On the other hand, however, everything has been revealed, insofar as man's eyes are opened concerning his own existence and he is once again able to understand himself."[41] Revelation is taken to be personal and not at all propositional, and to involve nothing by way of the communication of infallible information. Therefore, Bultmann goes on to explore existential subjectivity rather than the content orthodoxy has always been interested in, and he cares little about the content of what the apostles teach or the history that the evangelists record. That simply does not matter except as it can be shown to relate to existential experience. The next logical step, of course, is to eliminate insistence upon the uniqueness of Christ in this wholly existential affair of revelation and dekerygmatize as well as demythologize the gospel.[42] Revelation, in such a view, belongs to a person's inner history and not to the outer realm of fact and truth.

The more typical way of abandoning the objectivity of revelation in our day is to think of it as expanding human consciousness in relation to what God is supposed to be doing in the secular movements of our time. God is not seen as the object of experience so much as mysteriously present in all human engagement in creative tasks. Revelation is correlated with the inner drive of the human spirit toward fuller awareness, raising these powers to a higher pitch of activity. It is present as direction and stimulus, not as truth and content, as transformation, not information. Somehow enlightened by God, the individual is enabled to speak with new confidence about the human situation and locate new solutions for its problems. Revelation serves to stimulate the imagination and enable us to break through to higher stages of human consciousness. Understandably, this way of thinking about revelation is not greatly impressed by an appeal to the actual teachings of the Bible where they are inconvenient to whatever secular insight and agenda are in vogue.[43]

In his *Models of Revelation*, Avery Dulles suggests that we think of revelation in terms of the set of symbols contained in the biblical documents, symbols like the cross and resurrection, which are richer than bare propositions in the way they reveal God and his plan. In saying this, it seems relatively clear that Dulles does not mean to cut these symbols off from their historical and propositional anchors within biblical revelation but to see them as more than facts and concepts, as indeed they

---

41. Rudolf Bultmann, *Existence and Faith*, 85.
42. Schubert M. Ogden (*Christ without Myth*) registers the same criticism.
43. See Dulles, *Models of Revelation*, chap. 7.

are. Yet there remains a certain vagueness about the symbols. Are we bound to the truth-symbols as infallibly defined by the Scriptures? It seems as if Dulles wishes to leave this somewhat vague, thus avoiding controversy on questions of miracle, in the case of events, and literalism, in the case of the doctrinal content.

If we extract the symbols from the Bible and divorce them from their scriptural and historical contexts, there is a real danger that they will be construed in arbitrary ways, undisciplined by the Bible itself. The cross becomes the symbol for all suffering poor, not of vicarious atonement; the resurrection comes to signify new life, not the bodily resurrection of Jesus. God is the symbol of the depth dimension in human life; he is not the living God who made heaven and earth. Although we appreciate the emphasis on God-given metaphors and agree that they are richer than bare propositions, we are nervous when seeing a theologian back away from their factual and cognitive content, given the widespread retreat from content in the liberal movement. In our modern context, we cannot afford to be vague about what we mean by revelation. Nothing less than the clarity of the gospel is at stake.

What has gone wrong in nonconservative modern theology across the board is the retreat from content-full revelation, with devastating results for dogmatic theology. Instead of seeing revelation in terms of a balance between the objective and the subjective, as the Bible invites us to and as historic theology always has, the modern emphasis practically drops the objective side (what has been revealed) and leaves revelation as a subjective matter (what is experienced).

The Reason for the Shift away from Content

One could explain the dramatic shift away from content by listing a series of factors that incline modern minds this way. They include: Immanuel Kant's dogma that one can have no knowledge of the transcendent such as the Bible claims to deliver; numerous objections to one or another of the biblical concepts; the belief in the fallibility of the Bible as propounded by liberal criticism; and rejection of the imperialism of any claim that makes Jesus the only way of salvation. But when it comes right down to it, there is only one reason for the rejection of content in revelation: many moderns are not willing to have dictated to them how they must think and how they must act.

The idea that human beings must approach God on God's terms, implied by the second commandment, not in ways they themselves define, is simply unacceptable to the autonomous people of today. We face such a resistance to what the Bible teaches that the battle necessarily takes place around the issue of revelation and inspiration. Although there are some real problems to face, the shift to the subjective in revelation is a simple reflection of the widespread unwillingness to bow to the God who speaks authoritatively in the Scriptures. The idea that the Bible has the right to limit human freedom of thought and action is hated by many. It must be crushed and eliminated.

For the humanistic liberals, it is subjective revelation or no revelation at all. The objective content is not simply overlooked and omitted, but despised and rejected. Although it is true that a better balance is needed, conversion is needed even more. A large number of modern theologians are not prepared to accept the restriction (as they would see it) represented by full biblical authority and are passionately dedicated to denying it. It is the content rather than the fact of special revelation that is objectionable. When the Bible says something pleasing to the ear of autonomous people, for example, that love is important or that Christians should be one and put aside all differences, they, like classical Christians, treat the Bible as an oracle. But when biblical content discloses such truths as vicarious atonement, a supernatural deity, miracles, prophecy, incarnation, resurrection, Satan, and other beliefs out of favor with modern people, then the Bible is denounced, reinterpreted, or reconstructed.

Bultmann, as usual, provides the easiest illustration of this because he is so honest and straightforward in his views. What the New Testament teaches he deems mythical and incredible for modern people. He believes that the only possible way to make any meaningful sense out of the material is to existentially reinterpret it. The content of the biblical gospel, according to Bultmann, can be traced to the mythology of Jewish apocalypticism and proto-Gnosticism and is not credible to us today. We have to strip away the mythological framework and get down to the existential power of the myths that offer us salvation through an encounter with God who "acted" (whatever that means for Bultmann) in Christ.[44] A few other examples show that Bultmann's general approach, which is in utter revolt against the biblically defined gospel, is representative rather than atypical.

Edward Farley is quite explicit in his third reason for rejecting the Scripture principle. It is bound to a theistic way of viewing reality that he finds unacceptable. The problem of evil and the reality of human freedom rule out the existence of a God such as is presupposed by the biblical concept of revelation and inspiration.[45] The school of process philosophy determines results from supposedly rational procedures and does not

44. Rudolf Bultmann, *Kerygma and Myth*, chap. 1.
45. Farley, *Ecclesial Reflection*, chap. 7.

hesitate to deny Scripture if the text proves unsuitable.[46] In liberation theology, there is enthusiasm for the revolutionary, prophetic line of thinking uncovered from the exodus or from one way of reading the Jesus story, but there is little reluctance to reject and denounce those parts of the Bible that jeopardize desirable conclusions. Norman Gottwald, for example, celebrates the Mosaic liberation trajectory embodied in an early Israelite peasant revolt, but is highly critical of the royal consolidation under David when all of this was suppressed and forgotton.[47] Paul D. Hanson is eager to see God as "dynamic transcendence," which means not tying him down to old scriptural pronouncements, but leaving him free to be up to date and flexible.[48]

The central point is that the Bible teaches things that modern people have difficulty receiving. Many conclude that the only way to deal with this is to qualify the Bible's authority and deny its infallibility. After all, how can we believe in creation and fall after Darwin? How can we accept the Bible's teachings concerning women and homosexuality? How can we take seriously the incarnation and salvation through the blood of Christ alone? The cleanest way to deal with all these difficulties is to retreat from the notion that God's revelation involves necessary and trustworthy content. This is what a host of modern theologians have done.

Although the cost is high (the entire basis of doctrinal and ethical theology in any traditional sense disappears), the liberal theologians have considered it worth paying. This leaves them free to pursue doctrines of their own making and preference. The great roadblock, the full authority of the Bible, no longer stands in their way to keep their subjectivity in line. Construing revelation as an event without binding content allows no real chance for one's own doctrinal inventions to be refuted or considered heretical, since the basis for any such judgment has been eliminated.

Our harsh criticism of what we see as an unworthy retreat from God's truth does not mean that we are unsympathetic with the difficulties in believing certain aspects of biblical and traditional church teachings. We do not want people to think that they must swallow orthodox concepts just because they are traditional. We believe that one must be intellectually honest and that faith's honest questions ought to be sensitively addressed. What we oppose is handing over to autonomous human beings the right to specify the conditions of their faith in God. That right belongs to God alone.

46. See the critique by Royce G. Gruenler, *Inexhaustible God*.
47. Norman K. Gottwald, *Tribes of Yahweh*.
48. Paul D. Hanson, *Dynamic Transcendence*.

Real Revelation with Salvation Intent

In the shift away from the objective content of revelation, the truth foundations of the Christian gospel are swept away and the validity of the gospel is placed in doubt. We face a dilemma not unlike the one Luther faced: Are the gospel and salvation based on the Word and work of God or founded on human wisdom and church tradition? Is Christian theology a clear rendition of the Word of God given in the Scriptures, or is it the highest and best of human opinions?

Emphasizing the objective side of revelation and the authority of the Bible has nothing to do with bibliolatry or rationalism. It has to do with keeping the church securely founded on the apostolic scriptural witness that is essential to its life and work. The church is in danger when it no longer hears the message of the Bible as authoritative. It soon forgets what it believes and what its purpose is in the world, making it easy prey for whatever philosophy is dominant at the moment. Everything becomes blurred when the prophets and apostles fall silent.[49]

Therefore, we call for a return to the biblical pattern of revelation, which includes content-full communication as well as personal communion. The Bible presents the acts of God and the response of faith, the words of God and the call to obedience, the objective and the subjective. It tells us about God and brings us to God. We have no interest in downplaying the subjective dimension of revelation. Quite the contrary, we consider the work of the Spirit absolutely crucial for recognizing and understanding revelation. What concerns us at present is the way in which so many modern theologians have walked away from the sure content of the Christian gospel revealed in the Bible. Revelation, according to the Bible and historic theology, is not merely subjective and existential, but a meaningful disclosure of the gracious God who acts and speaks. It supplies us with crucial perspectives about the character and purposes of God, given in creaturely modalities that we can understand and that enable people to be reconciled to God. Revelation enables us to become acquainted with God so that we might meet and know him. It is critically important not to lose this conviction.

The Bible presupposes that God is able to reveal himself and specific truth about divine plans for us. God has done this preeminently in Jesus Christ and in other forms of speech and historical action. There is every reason to include, not exclude, the Bible as a particular and essential form of the pattern of revelation. Not only have countless Christians experienced the Bible as a special vehicle of the knowledge of God and

---

49. James D. Smart (*Strange Silence of the Bible in the Church*, 10) considers this the crisis underlying all other crises the church faces.

the occasion of freshly encountering God and learning about him, but the pattern of revelation as presented in the Bible everywhere assumes that God has communicated to us in human speech, thus rendering the relationship between God and people fully personal. As Howard Marshall puts it, "To say that God cannot make use of words and statements to reveal himself is to go against all that we know of persons and how they relate to one another."[50]

Verbal communication is the marvel of human existence. The capacity to give and receive meaning by means of language is a priceless gift. It enables us to encode what we want to communicate and makes possible rich cultural cooperation and development. That God might employ language in his revelation to us is something we would hope for. That God has actually done so is something that Christians can only celebrate! God has done so, however, not primarily to convey a catalog of religious information as such. The revelational goal is not perfect religious thought, but wholeness of life renewed in Jesus Christ by the Spirit.

As William Abraham has ably shown, there has been an unfortunate cultural shift across church history from "canon" to "criterion," from "ecclesial canonicity" to "epistemic normativity." Rather than the Bible being essentially "a criterion of rationality," an "epistemic norm," the early church saw the Bible more ecclesially as a means of grace, as revered materials divinely provided and intended as a mode of initiating persons into actually sharing the divine life. Wisely, Abraham hopes "to recover a way of thinking about canon which is soteriological rather than epistemological in outlook."[51]

The biblical text is not an end in itself. While it contains vital content absolutely crucial to Christian faith, content not to be reduced to vacuous symbol or existential stimulation, its central function is to make us wise unto salvation. Beyond the issue of information, the central function of Scripture is to lead to our spiritual transformation.

---

50. I. Howard Marshall, *Biblical Inspiration*, 15.

51. William J. Abraham, *Canon and Criterion in Christian Theology*, 8, 27, 466. R. Larry Shelton reports: "Wesleyans have seen Scripture as a 'means of grace' through which the Spirit functions to carry on the life-giving ministry of Christ" (in *Reading the Bible in Wesleyan Ways*, ed. Callen and Thompson, 11).

The Biblical Witness

Having sketched the pattern of revelation with broad strokes and having suggested that it is proper to think of the Bible as a product of revelation and a component of God's revealing activity, we now want to focus on the matter of the greatest interest to us in this book. We will look in greater detail at the evidence that supports the concept of a Scripture principle. What sort of doctrine of inspiration is supported by the Bible's own witness to itself?

There are really two important questions for us to answer. The first, the more general one, has to do with the church's decision to accept the bipartite (Old and New Testaments) Christian Bible as the canon of inspired Scripture, a decision already reached by Irenaeus by AD 200. Was this momentous decision a sound and good one, and should the church today affirm it? It could be argued that it was not appropriate for the Christian community to accept as Scripture the Old Testament, which in some ways suits the Jewish community better in that it presupposes an ethnic group, not the universal community gathered around Jesus Christ. It may have been natural for the earliest Christians who were Jewish to accept the Old Testament as inspired Scripture, but does it follow that the church today also ought to do so?

Why would a faith community under grace want to place itself under the Old Testament law? Furthermore, what evidence is there that Jesus and the apostles anticipated a New Testament canon or expected Christianity to become a religion of a book? Of course, there were historical factors that led the later generations of Christians to a bipartite Scripture principle, but that does not require us to follow suit. It may be that a Christianity that viewed the New Testament as a human collection and not an inspired canon would be in a better position to understand the gospel and proclaim it for our time. Can the Bible itself help us decide whether the church had been right and was wise to accept the Old and New Testaments as the written body of the Scripture principle?

The second, more specific question relates to the kind of Scripture principle the Bible commits us to. Is the Christian idea of biblical inspiration and authority identical to the Judaic understanding, or different? Does it involve strict inerrancy of detail and leveling of all the material, or is it more flexible? Classical Christians agree on the validity and importance of the Scripture principle, but they do not agree on precisely what is entailed by it.

In order to find some answers to these questions, we will need to sift carefully through biblical teaching on a Scripture principle. Because most of us who conduct such investigations already have convictions about the Bible, the challenge is to approach the data fairly and openly. Sadly, while it is common to judge that the liberals refuse to see the strong claims in the Bible in favor of the Scripture principle, it often is not recognized that conservatives quote the Bible's claims in the interests of their own preset dogma of biblical inerrancy.[1] But what is the biblical witness when separated as much as possible from preset dogmas on the matter?

We will not attempt a technical presentation of the biblical witness, but we will instead aim at a judicious grasp of the overall picture. We also will try to be quite scrupulous in noting what certain verses do and do not claim, and observe where they occur in the progressive development of the biblical account. Further, we are interested in the use of Scripture as well as the doctrine of Scripture as displayed in the Bible. Too often the valuable evidence contained in the way the New Testament

---

1. Norman L. Geisler (*Decide for Yourself*, chap. 1) gives a good example of how not to sift the evidence in this case. He solicits a list of proof texts scattered here and there in the Bible and leaves the impression that one can determine the "Bible's view of the Bible" from reading them. Geisler knows the goal he has to reach and cites a few texts that give the impression that he reached it inductively. The appearance is inductive; the reality is deductive.

writers handle the Old Testament is passed over in this connection, as if all that needed to be consulted were the so-called doctrinal verses. But the evidence of actual use must not be passed over in this kind of study because it fills out what the direct claims were taken to mean by those who made them and prevents us from speculating about their meaning in the abstract and in the interests of our own systematic theology.[2]

The ground can be covered most economically by considering three areas of evidence: (1) the Old Testament witness to "itself"; (2) the New Testament witness to the Old Testament; and (3) the New Testament witness to "itself." We put "itself" in quotes because we recognize that the Old Testament did not exist as a formal canon at the time its books bore the witness to which we refer, nor did the New Testament.

The Old Testament Witness to Itself

In the Old Testament, we find strong indications of a canonical process in motion. Various kinds of writings are surfacing and beginning to be shaped into a Scripture principle. Almost from the first, in the ministry of Moses and the Sinaitic covenant, a document is forming that will serve as a vehicle of religious and social duration for Israel, the people of God. Since this vehicle is something structural and not accidental, it was natural for the Jews of a later date to conclude that God had been giving them his Word in the form of written texts. Of course, there are many questions the books of the Old Testament do not answer for us. For instance: Which books precisely? Which text of each? What kind of authority? Why are biblical authors often anonymous? Nevertheless, the Scripture principle as we now know it is firmly rooted in this rudimentary way in the Old Testament.[3]

Of particular importance is the way the figure of Moses is presented in the Pentateuch. He is the prophet of God and mediator of God's law. "With him I [God] speak face to face—clearly, not in riddles" (Num. 12:8). Moses was God's prophet by whom the Lord brought Israel out of Egypt (Hosea 12:13) and the first and most eminent spokesperson in a series of prophets who would follow (Deut. 18:15–22). He is described as writing down the law of God in a book as a permanent testimony to Israel (Deut. 31:24–29). Through Moses, as Paul would later say, Israel received the oracles of God (Rom. 3:2). Moses was a mediator of reve-

2. In his stimulating article "The Authority of Scripture according to Scripture," (222n62), James D. G. Dunn maintains, "in order to clarify what the doctrinal passages mean, we must observe how Jesus and the NT authors used the OT."

3. Brevard Childs has established this point with force and conviction in *Introduction to the Old Testament as Scripture*.

lation, and writing down the Word of the Lord was an integral part of his office. At Sinai, he wrote down the words of the Lord, called the Book of the Covenant, and this document attested the treaty between God and Israel, as was the custom in the suzerainty treaties of the period.[4] This would seem plainly to be the root and origin of the later Scripture principle, which cannot be written off as a late and extraneous decision of the church.

Later books in the Hebrew Bible refer to Moses as the author of written revelation. This is particularly true of the postexilic books (Chronicles, Ezra, and Nehemiah), which appeal to the law or the book of Moses as a written text bearing divine authority. Psalm 119 is a lengthy eulogy to these Scriptures and breathes a spirit of joy and gratitude because of the gift of God in this respect. Preexilic historical books also refer to Moses, but less often to his literary activity, which the preexilic prophets never refer to explicitly.

Evidently, the Pentateuch was formed over many centuries, and Moses, although not the author of it in at least its final form, was the instigator of the literary activity that produced it.[5] It is not necessary for our present purposes to declare a firm opinion on the authorship of the Pentateuch, which is a matter of debate among Scripture specialists. It remains true, in any case, that Moses is said to have mediated a revelation and a covenant that issued in an authoritative document. This is witness to the fact that Israel was conscious of God giving the nation written Scriptures. The Scripture principle, then, is native, not alien, to the basic nature of Israel's relationship with God, a point of utmost importance.

Given the presence of a document of revelation, it does not follow that it is altogether immutable and inflexible. Treaty documents of the ancient world were authoritative for the original circumstances, but they could be altered at the behest of the sovereign. The Lord, in this case, was free to revise or update treaty provisions as need be.[6] We see such alteration in the two versions of the Decalogue and in the filling out of the Pentateuch over time as the original Mosaic nucleus was expanded. It is also implied by the manner in which the classical prophets interpreted the Mosaic material in fresh ways and applied it to new situations. Obviously, they did not consider the text closed to new points of signification arising from fresh reflections of their own. The Old Testament, in fact, does not support in every respect the Judaic Scripture principle, which came to involve rigid immutability. From the promise to Abraham to bless all

4. Meredith G. Kline, *Treaty of the Great King*.

5. A moderate, sensible theory is offered by William S. LaSor, David A. Hubbard, and Frederic W. Bush in *Old Testament Survey*, chap. 6.

6. Meredith G. Kline (*Structure of Biblical Authority*) speaks about the updating of treaty documents.

the nations through the prophetic anticipation of a new covenant and changes in the people's relationship with God in the messianic era, we have a forward-looking and revisable trajectory, one open to the future. It is not a closed text, complete and forever sufficient in itself.

In the prophets of the Old Testament, we encounter a group of people who saw themselves, in the tradition of Moses, able to mediate God's Word to the people. They were conscious of having received a calling and commission from God and spoke out boldly the words God gave them. They were servants to whom the Lord had revealed his secrets (Amos 3:7). They believed that God had put his words in their mouths and that they stood in the council of the Lord (Jer. 1:9; 23:22). They spoke the very word of God to the house of Israel (Ezek. 2:1–7). They saw themselves not as radical innovators but as ministers of the Mosaic covenant given much earlier, and their responsibility was to call the people back to the covenant agreement whose conditions they were forsaking. One could call them conservatives, concerned to call the people back to the original law of God (Hosea 4:1–2). Surely, what we have here is a strong claim to verbal revelation, a claim that bears directly upon our subject.

Given the assumption of a verbal revelation, a few qualifications are in order. First, when Jeremiah claims that his message is of God, it is not fair to lift this claim out of context and apply it arbitrarily to another book, like Chronicles, that Jeremiah does not have in view. Often conservatives, eager to enhance their belief, transfer to other texts strong claims originally referring to specific prophetic oracles. This is not responsible practice.

Second, even though the prophets claim divine authority for their messages, a certain human element often appears in them as well. Micah predicted the fall of Jerusalem at the hands of the Assyrians (Mic. 3:12), but this was not to happen, because the Lord intervened to save the city (Isa. 37:35), a point noted later in the trials of Jeremiah (Jer. 26:19). Because of the freedom of God, even a clear prophecy can turn out to be void if God decides not to do the thing predicted. The prophets did not have so divine a viewpoint as to make their words absolute.

Third, the claims that the prophets make refer primarily to their preached oracles, not to the texts we now have. They usually were preachers rather than writers, as far as we can tell. References to their written work are rare. We do not know exactly how the preaching of Amos or Hosea reached written form, including whether they or others took responsibility for the eventual writing. Isaiah instructs his disciples to preserve the testimony for a future time (8:16; 30:8). Jeremiah had Baruch write down his words on a scroll (Jer. 36:2, 4, 8), but the book of Jeremiah contains more than that, including connecting tissues in the form of historical narratives, as do Amos and Isaiah. It is impossible to avoid the conclusion that people other than the prophets themselves played a role in shaping the scriptural documents that incorporate the originally preached prophetic messages, a role that would have included decisions about ordering the material and precise wording to bring out the essential thrust.

We know virtually nothing about these people who worked on Scripture. We can think of them as faithful disciples who wanted to be sure that the burden of the prophets was remembered in the future. From internal evidence, it would seem likely that they felt free to adapt some of the oracles to new situations in their ordering and phrasing of the material. In any case, the prophetic claim to verbal inspiration does not apply directly to their important work, which must be considered in some other way.

Our own view is that the canonical momentum is clear enough to justify seeing the work of later writers in terms of the gifts of God to Israel by anonymous scribes who shaped and consolidated the texts. The popular idea that biblical books were normally the work of a single author writing under the inspiration of God does not fit the complexity of many biblical books that seem to have multiple authorships. We should rid our minds of the notion that the scriptural writers wanted to make a name for themselves and wrote as individual authors rather than as representatives and servants of the community.

Divine inspiration marshals more than the short list of famous writers we can name. It calls into service a whole company of gifted persons who contributed in different ways to the ultimate product, and did so anonymously for the most part. We must be satisfied with a condition of their lower visibility.[7] This fact notwithstanding, the crucial point remains that in the prophets we have a very strong claim to verbal revelation in human language and one that supports the Scripture principle in a very obvious if not unlimited way.

In the so-called Writings of the Hebrew Bible—books such as Psalms, Job, Proverbs, and Ecclesiastes—there are far fewer claims of divine revelation, only occasional references at best. There is nothing to compare with the claims we saw in the Pentateuch and the Prophets. The author of Ecclesiastes considered himself a wise teacher, a writer of words of truth, but nothing more (12:9). Many readers have considered this book a product of secular experience—see even the original Scofield Bible notes. The writer of Job likely would have been astonished to find his book later placed alongside the law of Moses and the prophecies of Jeremiah. Probably the sages of Proverbs would resist the suggestion

---

7. Bruce Vawter (*Biblical Inspiration*, 104–13) discusses anonymity in the context of a social concept of inspiration.

that their aphorisms are legally binding in the way that the Ten Commandments are. They would not have considered their work revelation in the manner of the other writings.

The point is that in the Old Testament collection there are different kinds of literature, some that make a powerful claim to divine origin and others that do not, some that stand on the high ground of revelation and others that occupy a lower position. Conservatives in particular need to realize that not all Scripture is prophetic oracle or Decalogue. Many texts express the Word of God, but some are content to perform lowlier tasks, such as giving utterance to a spiritual struggle or expressing an honest doubt.

From the Writings can be learned two lessons in regard to the Scripture principle. First, we do not know exactly why or how some of the books of the Old Testament came to be included in that canon. We can only assume that the canonical trajectory that is visible elsewhere in the Testament is at work here too and that God guided his people in the recognition of his work. Second, we must be prepared to allow biblical books to retain their particular character and claim and not force them into any other mold. It is proper to regard Ecclesiastes as God-given Scripture, but it should not be read like Amos or Deuteronomy. We must assess from Ecclesiastes itself what claim the author wishes to make and read it accordingly. This particular book does not assume the form of divine command, and it must not be distorted in that direction.

It is plain from reading Proverbs that the intent of the book is not to formulate divine commandments but to advance wise counsel for the practical living out of faith. Without doubt, the proverb writers and the psalm singers believed that their work conveyed truth about God and his will, and their preservation in the canon endorses this conviction. But the truth that calls us to dialogue and decision is a different kind of truth from the truth of command and demand. It is essential that we read the literature appropriately as it was actually intended and not try to change and improve it.

In summation, the Old Testament witness to itself yields several insights. First, a process of Scripture collection and formation was in motion from the very beginning of Israel's existence, which proves that the later Scripture principle is not a distortion or misdevelopment but a predictable result of the momentum of Israel's faith. It is irresponsible for modern scholars to disregard this fact and refuse to take seriously the fact that these documents are properly taken as the normative Scriptures of Israel, not just pieces of ancient literature. The claim for the authority of Scripture is as good as the claim for God revealing himself in the history and experience of Israel. If we accept one, we should accept the other as well. Israel's awareness of being called to be the people of the Lord is congruent with the awareness of being in possession of Scriptures that convey the knowledge of the Lord's will. The Scripture principle is inherent in the faith of Israel.

Second, just as the ways of God in general are inscrutable (Rom. 11:33), so in the provision of Scripture there is much that we cannot observe now. The community of faith played a role in shaping and defining the Old Testament. Many anonymous persons were active in its preparation. We cannot think of the inspiration of the text in simplistic terms. Its locus must have been much wider than just a special illumination of the final redactor. The formation of Scripture is almost indistinguishable from the formation of tradition in Israel, and its inspiration must have been a process involving a great many people and taking place over a longer span of time than we have been accustomed to thinking. To do justice to the biblical text, we have to posit God's leading in its preparation in ways that do not lie on the surface for easy viewing. The final composition, crucial though it is, was not the only important moment in the event of inspiration.

Third, given the diversity in claims noted, we have to distinguish between kinds and degrees of inspiration. The Old Testament contains within it many kinds of writing—poetry, proverb, law, oracle, story, parable, and prayer. They are not all alike and do not carry truth in exactly the same way. The speech of Deborah in Judges stands on a different plane than the speeches of Ezekiel. In one text God may be the speaker; in another text human advice seems to be offered. The Bible, as the very term ("books") implies, is a library, a God-given reader for the people of God. Inspiration does not secure only one kind of text, but many kinds. Out of respect for them all, we need to make proper distinctions and be careful how we read and listen. Like the church, the Bible resembles a body having many members, and not all of them are the same. They perform different functions, some humbler, some nobler. Our aim should be to take the record in its entirety, comparing one part with another, to come up with the truth in its fullness.

The New Testament Witness to the Old Testament

By the time of the New Testament, the Scripture principle was firmly established in Jewish minds and was part of the symbolic universe of the early Christians. The writers of the New Testament cite the Old Testament frequently as support and illustration of their own teachings. Their minds were steeped in the language and thought of the Scriptures, and they expressed the gospel of Christ in these terms.

What understanding of the Old Testament did they hold that led them to do this? To answer this question exhaustively, one ought to examine each New Testament book critically, taking note of every nuance. There are differences in the way in which Matthew, the author of Hebrews, Paul, and John use the Old Testament. But there is a common pattern underlying the whole. It involves standing a little farther back from the text than the biblical specialists do and getting a view of the whole that is important for our purposes here.

When we look at what Jesus and the apostles say about Scripture and take account of how they use it, we see a clearly dialectical attitude. On the one hand, they endorse it as the written Word of God, and on the other, they read and interpret it as if it were a pre-messianic text coming to fulfillment in their time. They endorse the Old Testament in a messianically qualified way. This is nicely summarized in a saying of Jesus: "Do not think that I have come to abolish the law or the prophets; I have come not to abolish but to fulfill" (Matt. 5:17). Being no heretic, Jesus endorsed the Scriptures of the covenant, but also being God's emissary of the new age, he explained what God was now doing through him as their fulfillment. This saying of Jesus represents the dialectic everywhere evident.[8] As Jews, the earliest Christian believers accepted the Old Testament as inspired Scripture, and as messianic Jews, in their use of it they qualified it in relation to the new phase of God's kingdom that had dawned. The Old Testament is the written Word of God intended to be read in the light of Jesus Christ.

This dialectic reveals why it is so important not to neglect either the doctrinal verses or the use to which the Old Testament text is put by the New Testament authors. If we look only at the claims, we will end up thinking that Jesus is some kind of Pharisee in the rigidity of his attitude. If, on the other hand, we examine only his use of the text, we may gain the impression that he is the first liberal Christian, critiquing and correcting the Bible at every turn. The fact is that Jesus and the New Testament writers respected the Old Testament text enormously as God's written Word and qualified it only in view of the new messianic situation. Jesus is a progressive-conservative in a sense and should not be used by any modern church party in a dishonest way. B. B. Warfield uses Jesus to pitch the doctrine of inspiration too high, and Ernst Käsemann uses him to pitch it too low. To get it right, let us look at all the data.

The Endorsement of the Old Testament

Let us look first at the way in which Jesus and the apostles endorsed the divine authority of the Hebrew Scriptures. Jesus himself believed

8. Joachim Jeremias, *New Testament Theology*, 27, 82–85.

that the will of God was revealed in the Scriptures, which stood above all merely human tradition. He criticized the Pharisees harshly for making the written Word of God void through their traditions (Mark 7:1–13). He believed that the Scriptures must be fulfilled and that they were being fulfilled in his ministry (Luke 4:21). He parried the temptations of Satan by appealing to the Scriptures and quoted from them as if God were speaking the very words (Matt. 4:4–10; 19:4–5). That Jesus possessed a remarkable sense of his own authority under God only underlines the impressiveness of this attitude. It seems clear that respect for Scripture was not something he feigned because people in his day shared it; rather, it was a conviction that he cherished.

Jesus used the Scriptures in many distinctive ways, just as we do today. Sometimes he cited texts because they were familiar to him and they said what he wanted to say, like the echo of Isaiah 5 in his parable of the wicked tenants (Mark 12:1–12), or the allusion to Isaiah 35 and 61 in his answer to the disciples of John the Baptist (Matt. 11:5). Then there was a confirmatory use, by which he sought to show how things that were happening now fulfilled the Old Testament in some important way, as when the response to his parables evoked a reference to Isaiah's experience of the same blindness (Matt. 13:10–17; Isa. 6) or when his sermon at Nazareth included a pointed reference to Isaiah 61 (Luke 4:16–21).

There was also an argumentative use of Scripture, where a text was used to prove a point, as in the temptation narratives when Jesus quoted the Bible to refute Satan (Matt. 4), or when Jesus cited the law itself in order to answer the question about the greatest commandment (Matt. 22:37, 39). He also used the Old Testament in a challenging way, in polemical contexts, to force an issue of decision: Have you not read? What do you think? What do you make of this? (Mark 2:25; 12:10, 26). Jesus used the Old Testament to turn the tables on his opponents. Always he appealed to the Scriptures as the resource the Father had given Israel as his Word.[9]

Although we do not wish to blunt the force of this point, recent polemics have distorted it in the direction either of denying or exaggerating it. In reference to the latter tendency, we would like to add some points of clarification and caution to guard against misusing the evidence. First, Jesus's quotations from the Old Testament do not reveal a meticulous and mechanical concern for the original text, suggesting that for Jesus it was the message conveyed rather than the precise wording that con-

9. John A. T. Robinson, "Did Jesus Have a Distinctive Use of Scripture?" in *Christological Perspectives*, ed. Robert F. Berkey and Sarah A. Edwards, 49–57; R. T. France, *Jesus and the Old Testament*.

cerned him. Second, although grateful for what God had said to past
generations in the Scriptures, Jesus was particularly excited about what
God was doing and saying in the present. Anyone in the kingdom, he
said, was greater than the greatest prophet of God in the past (Matt.
11:11). Third, although we do not believe that Jesus ever broke the law
or intended to, he was more concerned to be loving than to be seen as
strictly adhering to the letter of the law. Healing on the Sabbath and
letting his disciples pick a few heads of grain to eat on that holy day did
not constitute breaking the Sabbath for Jesus. He certainly knew that
it did mean that for others who concentrated on the details of legal observance. For him, however, the Word of God was gospel, not legalistic
code, and he resisted handling it in any other way.

Fourth, the evidence does not permit calling on Jesus of Nazareth to
settle the modern debate over biblical inerrancy. This discussion involves
whether in the original autographs of Scripture any mistakes occur and
what mistakes would qualify as errors. Although we do not consider this
a foolish debate in itself, we do object to the often repeated claim that
Jesus taught the answer to it, as if he were on one side against the other.
Of course, Jesus had complete confidence in the Scriptures, and even
appealed to them for such an obscure fact as the fate of Lot's wife; but
it is stretching the evidence to suggest that Jesus can be appealed to in
order to settle a debate over questions of original autographs, authorial
intention, the status of the New Testament—issues not directly addressed
by him. These are questions that we have to deal with and that cannot
be short-circuited by an anachronistic appeal to Jesus.

Fifth, along similar lines, the conservative party cannot capture the
authority of Jesus in disputes over biblical criticism, although it is tempting to try. Because Jesus cites a psalm of David or a prophecy from the
book of Isaiah, it does not follow that he is placing his divine authority
on the line for the precise literary authorship of these texts. In quoting
them, Jesus always calls attention to what the Scriptures teach and not
how they came to be written in the final redaction. It is an abuse of
Jesus's authority to use it for our partisan purposes. It is more natural
to think that when Jesus cites the Old Testament, he does so according
to the accepted conventions of his time and not in order to refute some
aspect of higher critical speculation in modern times. We object to any
such misuse of Jesus's authority. The literary composition of Isaiah, for
instance, is an issue to be settled by Old Testament scholars weighing the
evidence, not by a spurious appeal to unrelated comments of Jesus.

There is one further mistake to avoid when making an appeal to Jesus's
high view of the Old Testament. It is the temptation to reverse the proper
relationship between Jesus and the text. Conservatives regularly use Christ's
witness to the Scriptures as a kind of irrefutable proof of their position.

"He said it—do you believe it?" It is as though Jesus were a kind of John the Baptist witnessing to something even higher than himself and wanting to be the key link in a chain of theological logic. In fact, it is the other way around. The Scriptures bear witness to Christ and derive their authority for Christians from that fact (John 5:39). Of course, Jesus's view of the Bible is important for us when we try to ascertain what our own view should be, but it should not be used as an independent proof to establish objectively the authority of the Scriptures apart from faith in Jesus.[10]

Like Jesus, the apostles also make a clear endorsement of the Old Testament, continually quoting from it as the Word of God. The Scriptures are "inspired by God" (2 Tim. 3:16) and are called the "oracles of God" (Rom. 3:2) and "prophetic" (Rom. 1:2; 16:26–27). They can be represented as the Spirit speaking (Heb. 3:7). At the same time, we must not exaggerate the evidence. Paul can write Romans and Galatians without bothering to discuss a doctrine of Scripture. Even in a text like 2 Timothy 3:16, there is no mention of original autographs or inerrancy or anything theoretical. The whole emphasis is on the practical profitability of the copy of the Old Testament that Timothy was using. The comments are very low key and do nothing to prove the strict conservative view of "inerrancy." Paul does not discuss the nature of inspiration or the degree to which the Scriptures are reliable in order to achieve their practical goal. He is not interested in our modern debates about inerrancy and sticks to the profitability of the Scriptures in the practical realm. The only way 2 Timothy 3:16 can be used as a proof text for the modern discussion of inerrancy is by first reading a modern view back into it.

To take another case, when Peter affirms that prophecy originated not in the human mind but from the impulse of the Spirit, he is referring to the prophecies uttered and then to the prophetic Scriptures, but not to Scripture in general, much of which is not prophetic. He is not making a judgment about the entire Old Testament, and it is a considerable twisting of his words to apply them to the whole Christian Bible. Nor should we be too quick to conclude that when the phrase "it is written" is employed, it necessarily means that God is speaking. Paul uses the formula in 1 Corinthians 3:19 in citing a speech of Eliphaz, one of Job's friends who did not always tell the truth. We need to be fair and accurate in our use of this material.

Misuse aside, it is of the utmost importance that we recognize that, for Jesus and the apostles, the Old Testament is God's written Word and we ought to acknowledge it. If Jesus's authority means anything to us, then it means something here.

---

10. James Barr (*Fundamentalism*, 72–85) registers an effective protest against this practice.

The Messianic Qualification of the Old Testament

Looking at the other side of the dialectic, let us consider the messianic qualification that Jesus and the apostles placed on the Old Testament. They saw the text structured around the promise of God that was in the process of being fulfilled in the coming of the Christ. They viewed its authority not as an unconditional work standing alone but as a stage in God's revelation moving toward the coming of the Messiah and the divine kingdom. In this way they identified themes of continuity, areas of fulfillment, and even points of negation. Jesus could do this because of his sense of unique sonship and the coming of the new age in which ears were blessed to hear what the prophets had longed for (Matt. 13:16–17).

Let us consider a few concrete examples of the messianic use of the Old Testament. Jesus knew what God's original intention for marriage was and felt free to declare null and void the Mosaic permission of divorce in Deuteronomy 24. He could say that the law of Moses was provisional, temporary, and no longer in effect (Matt. 19:3–9). In his Nazareth sermon, Jesus dropped out the whole element of judgment in a text he was using (Isa. 61:1–2) because it was the other half of the text that was relevant and true for the current situation (Luke 4:18–19). He would not accept criticism of his Sabbath activities because he was sure of what God had in mind in ordaining the Sabbath and thus how it should be observed (Mark 2:27–28).

Jesus said that anger was as bad as murder and that oaths were not to be used anymore. He seemed to critique the tradition of clean and unclean foods. It is important, of course, not to misunderstand what Jesus was doing. It would be a travesty to depict him as anti-Torah in the slightest. He reinterpreted but did not break any of the commandments. He could distinguish between the greatest commandments and the slightest, and then say, "You ought to do the one without neglecting the other" (Matt. 23:23 paraphrased). Nevertheless, without ever denying that the Scriptures were the Word of God when they were given, Jesus could say they were not the Word of God to the present situation, in which the kingdom of God was coming near. He recognized a covenant relativity in relation to certain texts and thus shocked some of his hearers who had no room for such a limitation.

What Jesus was doing was reading the Scriptures in the context of the dawning kingdom of God and seeing them in the light of this wonderful fulfillment. Divine revelation was being updated and advanced before people's eyes, and hidden depths of the Scriptures were coming to light. Such messianic exegesis was another way of raising the christological question: "Who do you say that I am?" (Matt. 16:15). If people granted that Jesus was the Coming One, they would see the new dimensions he was pointing to in the text; but if they did not, they would refuse both him and his exegesis. Although they knew the Scriptures well, certain Pharisees would not take his claim seriously and could not see what the Scriptures were really saying (John 5:39–40). Focused on the text as immutable object, they were not open to consider the possibility of a fulfillment that might transcend their traditional reading.

Jesus endorsed the Old Testament, but he did so in a qualified way from the Messiah perspective. He did not consider a text of the Old Testament to stand necessarily on the same plane as the message of the kingdom, and he did not think of all Old Testament texts as having immutable truth value for all succeeding generations. In that sense, his Scripture principle was more flexible than the Scripture principle of orthodoxy often is. Fortunately, our practice is often better than our doctrine.

It is important to notice that Jesus did not see himself under the Old Testament the way other Jews of his time did. In fact, he placed himself over it and saw it leading up to him and witnessing to him. He had messianic authority apart from the Scriptures and felt free to use the text accordingly. The text alone did not determine what he had to say at every point. Had Jesus and the apostles thought that everything the Old Testament taught was currently binding on them, there could have been no Christian gospel as we now have it. If we disregard the messianic qualification that Jesus placed on the Old Testament, we run the risk of Judaizing the church and its message. There is a considerable difference between the excellent work of Marvin Wilson in *Our Father Abraham*, which calls today's Christians back to their legitimate Hebrew roots, and trying to Judaize the church in anacronistic ways that Paul resisted from the beginning.

The apostle Paul was also conscious of a divine call to minister in the new covenant in the service of Christ and was aware that this gave him freedom and authority to rethink the meaning of the Old Testament in the light of the new situation. From his encounter with the risen Lord, Paul could see that the Scriptures were a premessianic trajectory pointing forward to the age in which he was now living. He could say, "They were written down to instruct us, on whom the ends of the ages have come" (1 Cor. 10:11). He could see in them depths of meaning he had completely overlooked as a Jew. Christ had transformed everything for him, including his use of the Scriptures.

Now, when reading the story of Moses placing a veil over his face, Paul could see the great contrast between the age of law and the age of grace (2 Cor. 3:4–18). In the story of Hagar and Sarah, he saw a typology of Jew and Christian, law and grace (Gal. 4:21–31); in Israel's wandering in the desert, he could find lessons for the church (1 Cor. 10:1–6). In the singular form of the collective noun "seed" he could see an intimation of Jesus Christ (Gal. 3:16). In many cases the crucial meaning was provided not by the text itself but by the messianic fulfillment around which the text was adapted and fitted. Even more radically than Jesus, Paul would say that circumcision is no longer required for the people of God, and the law of Moses has a different quality of authority than it did earlier. The seventh-day Sabbath was no longer insisted upon, and laws about clean and unclean foods were shelved in the gentile mission. The book of Hebrews boldly asserts that the old covenant has become obsolete, and the sacrifices in particular are abolished (Heb. 8:13; 10:9).

Just because these developments are familiar to us, we should not overlook their importance. These practices were clearly taught in the Scriptures and dear to the life of the biblical community, yet they were abandoned. The reason can only be that the coming of Jesus into the world relativized the Old Testament in certain respects and made parts of it no longer in effect as the Word of God for Christians. Paul would certainly have rejected the charge that he was guilty of twisting the text when he interpreted it afresh in terms of Jesus. He would also have rejected the assumption underlying that charge, namely, that the only meaning of a text is its exegetically established original meaning.

It is obvious from Paul's modes of interpretation and his selectivity and adaptation of the texts he cited that he was concerned above all to preach Christ from the Old Testament. For him, the text had collided with the messianic event, creating a host of new insights that he was breathless to share. The significance of this for Paul's doctrine of Scripture is that he did not simply equate the text with the Word of God for today or consider it to have an independent authority on its own. It had been promulgated in the period of redemption prior to the coming of the Messiah, which made it relative to gospel authority. Now the Old Testament was free to function as the servant of the gospel and to be the occasion of some fresh themes. It should no longer be read just on its own, but correlated with the fulfillment of Christ.

It might be amusing to imagine a "battle for the Bible" in the first century, with the conservatives insisting on the final authority of the text in relation to, say, dress requirements, and the liberals maintaining that the gospel has taken us beyond that. The Jews of that period found it shocking that the early Christians would dare to claim superior truth to that of the Torah. Would today's conservatives be comfortable defending Paul against the loyalists who held firmly to the infallibility of the Old Testament? It bears consideration.

The New Testament, then, regarded the Old Testament as Scripture, as the Word of God given in the premessianic period, now to be read in the light of Jesus Christ. It was in every respect trustworthy and valid for the time when it was issued, but it had to be thought out again as the Word of God for messianic believers in the present age. This conclusion ought to give just about everyone something to ponder. In the first place, religious liberals need to explain why they take a lower view of the Old Testament than Jesus and the apostles evidently did. It is hardly adequate to say that it was appropriate for them because they were Jews but inappropriate for us because we are not. Something so close to the center of the original gospel cannot be dispensed with so summarily. Obviously, Christians will want to follow Jesus in this matter.

But, in the second place, conservatives will need to explain how they handle the messianic qualification of the Old Testament. They do not live like Jews; they do not heed much of the dietary and other ethnic instruction taught in the Jewish Scriptures. In fact, they orient themselves to Jesus Christ, not to the Old Testament independent of him. Thus, it is not the Judaic Scripture principle that they accept, but a Christian one in which the Old Testament is a premessianic trajectory finding fulfillment in the gospel and not possessing absolute and independent authority. Of course, each Old Testament provision was the Word of God in a historical sense (God gave it to ancient Israel), but it is not necessarily a Word addressed to us. The text is infallible in this special sense for us, but not in the sense that it was infallible for Jews, that is, literally and immutably. It is time that contemporary evangelical Christians become clearer about what they actually mean by their proud slogans.

If we take seriously the New Testament use of the Old Testament, as well as its "doctrine" of it, another relevant point arises for conservatives. It surely is proper to use the text the way that the New Testament uses it. How otherwise can we credibly claim to be following the New Testament counsel on Scripture? This must mean interpreting the Old Testament christologically and, therefore, not always sticking closely to the original meaning of the text.

There are two exceptions, however, that we think should be allowed. First, rabbinic exegetical methods per se are not normative but are historically relative.[11] Paul's use of a small detail like a grammatical singular in Galatians 3:16 is not proof of detailed inerrancy but only evidence of rabbinic practice. To press this kind of point would be to commit Christians to the whole gamut of rabbinic techniques to which we have not been sympathetic, at least since the Reformation. Second, and most important, Jesus and the apostles enjoyed an authority and position in divine revelation that gave them a freedom to declare in what respects the Old Testament was or was not valid and relevant. Their exegesis

---

11. Richard Longenecker, *Biblical Exegesis in the Apostolic Period*.

depended on a revelatory stance that was unique to them.[12] Of course, we should follow them in the interpretation of the Old Testament that they made, but we cannot initiate new criticisms of the Old Testament, and we certainly cannot adopt a stance superior to the New Testament, the charter of our new covenant.

Keeping in mind these exceptions, Christians today ought to follow the New Testament in seeking to discern what significance an Old Testament text has for us now in the ongoing purposes of God. It may be that God will use the Scriptures in a way different from the original meaning as we are led by the Spirit in the light of Jesus Christ. Believing that the text is God's written Word does not put us in a box so far as the truth that God may teach us from the text. The Word of God is not bound. The New Testament indicates to us, by its own use of Scripture, that the text can give meaning on several levels and possesses a surplus of meaning potential that transcends the meaning it originally had. Our modern concern for scientific exegesis has impoverished our reading of the Bible, and we need to return to a precritical approach in which we are open to God's Word in more ways than one.[13]

The New Testament Witness to Itself

Even more crucial for the church is the question about whether the decision, however early, to make the set of writings we call the New Testament part of the Scripture principle was sound and appropriate. Was this a legitimate development given the intentions that Jesus and the apostles had for the Christian movement? We often mask this issue by assuming that a claim like 2 Timothy 3:16 applies to the New Testament as well as the Old Testament, when, of course, it does not. Where, then, is the evidence that New Testament Scriptures were supposed to come along and join in a bipartite Bible? Is not Christianity focused on the incarnation and the gift of the Spirit? Is it not sufficient that it be attested by a set of kerygmatic documents of human derivation? Just because we have always thought of the New Testament as inspired Scripture does not make it so.

Perhaps it is important that we correct this tradition and go to work delving critically behind the documents to the more original layers, in this way capturing the gospel as it really was. Belief in the Scripture prin-

12. Richard Longenecker, "Can We Reproduce the Exegesis of the New Testament?"
13. Moises Silva, "The New Testament Use of the Old Testament: Text Form and Authority," in *Scripture and Truth*, ed. Carson and Woodbridge, 147–65.

ciple, however, prevents us from doing this.[14] The majority of Christians probably feel that it makes no sense to reopen a question that has been closed for eighteen hundred years and is for all practical purposes not reformable. Besides, have we not heard the Word of God from the New Testament all this time—has it not proven itself as Scripture? It is just intellectual honesty that requires some of us to ask the question. Why was it that the church decided to go beyond Jesus Christ as the canon of revelation and add a New Testament Scripture principle? And how did the church know what books ought to be included in it?

There are several factors that support the ancient decision to receive New Testament writings as the canon of the church. One is the canonical process already in motion in the Old Testament and virtually in place by the time of Jesus. Another is the authority of Jesus himself and the apostolic structure put in place by the Lord. A third is the natural way in which the early Christians accepted the authority of the New Testament writings. The underlying factor always to keep in mind is the canonical process that produced the Old Testament. Now that the quenched Spirit had returned through the ministry of Jesus, the expectation would be kindled of fresh revelation and the possibility of new inscripturation. The reason the New Testament Scriptures were so readily accepted in the primitive church, without there being any direct effort to achieve it, is that inspired writing had been the complement of revelation under the old covenant; thus, the same factors at work in the new covenant occasioned no surprise. God had given his written Word to Israel in the context of their salvation history and was engaged, it could be assumed, in providing the written complement of new covenant revelation.

Revelation, in the Judeo-Christian tradition, generates Scripture, and Christian minds were instinctively prepared and predisposed to receive it. Just as the Old Testament message called for fulfillment in the New, so Old Testament Scripture anticipated a written complement to itself should the need of generational passage arise, the purpose in each case being the maintenance and stability of the believing community. Given the delay of the return of Christ and the open-ended nature of church history, the importance of new covenant Scripture was as great as or even greater than it had been in the premessianic period. Furthermore, the prophets and apostles in the New Testament church enjoyed not only equal status with their Old Testament counterparts but even greater dignity and authority because of the surpassing splendor of the new covenant they were administering (Matt. 11:11; 2 Cor. 3:4–18).

14. Schubert Ogden (*Point of Christology*, 103–4) is quite adamant that we relocate the canon from the New Testament text as such to the earliest stratum of apostolic testimony we can uncover by critical means.

The emergence of New Testament Scripture was predictable by analogy with Old Testament experience and legitimated by the fresh flow of divine revelation. A resumption of the canonical process would be expected. The initial intimation of this was the action of Jesus in calling the apostles and promising the Spirit for their enabling, thus providing the vehicles of continuity for the ongoing life of the church. By means of this eyewitness testimony, the faith "once delivered to the saints" could be handed down in purity and integrity. Indications are that Jesus anticipated and planned for a period after his death and resurrection during which the Supper would be observed, the gospel preached to the nations, and judgment visited on Palestine. The apocalyptic interpretation of the New Testament, in which there is no room for a church age because the end was imminent, is incorrect. If anything, what the New Testament writers had to counter was precisely an eager and false anticipation of the parousia, which tended to frustrate the outworking of Jesus's gospel and the mission of the church. The kingdom had drawn near; the date of its consummation was not something human beings could know; therefore, disciples were to get on with the church's mission.

Because the eschatological reality was now present, "the length of the interval until the consummation is of no crucial consequence."[15] Anticipating this indefinite period, then, Jesus in his lifetime trained disciples, of whom twelve in particular were given a place of special importance. He called them to follow him, appointed twelve to be with him in a special sense, gave them private instruction, ordained them with authority, and sent them out to preach and heal (Mark 1:17; 3:14; 4:34; 5:37; 6:7). They knew that they were being trained for a world mission and that Jesus was preparing them for the time when he would no longer be with them.

No doubt, like the rabbis, Jesus would have handed his teaching over to his disciples and made it clear that it was their responsibility to hand it on to others. He spoke about the founding of this church or messianic congregation and the role of the apostles in its leadership and discipline (Matt. 16:18–19; 18:17–18). In the farewell speeches in John 14–17, Jesus prepared them for his withdrawal from the scene. After the resurrection, he sent them forth in the authority of the gospel to make disciples of all nations and to be special witnesses of all they had seen and learned (Luke 24:47–48). To help them in this ministry, Jesus promised the Spirit coming in power to enable them to be witnesses to the ends of the earth (Acts 1:8). The Spirit would help them know what to say in tight situations and help them recall the instructions Jesus had given them before his departure (Matt. 10:19–20; Luke 12:11–12; John

---

15. E. Earle Ellis, *Eschatology in Luke*, 19.

14:26). Furthermore, the Spirit would lead them into all truth and enable them to explicate the gospel in new circumstances and in answer to new questions (John 16:12–13).

Although it is true that these promises do not explicitly refer to the writing of Scripture, "they provide in principle all that is required for the formation of such a canon, should that be God's purpose."[16] It is most natural to believe that these promises of remembrance and guidance into new truth have found their most far-reaching fulfillment in the New Testament Scriptures. In effect, Jesus preauthenticated the New Testament canon as the Scripture of the church when he called the apostles to be with him and promised the Holy Spirit to guide them.[17] The easiest place to see this being worked out and confirmed is in the writings of Paul, whose claims to authority are far-reaching and nuanced. Although not one of the original twelve disciples, Paul was commissioned by the risen Lord, and his apostleship was accepted by the rest (Acts 26:16–18; 1 Cor. 9:1; 15:5–11). His understanding of this commission and the kind of authority entailed by it is most germane to our thesis.

Significantly, the wording of the commission of Jesus to Paul contains allusions to prophetic calls in the Old Testament to Ezekiel, Jeremiah, and Isaiah, and it gives some indication of the way Paul saw his ministry. He believed that the Lord had set him apart prior to his birth to be an apostle to the Gentiles, that the gospel that he preached was not human in origin but came by revelation of Jesus Christ, and that he had been graced with this calling (Gal. 1:11–12, 15–16; 2:9). His task was to lay the foundations of the church and make the Word of God fully known (1 Cor. 3:10; Col. 1:25). Paul had received a stewardship of the grace of God to preach the unsearchable riches of Christ and could speak out boldly because of his office (Eph. 3:1–10; Rom. 15:15–21).

The signs of a true apostle were evident in Paul's ministry. He had been given authority for the upbuilding of the churches (2 Cor. 12:12; 13:10). Paul saw himself, and was seen by others, to be standing in the circle of primary apostles especially called to proclaim the message of Jesus and the kingdom. He could compare himself favorably with Moses as one who was mediator of even greater divine revelation (2 Cor. 3:5–18). For this reason, Paul expected people to heed his words and written communications. He felt competent to issue commands and expected them to be observed (1 Cor. 14:37) because they were instructions given "through the Lord Jesus" (1 Thess. 4:2). He wanted believers to "stand firm and hold fast to the traditions that you were taught by us, either

16. John W. Wenham, *Christ and the Bible*, 113.
17. Edward Farley refers to "the myth of apostolicity," but it is a reality well founded in the historical documentation. See his *Ecclesial Reflection*, 119; and Hans Küng, *The Church*, 344–59.

by word of mouth or by our letter" (2 Thess. 2:15). His authority ought to be respected, whether mediated in person or by means of written communication; his letters were to be read in all the churches (Col. 4:16; 1 Thess. 5:27).

It was natural, then, that the Pauline corpus would be revered and heeded as New Testament Scripture in subsequent Christian generations and be placed alongside the Old Testament (2 Pet. 3:16). Our Lord's intention was that, after his death, there should be authoritative persons to communicate the truth and spread the Word. This was abundantly fulfilled. It is wrong to hold that this whole picture of apostolic authority was an invention of the church in the subapostolic age, something done to justify itself in controversies with the Gnostics.[18]

To get a clearer impression of how apostolic authority worked, let us consider the following points. First, Paul places an eschatological proviso over himself: "Now I know only in part" (1 Cor. 13:12). He is conscious that not all knowledge has been given to him. Exhaustive knowledge and comprehensive infallibility belong to the future age after the parousia. Therefore, there are times when he can only issue some advice based on what he acknowledges to be his opinion (1 Cor. 7:25, 40). Sometimes he had no word of the Lord on a matter, no special insight from above. In reply to criticisms of him, he is content to leave the matter with God, the righteous judge who will make everything clear (1 Cor. 4:4–5). Referring to some who disagreed with him, Paul expresses the hope that in time they will see it differently (Phil. 3:15). This is not the picture of the apostle one often encounters, a man dogmatically sure about everything. Of course, he is not suggesting that the truth value of his plain teachings is in doubt, only that there is a partiality and fragility to what we humans are grasping. His modest attitude allows us, his readers, to argue controversial matters with him and not feel guilty. I think he would welcome that, as long as our attitude is modest and respectful.

Second, Paul was frank and open about his human weaknesses and did not try to hide them behind his apostolic office. He knew himself to be a frail earthen vessel and not a superman, as some of his opponents imagined they were (2 Cor. 11:5; 12:11). He experienced the weakness of the cross and the grace of God in that context (2 Cor. 11:30; 12:9–10). Jesus made use of weak people who were often unbelieving and full of misunderstanding in order to praise the power of God in and through them (2 Cor. 4:7). This dimension of human weakness can be seen as a factor in Paul's writings as well. We hear one side of a conversation when we read Galatians or Corinthians and have to think hard to figure out what Paul is teaching and what, in our context, we should be learning.

18. Rosemary R. Ruether, *Church against Itself*, 96–121.

Sometimes there can be a question about whether it was Paul or his opponents who said something (1 Cor. 7:1) or what he meant in a verse like 1 Corinthians 4:6 or 1 Timothy 2:15. How we would like to ask him if he thought hairstyles would always be a sign of the male-female distinction (1 Cor. 11:4–5) or if he meant that a woman should never be the main pastoral leader (1 Tim. 2:12). The epistles of Paul do not resemble Scriptures sent directly from heaven but are more human than that. His authority as an apostle speaks to us through the weakness of human flesh, and we must not be ashamed of this or try to cover this up.

Third, Paul does not very often exercise his authority in an authoritarian manner. He much prefers to exhort rather than command. Of course, he has authority he can use, and does so where the gospel is at stake, but more often we find him quite conciliatory and collegial. It is rather typical of Paul to say, "I do not say this as a command" (2 Cor. 8:8). More than twenty times in the letters, Paul exhorts people to do things rather than commanding them to. For instance, "We might have made demands as apostles of Christ. But we were gentle among you" (1 Thess. 2:7). This says something about Paul's desire to have people respond to him as equals and not subordinates. He does not want to "lord it over your faith," as he once put it (2 Cor. 1:24). As his brothers and sisters, believers were not slaves of his but mature sons and daughters of God who must not fall back into slavery—including to him. He wanted people like Philemon to act freely out of their own faith resources, and for that he had to woo, not threaten, them. He "preferred to do nothing without your consent, in order that your good deed might be voluntary and not something forced" (Philem. 14).

Paul wanted Timothy to observe his teaching and conduct and learn from them as an example, but he also wanted him to be his own man in the ministry (2 Tim. 3:10–4:5). He wanted believers to have the mind of Christ and be able to discern the will of God for themselves—after all, they would not always have Paul around to ask. He did not want people to be under him as Jews were under Moses. There is a liberty in Christ they needed to experience, and one way of doing so was to take up the theological and ethical subject matter and think it through for themselves. We do not think Paul would be pleased if people were to interpret him legalistically rather than engage him in dialogue.[19]

Fully half of the New Testament, however—the four Gospels and the book of Acts—contains almost no direct claim to apostolic authority, even though these books are absolutely crucial to the apostolic criterion. Have we been mistaken to consider them Scripture, if all they appear

19. Peter Richardson, "'I Say, Not the Lord': Personal Opinion, Apostolic Authority and the Development of Early Christian Halakah."

to be is human testimony? What we confront is fascinating. On the one hand, the Gospels, like John the Baptist, are content to bear witness to Christ and do not feel the need to call attention to themselves as apostolic witnesses. On the other hand, also like John the Baptist, their credentials to do so are exceptionally good. As Jesus said of John, there was none greater in the old covenant than he (Matt. 11:9, 11). When pushed to defend himself, John chose to identify himself with the voice crying in the wilderness preparing the way of the Lord (John 1:23). What seems clear is that the material concern of the four Gospels is to let the authority and light of Jesus shine out of their pages and not to complicate the issue by making claims for themselves. We can assume that in the age when they were written, about AD 70, it was the authority of Jesus that people were concerned with; the authority of the four Gospels as texts was not the subject of controversy. But with the rise of false Gospels in the second century, both issues became crucial.

What emerges from reading the Gospels is a strong claim for the authority of Jesus Christ. The records wish to confront us with the One whose word will never pass away (Matt. 24:35) and whose authority is on a plane with God's own (Matt. 7:28–29). The four Gospels in their setting are not concerned to prove their authority as texts; rather, they make known Christ's authority and saving power. It is his authority that grounds the authority of the New Testament, not the reverse. It is Jesus whom we receive and honor when we receive and respect these apostolic writings. As Jesus said to the disciples, "Whoever welcomes you welcomes me, and whoever welcomes me welcomes the one who sent me" (Matt. 10:40). The basic aim of the Gospel writers is to put people in touch with the reality of the risen Lord by telling of his earthly career. As far as internal evidence goes, we are not told the identity of any writer or instructed to regard them as apostolic. Although their identities may have been well known, they remain modest on that score and give prominence only to Christ himself.

The way Matthew begins his Gospel, "An account of the genealogy [genesis] of Jesus the Messiah" (1:1), and the way he structures his book around great blocks of teaching and actions, ending with the solemn commission and command "teaching them to obey everything that I have commanded you" (28:20), sound rather scriptural. It is as if he wanted his readers to regard his book as Christian Scripture, as, in fact, Christians have always done. The authority of Mark commends itself by means of a great vividness of style that strongly suggests the writer is giving us eyewitness testimony of the drama recorded. The writer of Luke-Acts also seems to know the history firsthand. The "we" passages in Acts suggest that the writer was Paul's traveling companion, and he claims to have used eyewitness sources for the life of Christ (Luke 1:1–4).

Whoever wrote John must have been a Jew of Palestine, an eyewitness of what he describes, and very likely the beloved disciple, the apostle John.[20]

On the other hand, the same four Gospels that display such reticence in defending their own authority as texts could likely have done so decisively had they been forced to by controversy. A strong case can be made that two of them are apostolic in the strict sense, and two indirectly apostolic. In the case of Matthew, not only is the ascription "according to Matthew" present in all existing texts of the Gospel, but the testimony of Papias, dating from early in the second century, refers to Matthew as the writer of a Gospel. The main objection to this strong external evidence is the conjecture that Matthew the apostle would not have used Mark's Gospel as a main source, assuming he did so. But this objection would not hold if the Gospel of Mark was based upon Peter's teaching, as Papias says, and if Matthew admired Mark's Gospel as a worthy statement. Robert H. Gundry has recently defended the apostolic claim of Matthew's Gospel.[21] As for Mark, the early witnesses agree both on Mark as its author and on his association with Peter in the production of the Gospel. We know a number of things about Mark from the New Testament, one particularly interesting item being that John Mark was "servant" or "assistant" to Paul and Barnabas (Acts 13:5), a term that often means a person who handles documents (Luke 4:20). To such servants Luke himself makes reference (Luke 1:2) in relation to his own eyewitness sources.

Luke, for his part, was no eyewitness of the earthly ministry of Jesus, but he claims to have had access to narratives written by those who were. The early external testimony identifies Luke as the author, and the evidence of Acts itself suggests that it was Luke the companion of Paul who composed it. The silence of Acts on the death of Paul and on the destruction of Jerusalem strongly supports Luke's authorship in the early 60s of the first century. As for the Gospel of John, J. A. T. Robinson has argued at length for the evangelist being the beloved disciple. The Fourth Gospel, contrary to prejudice, is as good a historical source as the Synoptics are, and sometimes better.[22]

The formation of the New Testament canon, then, was a natural and gradual process, as books like the epistles of Paul and the four Gospels were accepted and used. We should not think of "canon" as a list of books in a formal document (obviously, this is something that comes later), but as a process during which the various books came to be read

---

20. B. F. Westcott, *Gospel according to St. John*, v–xxviii.
21. Robert H. Gundry, *Matthew*, 609–22.
22. J. A. T. Robinson, *Redating the New Testament*, 259–311.

and were found to be of scriptural substance. We can see this happening in the New Testament itself and immediately after. In 1 Timothy 5:18, a text from the Old Testament and a saying of the Lord's now found in Luke's Gospel are placed side by side and introduced by the phrase "the scripture says." In 2 Peter 3:16, the epistles of Paul are mentioned in the same breath with Old Testament Scriptures and equated with them. The Didache quotes from the words of Jesus, apparently from a written Gospel, placing them on a level with Old Testament texts.

In such references we see the beginnings of the New Testament canon, even though this is not yet the way it was spoken about. By 170 AD (at the latest) "not only was the concept of New Testament Scripture firmly established, but the main contents of the new canon were undisputed, namely, four Gospels, Acts, thirteen letters of Paul, 1 Peter, and 1 John. Complete unanimity had not yet been reached about the other books, but there was no doubt as to the existence and main contents of an extended canon."[23] The early church was, as Luke describes it, devoted "to the apostles' teaching" (Acts 2:42), not only at first but also in the subapostolic period. What we call the New Testament canon was the final result, the crystallization of the process in which the early Christians recognized the authority of apostolic writings.[24] Of course, it is true that the process is not altogether clear. We see the general pattern without much of the detail. But we surely can conclude, against Harnack, that the creation of the New Testament was a proper, not an improper, development that proceeded naturally and appropriately from the apostolic essence of original Christianity.

The move from apostolic authority to recognition in local churches to wider recognition of the canon is smooth, even though it took time and cannot be traced in the detail one might like. The evidence, although good and sufficient for reasonable people, is not overpowering and compels us to refer to the leading of the Spirit and the providence of God. There are, on the one hand, the objective factors we have referred to: the Scripture principle manifest in the Old Testament, the structure of authority set in motion by Jesus, and the calling of apostles to be ministers of the Word. And there is the subjective factor in the process, whereby the Christian communities evaluated the documents they received and listened for the voice of the Shepherd in them. In this way, a de facto New Testament was formed.

The rise of heresies in the second century hastened Christian thinking about canon since it was now important to make explicit what had

---

23. Wenham, *Christ and the Bible*, 122.

24. Theo Donner, "Some Thoughts on the History of the New Testament Canon"; and F. F. Bruce, "Tradition and the Canon of Scripture," in *Tradition*, 129–50.

been only implicit in the practice of the churches. Christian experience did not create the canon, which had been set in motion by the objective factors already mentioned, but did confirm it and give it communal backing. John Calvin taught correctly that there are "sufficiently firm proofs" at hand to establish the credibility of Scripture, but that, in the last analysis, the witness of the Holy Spirit in believers is stronger than any proof and gives the kind of firm confidence in the Bible that has always characterized Christians (*Institutes* 1.7–8).

Even if we were less sure than we think we can be about the apostolic authorship of some of the New Testament books, we still can trust God to have overseen the provision of an adequate foundational record of his revelation through Jesus. The experience of truth and reality in the Scriptures, real in the context of worship and devotion, can help us by confirming that God has in fact provided for us in this way.[25] But why, if the Spirit dwells within us and the law is being written on our hearts, do we need an external letter such as a New Testament canon to guide us? It is because of the now and the not-yet of the kingdom of God. Until the coming of the Lord, the Scripture principle is needed to keep us on track theologically and ethically, and this is why it is incorporated into God's dealings with us in both the old covenant and the new. Scripture helps to ensure the integrity of the categorical structure of the faith and to prevent it from being distorted so that it cannot function effectively. True, the canonical process was spurred on by the heretical challenge of Marcion in the second century, but that crisis did not create the process. It was happening already and was already well advanced.[26]

Some Conclusions about Inspiration and Authority

The Bible does not give us a doctrine of its own inspiration and authority, a clear doctrine to answer all the various questions we might like to ask. Its witness on this subject is unsystematic, somewhat fragmentary, and enables us to reach important but modest conclusions. It clearly does support the central place of the Scripture principle in Christianity. The evidence suggests that it was God's will that written revelation in the form of Scripture should emerge out of the traditions of Israel and the church to preserve the substance of the faith for posterity. This appears most clearly in the way Jesus and the New Testament writers handled the Old Testament as the Word of God, and in the way the apostles

---

25. The canon seems to have revealed itself to the church as it used the available writings in the context of life and worship. See Geoffrey Wainwright, *Doxology*, 168; and Carl F. H. Henry, *God, Revelation, and Authority*, vol. 4, chap. 18.

26. Jaroslav Pelikan, *Christian Tradition*, 1:59, 119, 120.

described themselves as heralds and witnesses of the Word. What has been given is trustworthy and ought to be received obediently in a spirit of faith.[27] Christianity without a Scripture principle is a figment of the liberal imagination, something that was not meant to exist. The idea that the Bible is a collection of fallible human documents whose authority is on a par with other sources of information is a modern idea out of keeping with the nature of the texts themselves and the way they have always been seen.[28] Without belaboring the issue, the Bible itself supports the view that Scripture is a product of divine revelation and to be gratefully received.[29]

A second conclusion to which the evidence leads is the practical purpose of the Bible as a book that testifies to salvation in Jesus Christ. As the Thirty-Nine Articles say: "Holy Scripture contains all things necessary to salvation, so that whatsoever is not read therein, nor may be proved thereby, is not to be required of any man, that it should be believed as an article of the faith, or be thought requisite or necessary to salvation" (VI). The Bible is basically a covenant document designed to lead people to know and love God. As such, it has a focused purpose and concentration. This is the kind of truth it urges us to seek in it, and this is the context in which its truth claims ought to be measured. Even though the Bible versions in their present forms are not flawless, and there are many things in them that are puzzling and admit of no obvious solution, the Bible is not prevented from carrying out its designated purpose. It was "written for our instruction, so that by steadfastness and by the encouragement of the scriptures we might have hope" (Rom. 15:4). The Bible's treasure and wisdom are oriented to presenting Jesus Christ, the embodied wisdom and power of God. We should never define biblical authority apart from this stated purpose or apply to it standards of measurement that are inappropriate. God speaks through the Bible, not to make us scholars and scientists, but to put us in a right relationship with God and to give us such a religious understanding of the world and history that we can grasp everything else better.

Citing 2 Timothy 3:16–17, the Second Vatican Council was wise in asserting that the Scriptures teach "firmly, faithfully, and without error that truth which God wanted put into the sacred writings for the sake of our salvation" (*Dogmatic Constitution on Divine Revelation*, chap. 3).

27. Herman Ribberbos, *Studies in Scripture and Its Authority*, 20–22.

28. As in Edward Farley, C. F. Evans, and James Barr, and in such older liberal authors as Harry E. Fosdick, *Guide to Understanding the Bible*; and Harold DeWolf, *Case for Theology in Liberal Perspective*, chaps. 1–2.

29. Like Karl Rahner (*Inspiration in the Bible*), we see Scripture as an intrinsic part of God's formation of the church and his rule over it. The inspiration of Scripture is an element in the definitive establishment of the church and a way to guide it in faith and life.

The importance of grasping the purpose of the Bible is obvious once we consider that the interpreting of any book depends on the kind of book it is, whether a novel or a cookbook or a dictionary. If the Bible is the covenant book of the people of God, then it exists for them and for their religious (in the broad sense) needs, not primarily for literary critics, historians, geologists, or text critics. It is the witness to the agreement we have with God through Christ. What we expect to learn from it is teaching, reproof, correction, and instruction in righteousness to make us the kind of mature disciples and servants of the Lord we want to be (2 Tim. 3:16). Knowing how inspiration happened or whether the original texts were or were not free from what someone might regard as a flaw is not necessary for us, and the Bible does not tell us these things. What it does do is confront us with the living God and involve us in a relationship with him through our faith. About this, the Scriptures are clear and plain, and their profitability for the life of faith evident and empirical.

Another conclusion the evidence points to is the complex character of the Bible as the Word of God. It contains many kinds of literature and several levels of claim to authority. The truth appropriate in a psalm or a proverb, in situated command or a parable, is discerned by reference to the genre in question. We will want to notice whether the author claims to be delivering a prophetic oracle or a piece of advice, an apostolic commandment or an agonized question. Although God is the ultimate origin, we might even say author, of the whole Bible, God is not the speaker of every line in it except in an ultimate sense, so that we must give thought to who is speaking and what is being said to us in each place. What is God saying through the psalmist crying out in this way, or through the scribe arranging the narrative in this manner, or through the author of Ecclesiastes giving expression to his doubts the way he does?

We need to avoid being too simplistic when we utter slogans like "what the Bible says, God says," when a glance at almost any page will show how unsimple such a conviction is in practice. The simple thing we can say about the Bible is that it is the text in which the Word of God can be heard and the will of God discerned. What is not simple is cashing in on this assurance. We have to take the portion we are reading in relation to the larger organic structure of revelation and observe the kind of claim the immediate text is making on us once it is broadly considered.

A conclusion we can draw from the New Testament use of the Old Testament, one that has great bearing on the interpretation of Scripture, is the dynamic nature of our encounter with the text. Jesus and the apostles did not feel limited to every jot and tittle of the text as laid down. They accorded utmost respect to the smallest detail, but they also read the text in relation to the present context and sought for the will of God in the interaction between the text and their own situation. We see how Jesus would drop out part of a text that did not apply to his hearers (e.g., in his use of Isa. 61 in Luke 4:18–19). Obviously, he did not just place himself under the text but considered whether and how the text applied to his present circumstances. We cannot use Jesus to prove that one ought to subject oneself at all times to whatever the Scripture text says. Even in the case of Jesus's own words, the Gospel writers take some liberties, particularly when they rephrase what he said and place his words in new contexts to bring out fresh meaning. The authority of the original is not being denied; rather, the text means something different in the new context.

The key point is this: the Word of God is not to be found simply by staring at the text of the Bible or by searching one's own religious consciousness, but it is found in the interaction between the two, from the coming together of revelation past and revelation present under the guidance of the Spirit. There is a freedom permitted us in our reading of Scripture that was lacking in the ancient Pharisaic and in the current fundamentalist settings. God's Word is related to the situation to which it was addressed, and to understand it properly, we need to search through it for the will of God for our own situation. God does not say exactly the same thing to every historical context, and we muzzle the power of Scripture when we refuse to ask how the Lord wants to use this Scripture in our hearing now.

God has spoken in the Scriptures, but God also speaks through them today in ways that the original writer may not have intended. In saying this, we are simply confessing our faith in the Spirit as alive and active in bringing out from the Bible the ever-relevant Word of the Lord. Therefore, we study the text with the greatest care and also open our minds prayerfully to God's particular Word to us. In this way, we do not exalt the letter over the Spirit or eliminate the written norms in favor of subjectivity, but allow the Word and the Spirit to function together.[30]

Finally, what does the Bible teach in regard to the claimed errorlessness of the biblical text, an issue debated so vehemently today, especially in North America? If God be the author of the Bible, does it not follow that the text must be free from any flaw and from all error? Can God lie? Did not Jesus use the Old Testament with such a total trust as to imply the total perfection of it? The argument from the nature of God linked to the evidence of the New Testament doctrine of inspiration appears to settle the issue decisively for many.[31] But the case for biblical errorlessness is not as good as it looks.

30. Chapter 9 will be given over to a model of dynamic, but biblically faithful hermeneutics.

31. Numerous conservative evangelical scholars still believe that it does. See John W. Wenham, *Christ and the Bible*, chap. 1. They can do so only, we believe, by reading the data selectively.

Of course, God cannot lie, but that is not the issue. God gave the Bible, not by mechanically dictating it (as all in this debate agree), but by transmitting the text through all manner of secondary authors. We cannot determine ahead of time what kind of text God would give in this way. We have to inquire into what it claims and what has actually been produced and transmitted over time. The orthodox Lutherans thought that the vowel points in the Masoretic text must have been inspired, but they were proven wrong by such an inquiry. God could have produced an errorless Bible, but we have to look and see if this is what he willed to do. What we might expect God to do is never as important as what he actually does. We might hope that God would reveal the list of canonical books, or ensure the perfect transmission of the text, but he did not perform according to human expectations.

From the affirmation of the inspiration of the Bible, we cannot deduce what the Bible must be like in detail.[32] This leaves us with the question, Does the New Testament, and did Jesus, teach the perfect errorlessness of the Scriptures? No, not in plain terms. E. F. Harrison made this point: "One must grant that the Bible itself, in advancing its own claim of inspiration, says nothing precisely about inerrancy. This remains a conclusion to which devout minds have come because of the divine character of Scripture."[33] It is not just that the term "inerrancy" is not used in the Bible. That would not settle anything. The point is that the category of inerrancy as used today is quite a technical one and difficult to define exactly. It is postulated of the original texts of Scripture no longer extant; it is held not to apply to round numbers, grammatical structures, or incidental details in texts and to be unfalsifiable except by some indisputable argument.

Once we recall how complex a hypothesis inerrancy is, it is obvious that the Bible teaches no such thing explicitly. What it claims, as we have seen, is divine inspiration and a general reliability, with a distinct concentration on the covenantal revelation of God. And when we examine the text in detail and note how the Gospels differ from one another, how freely the New Testament quotes from the Old Testament, and how boldly the chronicler changes what lay before him in Kings, this impression is strongly confirmed.

Why, then, do some scholars insist that the Bible does claim total inerrancy for itself? Some argue for inerrancy sincerely, hoping that it is true. They find reassurance in this hope. Some ask honestly, How would it be possible to maintain a firm stand against religious liberalism unless

32. Evangelical philosopher Stephen Davis (*Debate about the Bible*, 61–65) applies his logic to this and related topics.

33. E. F. Harrison in *Revelation and the Bible*, ed. C. F. H. Henry, 238.

one held firmly to total inerrancy? The logic of inspiration coupled with the demands of faith today were quite enough to convince some. Even so, looking at the actual biblical evidence available, we have to conclude that the case for total inerrancy just is not there. At the very most, one could say only that it is implicit and could be drawn out by careful argument, but this is disputable and not the basis for the dogmatic claims one often hears for inerrancy. In the last analysis, the inerrancy theory is a logical deduction not well supported exegetically. Those who press it hard are, in our judgment, elevating reason over Scripture.

A major reason evangelicals have experienced difficulty following inductive, and avoiding deductive, thinking on the subject of inspiration is that B. B. Warfield, to whom many still look, led the way. On the one hand, Warfield claimed to follow the inductive approach in arriving at his doctrine of Scripture and disowned a priori conceptions; but, on the other hand, when he sought to define inspiration, he lapsed into strongly deductive arguments to prove why something that was inspired would have to be perfectly errorless. His powerful desire to see the Bible in a certain way overpowered the empirical support for his favored view. This inconsistency surfaces again and again in his theological followers. The deductive tendency that would see inerrancy as a necessary corollary of inspiration works against honestly facing up to the data, both in the case of the claims themselves and in respect of many of the actual phenomena of the biblical text.

What we have to say, instead, is that inerrancy is not precisely claimed by the Bible for itself and must be regarded as a possible implication on which sincere persons disagree. Being an inference of great complexity and difficulty, inerrancy is also a belief to be handled with sensitivity and not one to be used as a battering ram to injure fellow Christians who disagree. The inerrancy hypothesis lacks exegetical foundations. Scripture does not explicitly affirm inerrancy; neither does it deny it in so many words. The whole question is a matter given over to the theological judgment of the church.

In an age when many theologians boldly deny the Scriptures, can we afford to allow a doctrine of Scripture that falls short of the strictest specifications? Is the experience of the trustworthiness of Scripture in bringing us to know and love God not sufficient to cause us to trust Scripture in every detail without limit? Where can one draw the line clearly between what the Bible faithfully teaches and what is errant? Considerations such as these move people to a view of the Bible higher than its own view of itself. A desire for religious certainty, the need for solid defenses, the logic of inspiration, the experience of God's reliability in the Bible—all of these move many to tighten up the doctrine of Scripture beyond what is seen in the text and claimed by the text.

So what should be done? There ought to be as much goodwill and cooperation as possible between those who believe that the strict view of inerrancy is important to hold and those who think that a contrasting view is truer and wiser.[34] For our part, to go beyond the biblical requirements to a strict position of total errorlessness only brings to the forefront the perplexing features of the Bible that no one can completely explain, and it overshadows those wonderful certainties of salvation in Christ that ought to be front and center. It makes us sitting ducks for the liberal critics like James Barr and postpones our ability to be certain about the Bible to that remote time when the experts will be able to say, "At last we have proved the Bible in every respect." Much wiser, in our opinion, is the willingness to stay with the more modest biblical claims and the ability to shelve those perplexing biblical difficulties without worrying so much about them. We all work with an imperfect Bible, whatever translation we use, and we do not forsake our confidence in it because of some implausible number in the Chronicles. All of us live with uncertainty, so why even give the impression that some proven defect could bring the whole house of authority down?

The Bible in the power of the Spirit has been true enough to bring us to know and love God in Jesus Christ. If this is what it claims and this is what it has done, then it ought to be enough for us. It is common for special interest groups in the church to make the Bible say more about their distinctive convictions than it really does. In this case, practically the whole church, being committed to the divine inspiration of Holy Scripture, has a stake in the doctrine of inspiration being very precise and very firm. Yet we must permit the biblical testimony to be what it is, namely, "obviously fragmentary and unsystematic."[35] It may be that a moderately phrased category of inerrancy is the best operating principle, given the modesty of Scripture on the subject and the theological atmosphere we now find ourselves in.

34. Richard C. Lovelace (in *Inerrancy and Common Sense*, ed. Roger R. Nicole and J. Ramsey Michaels, chap. 1) offers some rare historical wisdom on this question and how to proceed with it.

35. I. Howard Marshall, *Biblical Inspiration*, 30.

Inspiration and Authority

Now that we have surveyed the spectrum of revelation and the specific biblical witness to inspiration, the task before us is to explore some dimensions of a Christian doctrine of Scripture. What model of biblical authority is authorized by the testimony we have?

The first point to make is that the Scripture principle is inherent in and integral to the faith of Israel and the church, so much so that it cannot be severed without great damage to the total organism. It is not something incidental or tacked on anachronistically, but belongs to the dynamic of salvation history. The saving divine action has created both a community of the faithful and a reliable written witness to teach and guide that community. It would seem reasonable either to accept or reject the whole of salvation history with the Scripture principle, but not to hold on to remnants or separated limbs of the organism. If salvation history is credible, so is the Scripture principle. If it is not credible, neither is biblical authority. The two go together.

Edward Farley is clear; he sees the connection and rejects them both.[1] We see the connection and affirm them both. The plan of God for the salvation of sinners, given our reading of the evidence, includes the provision of a reliable written testimony to this redemption that is more than a product of merely human wisdom. It participates in the effective divine action on behalf of sinners. The person who can embrace the truth of salvation history will find it possible also to accept the gift of the Holy Scriptures, a gift that provides the message with

1. Edward Farley, *Ecclesial Reflection*, 153–65.

sound epistemological foundations. God supplied the old covenant, with authoritative documentation, and then the new covenant, with apostolic Scriptures to carry forward a true witness to the gospel. Had God left the message uninscripturated, it might have become irretrievably distorted and damaged. As it is, the truth has been enshrined in God-breathed Scriptures that ensure that the message will function effectively and appropriately.

The second point brings out what the Scripture principle means. It means that there is a locus of the Word of God in a form available to us. It means that the Bible is regarded as a creaturely text that is at the same time God's own written Word, and that we can consult this Word that reveals God's mind. It means that God has communicated authoritatively to us on those subjects about which Scripture teaches, whether doctrinal, ethical, or spiritual, and that we believers willingly subject ourselves to this rule of faith. More than merely human tradition and existential address, the Bible is the informative Word of God to the church. The text is not reduced to an expression of human experience and tradition, as in liberalism, but is a content-full language deposit carrying the authority of God.[2] Deciding what functions the Bible shall have in the church is not ours to do; it belongs to the authority of Scripture.[3]

Ernst Käsemann said, "Indeed—and whatever contradiction and annoyance I may cause by saying this—not everything that is in the Bible is God's Word. In the last resort, the contemporary controversy is about the truth or falsehood of this proposition."[4] He has placed a finger directly on the issue. In saying that not everything in the Bible is God's Word, one rejects the core idea of the Scripture principle that guarantees precisely that. Käsemann cares a great deal for the critical reading of the text; we agree, but ought to care most about what God is teaching us in and through the text, not the technology and often the speculative guesswork of the critical art of textual interpretation. The battle line falls right here.

The Scripture principle proper to Christianity is not identical to the Judaic Scripture principle. Most importantly, the bipartite Bible is structured in such a way as to identify the Old Testament as prefiguring narrative, not the last word on the purposes of God. The messianic age has dawned in Jesus the Christ, and the revelation associated with that age

2. James I. Packer (in *Scripture and Truth*, ed. D. A. Carson and John D. Woodbridge, 325–56) gives us a superb discussion of the kind of hermeneutics that operates out of a biblically defined doctrine of inspiration.

3. David H. Kelsey (*Uses of Scripture in Recent Theology*) would have us suppose that the proper function of the Bible in the church is the function that a person decides to grant it.

4. Ernst Käsemann, *New Testament Questions of Today*, 272–73.

takes precedence over the premessianic material. Scripture is not leveled in the way it is in the Judaic Scripture principle, but is searched and interpreted in terms of a christological presupposition. Naive rhetoric about biblical infallibility could easily lead to a tragic Judaizing of the Christian faith. There is a liberty that should be built into the Scripture principle. The existence of real differences of emphasis in the canon, such as between Job and Proverbs, prevents the Scriptures from becoming an authority for a petrified orthodoxy.[5] The work of the Spirit opens up the text so that it can serve the church in new ways to meet the challenges of today.[6]

What Is Inspiration?

For all the talk about inspiration, the term occurs only once in the Bible (2 Tim. 3:16), and even then without a definition. It appears to mean "breathed out by God," but the context also suggests a spiritual power possessed by the text that makes it so effective in the ways specified. Some have suggested that God dictated the words to the scribes of Scripture, whereas others propose flashes of insight and religious genius on the part of the writers and editors.

What kind of divine activity is affirmed by inspiration? A valuable clue can be found in the diverse products of inspiration present in the phenomena of the Bible. One kind of inspiration was prophetic and enabled the prophet to speak the word of the Lord with great authority and assurance. Another kind of inspiration was scribal and supported writers in researching and composing their work. Another lies behind the Wisdom literature, and another behind the poetic utterances. The obvious lesson to learn about inspiration from seeing what it produced is that inspiration is not one single activity but a broader superintendence over a process of Scripture-making that is complex.

It was wrong of Athenagoras to suggest that God used the biblical writers as a musician uses his flute. Mechanical analogies of this kind derive more from Hellenistic ideas of inspiration than from the Bible's picture of it, and they pose a danger to the real humanity of the Bible.[7] There is pressure to think of inspiration in mechanical terms because of the natural desire to have God speak directly in the Bible. It is tempting to construe the whole text as if it were prophecy, so that

5. Paul D. Hanson (*Dynamic Transcendence*) is afraid of this happening.
6. Don S. Browning, *Moral Context of Pastoral Care*, 93.
7. William J. Abraham (*Divine Inspiration of Holy Scripture*, chap. 1) is quite concerned that conservatives so often sound as if they mean to conceive of inspiration in mechanical and docetic terms.

one might consider every verse in it as if it were an oracle from on high. But this overlooks the simple fact that the Bible is more than prophecy, and although direct divine speech is part of the record, there are many other kinds of communication as well, some of them more indirect and ambiguous.[8]

It is probably best to think of inspiration as a divine activity accompanying the preparation and production of the Scriptures. We are not privileged to observe how in hidden and mysterious ways the Spirit worked alongside the human agents in the creative literary work, but we can plainly see the result of what was done. We have a book like Genesis that refers to the sources it used in composition: "these are the generations/descendants of" (Gen. 2:4; 6:9; etc.). Jeremiah contains not only prophetic oracles but considerable narrative stitching the book together. The historical books are completely anonymous and were likely the work of a large number of scribes and historians making contributions toward the final redaction. One does not get the impression that inspiration is a sudden activity in the isolated life of some famous writer known to us all. It seems to have been a quieter and more long-term affair, as traditions were shaped and texts brought to final form. We may speak of the social character of inspiration and of the complexity of its execution, involving the work and gifts of many people, most of them unnamed but doing their part under the care of the Spirit to achieve the desired result.[9] God was at work in the community to produce a normative text for the community.

We suggest thinking of inspiration in broader terms than is customary, less as the enlightenment of a few elect persons and more as a long-term divine activity operating within the whole history of revelation. Inspiration means that, while God gave us the Scriptures, there is to be some variety in how we must think of the individual units produced by the inspiration. Scripture exists because of the will of God and is a result of his ultimate causality. Even so, it comes into existence through many gifts of prophecy, insight, imagination, and wisdom that the Spirit has chosen to give. The most important point is that everything taught in the Scriptures is meant to be heard and heeded because it is divinely intended. Every segment is inspired by God, although not in the same way, and the result is a richly variegated teacher, richer for all its diversity. The differences are what enable the Bible to speak with power and relevance to so many different people in various settings, addressing the many sides of the human condition.

8. Paul J. Achtemeier (*Inspiration of Scripture*) has called attention to the inadequacy of the prophetic model for representing the biblical category of inspiration in its fullness.

9. Bruce Vawter, *Biblical Inspiration*, 162–66.

The Proper Use of the Bible

Before one actually considers the rules for the interpretation of the Bible, there is a prior attitude to deal with. Something needs to be said about the use of the Bible that is appropriate to the Scripture principle, about the preunderstanding that is the foundation of good hermeneutics. First, there should be a spirit of openness to the text. If the Bible is not merely a human product but is the Word of God, without exhausting that Word, then it follows that the believer will choose to accept the discipline of its teachings and seek to walk in the light of its statutes. Of course, the text can be studied in the academy from a scientific point of view that endeavors to evaluate the various claims the text makes in a somewhat objective way. Nevertheless, the Christian will want to move beyond what can be known by reason to the level of hearing God's Word in the text. The Bible, not merely the product of Near Eastern culture, is also the written Word of God and the canon of the church. Therefore, it ought to be approached in a spirit of faith, in the context of the believing community, and received as a reliable witness to God and his relationship with us. For the church to be apostolic means that it will live under the discipline of the normative Word of God.

This attitude brings one into conflict with the pretensions of much contemporary biblical criticism that often is suspicious of the text and prepared to overthrow it in the name of critical freedom. Criticism is faulty when it lords it over the text instead of submitting humbly to the text and serving it. It very easily becomes a technology of deconstruction that exalts the judgment of the scholar and demeans the authority of the Scriptures. Criticism is useful when it illumines the meaning of the Bible, and it is harmful when it seeks to overthrow what the text was given to tell us. No one can be wiser than the Bible, the book that owes its origin to the activity of God. As a divinely willed language deposit, the Scriptures are the place to stand in order to hear God speak and a central means of grace in the life of faith. They can be effective only when the reader approaches them in a spirit of openness and faith. The crucial thing is a determination to know and love and serve God under the authority of his Word.

The proper attitude to the biblical text also means being concerned about the text, both in the stages of its preparation, insofar as these can be exposed, and in the final form of the text. It could be that delving into the state of the tradition before it was brought into its canonical form might shed some light on the meaning of the final redaction. Since inspiration eventually secured the text in a canonical collection, the greatest attention must be given to the final shape of the Bible. We might speculate about the original parable as Jesus gave it, but when it comes down to it, what we have to read and preach is the parable in the redaction of a particular Gospel where, in the wisdom of God, it came to rest. It is this text that we trust, not any speculative reconstruction of a better form of the text. There is value in looking at the possible sources of the text because God was active at every stage in the process of Scripture making, but it is the final text that the Spirit ultimately gave us and where final authority resides.

Placing the authority, as Schubert Ogden does, in a more primitive layer of tradition than the New Testament itself really disowns the Bible as our authority and enthrones the human expert with all his or her biases as the last word.[10] Inspiration means that the proper place of a biblical text is in the canonical collection and that it must be read in this context. James Barr has a valid point when he suspects that this commitment to the canonical text really lowers our estimation of the value of the critical work done on the earlier stages. It does in fact lower it. What is implied is that religious authority does not attach to the guesswork of critics, but remains where God intended it to lie, in the Bible unaffected by criticism.[11] Belief in inspiration is indeed hostile to all forms of criticism that refuse to submit to the text and that prefer a reconstructed text to the text evidently intended by inspiration.

The appropriate use of Scripture, then, is that we approach it as our God-given norm, the rule of faith and practice. This is the Protestant principle. God has left the church with a body of normative tradition in an objective language deposit for the sake of the people God is forming for himself. Therefore, we look to the Scriptures to provide the definitive Word that can enliven and shape us. No other norm can do this for us. Biblical revelation is the criterion of Christian thought and action, a safeguard against human self-will. It stands as a witness to keep our feet in the orbit of God's will. It is not enough just to say that the Bible mediates an encounter with God, that in it we hear an echo of God's voice.[12] The Bible is, in fact, the inscripturation of God's Word and is a self-determining authority over the church. How it rules is not decided by the reader's taste but by the claims of the text itself.

Unfortunately, there is a body of opinion that wants to retain the freedom to critique Scripture and does not want to submit to its authority without reservation. Members of this body are prepared to use it as a source of information about the way in which people thought of God and themselves, but not as a source of divine truth. How, they ask, can we believe a text that presents notions foreign to our understanding and

10. Schubert M. Ogden, *Point of Christology*, 97–105.
11. James Barr, *Holy Scripture*, 130–71.
12. Hendrikus Berkhof, *Christian Faith*, 88.

lacking in credibility for us? They are not prepared to humble themselves and be instructed by the text on the assumption that it knows best. They insist on retaining the right to say that Scripture is only human and falls into error.

To illustrate how tempting it can be to take this view under pressure, Paul K. Jewett, a thoroughly orthodox Protestant theologian in every other respect, when faced with texts in Paul that seem to contradict his own convictions about feminism, rejects certain texts as representing only a human opinion of Paul, suggesting that some verses in the Bible are not divinely intended and not binding on us.[13] The logic of this approach to the Bible, of course, removes the basis for appealing to it on behalf of any conviction, including feminism. What Jewett should have done, to follow the normal orthodox method, was to respect the divine authority, even of a Word limited by its situation, and to ask what it may signify for us.[14]

This example of Jewett alerts us to the complexity of the norm of Scripture. It is not always easy to know how to appeal to the Bible, which can easily be used carnally to serve our selfish purposes. Biblical revelation is progressive in character, moving from premessianic to messianic revelation, and therefore it is imperative to take careful note of where a text occurs in the organism of Scripture. An Old Testament text may have been the Word of God to ancient Israel and not be God's Word to us now. We run the risk of Judaizing the church if we forget this. There are various levels of authority from one passage to another. There are commands and exhortations, parables and poetry, pieces of advice and expressions of ecstasy. Each of these carries an appropriate authority in a distinctive way. Some passages aim to instruct us in doctrinal truth. Other passages want to transform our lives by challenging us to the quick. Still others exhort us to get moving toward discipleship. The Bible does all these things and many more. It tells truth in every case, but not the same kind of truth. We must be alert to identify the kind of truth claim each passage makes on us and then be submissive to it.

Note two examples of a provocative kind. It is not necessary to understand the story of the fall of Adam as a historical, eyewitness account, which it could not have been. Even though the historical character must be preserved (Rom. 5:12), the story itself in Genesis 2–3 is probably an etiological inference drawn from the human experience of guilt and salvation in history presented in the form of what must have happened in the beginning to bring this about. The visual appearance of the in-

13. Paul K. Jewett, *Man as Male and Female*.

14. Willard M. Swartley (*Slavery, Sabbath, War, and Women*, chap. 4) takes an approach better than Jewett's.

cident need not be thought of as the heart of what is being asserted in the passage. The form of the narrative seems saga-like, which is, of course, a perfectly legitimate way of presenting such a universal truth about all human beings. Our whole human history is determined by the decision to rebel against God, and thus is presented in terms of the fall of humanity.

Similarly, in regard to eschatological assertions, belief in their absolute authority does not commit the reader to the interpretation of them as anticipatory, eyewitness accounts of what the future will be. This, in fact, lands us in a nest of problems we associate with date setting and prophetic crystal-ball gazing so common among prominent premillennialists and dispensationalists today. Rather, biblical assertions about the future are oriented to the present as well and are designed to bring out the opening up of the future in a symbolic way. Sitting at table in the kingdom of God has much more than a literal meaning. Statements about hell say more about the dreaded possibility of finally deciding against God than they do about the high temperature of that awful place.

We also need to keep an eye on wholeness, so as not to take a passage out of its canonical context. Biblical study has often focused too much on small units in the text and failed to examine the meaning of them in relation to the broader picture. Jonah, for instance, should not be read as an isolated book, but be viewed in relation to the later New Testament Scriptures that reflect on its meaning as a prophecy of Christ. Deuteronomy should be read in dialogue with Job and Ecclesiastes, which force us to see the whole question of wealth and piety in a deeper way. Of course, passages must be studied first in their own right, but eventually they ought to be placed in the framework of the whole revelation of God. This was the way of the older exegetical tradition that operated out of a firm conviction about biblical inspiration.[15]

Theological Reasoning in the Mode of Authority

If there is an identity between Scripture and the Word of God, then the data for theology should be sought in the vehicle of revelation first of all. Reason certainly has a role to play. It enters into the decision to appeal to Scripture initially, when the critical decision is made to accept the Scripture principle. It comes into play when we evaluate what the Bible teaches and when we consider how the truth can be intelligibly conveyed to searching minds. However, reason does not have the competence to overthrow biblical teachings once they have been established.

15. As Brevard Childs (*Biblical Theology in Crisis*, chap. 8) reminds us.

They cannot be ruled out just because they seem unreasonable, if in fact they are exegetically well supported. Theological thinking is not done in the context of perfectly free inquiry; rather, it continually goes back to consult the authoritative Book. In this it differs from ordinary sciences. It locates the primary evidence for its judgments in the vehicle of revelation. The fact that the Bible teaches about angels is enough to establish this reality, even if there were no other reason to believe they existed.[16] A hymn captures the proper mode of theological reasoning when it says, "Jesus loves me, this I know, for the Bible tells me so." We do not come to the Bible wondering if it will tell the truth. We already trust it to tell the truth. We come to discover what the truth is. Theology makes doctrinal houses from the bricks and mortar of biblical texts, and reason seeks for the consistency among them.[17]

Has such a view been a hindrance to the advance in knowledge? Does not Galileo symbolize the suppression of scientific ideas because they came into conflict with scriptural notions? Does it not require one to believe that Methuselah lived for nine hundred and sixty-nine years, even though this seems absurd? Science in different modes has forced us to reconsider traditional interpretations of the Bible. However, it also is true that Christianity provided presuppositions necessary for the rise of science and does not stand in the way of advancing scientific knowledge. Science poses questions to theology and compels us to consider or reconsider what we believe theology to be saying. This is all to the good. The Bible's purpose is to lead us to know and love God in Christ and grow to maturity in him, not to be a textbook giving scientific particulars that can be found by empirical research. It is a religious classic, operating in a specialized area, and not running competition to the sciences.[18]

The Coherence and Reliability of the Bible

Most people would agree that inspiration would mean very little if it could not guarantee a basic coherence in the Bible's teaching and a solid reliability in the Bible's narrative. The Scripture principle would be overthrown should the Bible turn out to be self-contradictory and fallacious. We have a right to expect coherence and reliability as Scripture claims to deliver, focused as its purpose is according to 2 Timothy 3:15–17. This means a coherence in the teachings pertaining to the cov-

16. Mortimer Adler (*Angels and Us*) defends the existence of angels as a rational belief.

17. Clark H. Pinnock, *Biblical Revelation*, chap. 3.

18. John W. Montgomery ("The Theologian's Craft," in *The Suicide of Christian Theology*, 267–313) discusses theological theorizing.

enant purposes of God and a reliability in the narration of the history of salvation germane to the purpose in view. It would, of course, be important to consider what kind of truth a given passage wants to convey and the cultural differences in the standard of measurement appropriate to apply. Essentially, we would want to be open to the Bible's freedom to be true however it chooses.[19]

The issue we are grappling with here has to do with the "perfection" of the Bible. Is it perfectly coherent in such a way that there are no conceptual incoherences? Is it perfectly inerrant so that there are no factual discrepancies? Because of belief in the divine inspiration of the Bible, Christians, from very ancient times, have felt that it must be so, that inspiration entails such a perfection even before reading the text. The difficulty is that today these inferences have been radically questioned and need to be examined.

Addressing ourselves first to the unity and coherence of biblical teaching, we have to face the challenge posed by a widely held current opinion that biblical theology is pluralistic and full of radical diversity, so much so that the Bible cannot be used as our teacher in the ordinary sense. In the past, of course, the unity of the Scriptures was assumed, and drawing out the systematic message of the Bible was the theologian's task. The contents of Scripture were believed to have flowed from God's mind ultimately, and with patience and hard work they would yield consistent doctrines. All this was implied by divine inspiration. When Martin Luther concluded that James was out of line with Pauline teaching on justification, his immediate reaction was to deny Scripture status to James. If Scripture is our inspired teacher, making us wise unto salvation, then we assume it will not confuse us or tell us lies. This is implied by the Scripture principle. The result has been that texts were read in the light of one another and never set in opposition to one another; what is obscure is viewed as secondary and considered in relation to what is primary, clear, and central.[20]

Now, however, there is a strong emphasis on the diversity of Scripture. With the increased stress on the human character of the text has come a vision of it as a developing human witness full of complex and even competing ideas. The Bible, therefore, cannot be appealed to with hope of achieving a coherent picture in a conceptual sense. The present trend goes back to the influential book by Walter Bauer titled *Orthodoxy and Heresy in Earliest Christianity* in which he maintained that the early church tolerated highly diverse and mutually exclusive beliefs and that

19. Anthony Thiselton ("Truth," in *The New International Dictionary of New Testament Theology*, ed. Colin Brown, 3:874–902) points out just how complex a category such as truth can be.

20. See James I. Packer, "Upholding the Unity of Scripture Today."

a clear sense of orthodoxy did not arise for several centuries. More recently, the book by James D. G. Dunn, *Unity and Diversity in the New Testament*, extends the thesis into the earliest period and contends that the New Testament itself presents several different kerygmas and doctrines, denying the existence of a normative Christianity in it. The result is the assumption that we can hardly appeal to the Bible to establish Christian doctrines and norms, leaving the whole exercise of theology in a hopeless muddle. The bottom line is that the method of classical theology, which involved piecing together the information supplied in various texts in order to construct a coherent theology, apparently lies in ruins. The manner in which an Augustine or Calvin did theology is closed to us now, and the results they reached are mainly of historical interest.[21] Small wonder that classical Christians tremble in the presence of biblical criticism. It is most threatening when such criticism attacks the assumption that the Bible can be appealed to as a norm for faith and practice.[22]

At the outset, it is important to ascertain just how radical the diversity is. Obviously, if the Bible presents a series of plain contradictions, the point is made, and orthodoxy had better pack its bags. But it is not as simple or devastating as that. Despite a degree of diversity, there is, after all, a tremendous unity in the Bible. Even though it was written over centuries, it yields a compelling set of doctrines that have occupied the minds of people unceasingly. Donald Guthrie sees no evidence that there were several differing gospels in the New Testament, or that the variations in emphasis were anything more than that. He is impressed by the deep unity of biblical thought and sees the rich variety as contributing to it.[23] In other words, part of the problem is exaggeration.

H. E. W. Turner showed in the Bampton Lectures for 1954 that Bauer's work was full of misjudgments regarding theological positions in the early church. Trinitarian orthodoxy is much earlier than the Nicene formulary.[24] As for the New Testament, nothing requires us to follow Dunn in concluding that the kerygma of the Synoptic Gospels is contradictory with the kerygma of Paul or John. Similarly, in Christology, although there is certainly a difference in emphasis in Acts as compared with John, for instance, it is not obvious that they contradict each other.[25]

Exaggerations aside, the rich diversity in biblical teaching adds to its profundity. Differences surface for most people when there is a dispute

---

21. Bernard M. G. Reardon, *Religious Thought in the Reformation*, xi–xii.
22. Van A. Harvey, *Historian and the Believer*, 24.
23. Donald Guthrie, *New Testament Theology*, 59.
24. H. E. W. Turner, *The Pattern of Christian Truth*.
25. D. A. Carson critiques Dunn in *Scripture and Truth*, ed. Carson and Woodbridge, 71–77.

in interpretation on some interesting question. On a controversial issue, such as war, one will notice the opposing sides quoting different texts to support their opinions. One side will resort to Old Testament statements that seem to support the right to defend one's country militarily, whereas the other side will appeal to the Sermon on the Mount to deny such a right. Quite apart from the misuse of texts, there does seem to be a variety of teaching on issues like war, forcing the reader to ask how the Bible as a whole should be understood and applied. Tight consistency is not what we find when we read the Bible. It is like listening to an orchestra rather than a single solo instrument, or a large choir rather than a solo voice.

This complexity arises from several features of the Bible. First, it is a progressive account of revelation given bit by bit over a long period of time, not all at once. In it we can trace the development of the promise of God as it was given to Abraham and then unfolded in stages, leading to its fulfillment in Jesus Christ.[26] Both unity and diversity are evident in the outworking of the divine plan of salvation. This becomes more apparent in the New Testament, where the old covenant is seen to have become "obsolete" in a certain sense and replaced by a new covenant (Heb. 8:13). Although it is not a contradiction that circumcision was called for in the Old Testament but not in the New, it does remind us that the unity of the Bible is not simple and obvious but makes room for changes. This means that we must assess the meaning of each part in relation to the whole and not lift passages out of context.

Another feature of the Bible that gives rise to complexity is the dialogue between witnesses in the text. As we noted, some real diversity exists between the several New Testament writers regarding the person and work of Christ, and we have no right to force one writer to say what another says. We have to respect the distinctiveness of each witness.[27] Everyone is familiar with the tension in the Bible between divine sovereignty and human freedom, twin truths that seem to stand alongside one another, defying resolution.[28] The Bible is like that. It does not suppress differences of emphasis or angles of vision and does not force them onto a single plane. It would seem to be the will of God that the Bible should set forth its truth in a richly textured way, and our duty is not to corrupt this policy by harmonizing the differences inappropriately.[29]

---

26. Walter Kaiser (*Toward an Old Testament Theology*) sees promise as the key to the developing theology of the Bible.

27. James D. G. Dunn (*Christology in the Making*) points to the diversity in New Testament Christology in his exaggerated way.

28. D. A. Carson, *Divine Sovereignty and Human Responsibility*.

29. G. C. Berkouwer loves to work with pairs of truths and resists rationalizing harmonizations. See the analysis of his work in J. C. De Moor, *Towards a Biblically Theo-Logical Method*. See also Barry L. Callen, *Caught between Truths*.

Still another feature of the Bible that yields diversity is the situational orientation of much of the material. It is easy to pit one book against another when each was written to meet a particular need, but it is not necessary to do so. It likely is more fair to suppose that each of Paul's letters, for example, represents a contingent expression of his coherent position. Diversity is bound to arise when the gospel is applied to different situations and cultures by different people with their own peculiarities and personal styles.

In this matter of the unity of the Bible, one is not forced to choose between accepting contradictions and striving feverishly to harmonize differences in a tight consistency. There is a third alternative—complementarity. As Bernard Lonergan has pointed out, two authors may bring out some very different points and still be in basic agreement on the central issues.[30] Matthew and Paul certainly say some very different things about the law, but what they say is compatible if we take into account the points of reference involved.[31] Karl Rahner recognizes differences in ecclesiology on the part of the New Testament writers but concludes that it is a unity amid diversity. The differences are rooted in the practical problems facing the various early churches that produced the documents.[32]

Are we being honest when we adopt a complementary model, arising, as it obviously does, from a belief in the Scripture principle and saving it from being proved false? There can be no doubt that this conviction has in the past influenced and does even now influence Christians to seek positive internal relations between texts and to reject outright contradiction between them. We would not deny that belief in inspiration supplies a hermeneutical guideline that encourages denial of apparent contradictions. It causes us to look for the underlying unity beneath every case of surface contradiction. Even so, from an empirical standpoint, it need not be the case that just because we have four Gospels that paint different portraits of the Christ, we therefore have four frames that could not be dealing with the same person.

Yes, in Paul and John and the author to the Hebrews we have three theologians with their distinctive vocabularies and categories. But no, this fact does not lead us to conclude that we are dealing with three truth systems that do not dovetail and complement each other. So long as we do not exaggerate the differences in the Bible, but take account of the purposes and pastoral settings involved, we do not find convincing any charge that the Bible is contradictory. Even in the extreme cases, it does not seem sensible to pit Jesus against Moses, or Paul against James.

---

30. See the chapter on dialectic in Bernard Lonergan, *Method in Theology*.
31. Brice L. Martin, "Some Reflections on the Unity of the New Testament."
32. Karl Rahner, *Foundations of Christian Faith*, 335–42.

Why does Rudolf Bultmann say that belief in the virgin birth of Jesus in Luke is incompatible with belief in the incarnation in John when no such thing is required? The church has always believed them both and not found them contradictory.[33] Why does Dunn assume that Paul could not have consented to what James said about justification? Of course, there is a contradiction in surface terminology and textual emphases, but not in theology deeper down.[34] If there are real contradictions in the Bible, it is not very obvious to us what they are.

There is a final consideration that counsels caution against rushing to conclusions and encourages patience in the presence of perplexing features in the biblical text. It is God's purpose in the polyphony of Scripture. The shallowness of the two extremes is striking. Confronted with two seemingly contradictory texts, one person will declare a contradiction whereas another will claim a harmony, but neither one really pauses in the presence of the dialectic to see what God may be teaching through this textual circumstance. Puzzling features are always found in great works of art, and it is always wise to wait until the deeper nuances that explain them reveal themselves.

The Bible is not coherent and unified in the way we might choose, but in the way God has chosen or at least permitted. The paradoxes and tensions there are able to lead us deeper into hidden theological riches. It is unnecessary to cut the Gordian knot by declaring contradiction or by rushing to artifically harmonize contrasting trends; either approach can cut us off from the deeper teachings that come only as we wrestle with the problems of unitive exegesis. There will always be some who propose that we drop one or another voice out of the biblical choir because they are not pleased with its contribution. But the church must always refuse to follow this suggestion, trusting rather that each voice was meant to be there and meant to add to the total effect of the treasury of God's Word.

We have no right to impose on the Bible the sort of coherence that may suit us and no right to force the text into a greater coherence than it has chosen to display. God himself apparently was not overly concerned about tight coherence when quite significant changes were introduced into the new covenant as compared with the old. It would not be right to pretend that Ecclesiastes does not deny the hope of life after death in order to bring this writer into line with New Testament writers. It does not follow that the apostolic directive in Acts 15 pertaining to dietary practices should be considered binding on us. The Bible is marked by

---

33. Rudolf Bultmann (*Kerygma and Myth*, 1:34) says, without proof: "The doctrine of Christ's pre-existence as given by St. Paul and St. John is difficult to reconcile with the legend of the virgin birth in St. Matthew and St. Luke."

34. James D. G. Dunn, *Unity and Diversity in the New Testament*, 251.

diversity as well as unity, and this is part of the rich package God has given us in Scripture.

The Factual Reliability of the Bible

Belief in the Scripture principle certainly predisposes one to trust the Bible and expect it to teach the truth. When encountering perplexing features in the Bible, it is instinctive for Christians to hope for some explanation or resolution. In this they are in line with the trustful spirit we see in the biblical writers themselves and with the historic confidence Christians have displayed toward the Scriptures over the centuries. Finding an error in the Bible would not necessarily discredit all of its assertions, but it would create some uncertainty about the Bible as consistently truthful. It is not hard to understand why there would be discussion about biblical inerrancy, especially in an age when the suspicion is abroad that the Bible is not trustworthy.[35]

At the same time, we must recall from the last chapter that the Bible itself does not teach a doctrine of inerrancy in so many words. Although we might grant that it teaches a broad and non-technical kind of inerrancy, it clearly does not teach a technical and strict version of it. Therefore, we ought to proceed with caution on this subject. Inerrancy, as Warfield understood it, is a good deal more precise than the sort of reliability the Bible proposes. The Bible's emphasis tends to be on the saving truth of its message and its supreme profitability for the life of faith and discipleship. It does not inform us about how we ought to handle perplexing features in the text.

That the New Testament does not clarify this issue is plain in that people today cannot agree even on the definition of the term "inerrancy." Much of our bickering stems from this inability to define the word effectively. Some make it a strict category, which necessitates a good deal of special pleading to show that minor discrepancies of one kind or another are not really so. Others find a great deal of room to move under this rubric. This latter view turns still others off on the grounds that, as ambiguous and difficult a term as it surely can be, it therefore should be dispensed with. Sticking with the simpler, less problematic language of the New Testament seems wiser to them than bickering over a word. If it often is not clear, even among those who use the term, exactly what inerrancy means, why impose it as some kind of shibboleth? It is obviously not the ideal term and should not be used to divide the Christian community.

---

35. Harold Lindsell (*Battle for the Bible*) stoked the fires of controversy that threaten to radically divide evangelicalism.

What, then, should we say about the reliability of the Bible and this question of inerrancy? First, we must proceed more carefully and stop being so dogmatic about it. All sides of the debate agree that the Bible is trustworthy in the fundamentals it seeks to teach. In telling us what God has said and done, it brings us to a saving knowledge of him and builds us up in our holy faith. Further, all are aware of certain perplexing features in the Bible that resist easy answers and require wisdom in knowing how to handle them, a wisdom in short supply among us, perhaps because of the pressure we feel from those denying the Bible altogether.

On one side, we have people claiming that, unless the Bible is perfectly inerrant in quite a strict sense, it cannot be trusted at all. Actually, they do not mean that our present texts of the Bible are inerrant, but the original autographs given long ago and not currently extant. What must ordinary Christians think of such an approach? They are being told, in effect, that they cannot trust the Bible in their hands because it contains potential errors. It forces them to place their trust instead in the scholars who are working to show why each of the hundreds of apparent errors are not real errors. Should they think seriously about it, it actually threatens confidence in the Bible they now have and substitutes a confidence that may one day be warranted when the scholars have finished their work—if indeed they ever do. Surely it would be an exaggeration to call this a high view of Scripture, since it does not allow us to trust the only Bible we have and possibly ever will have. And at the same time, our belief in the clarity of Scripture is also placed in jeopardy because we are told that texts that apparently say one thing may not say exactly that when all is known. All the while, we live in fear that a single point will prove inexplicable and thus eventually threaten to bring the whole of Christianity down on its head. There is not much wisdom here.

On the other side, wisdom is also in short supply. What is gained by going around claiming to have found so many biblical errors? What message is that calculated to give? And how sure are we that we want to call them errors anyhow? For one thing, it is well accepted that something formerly thought to be an error can, upon further research and reflection, turn out to be nothing of the sort. Besides, the question of error is so tied into the language game being played by the text that it seldom comes up in actual exegesis. The stated number of chariots may not agree with what is likely to have been the literal number, but that does not prove there was no truth in the number given in the biblical text. The person who announces the discovery that the Bible errs on the basis of a list of apparent errors is not likely to accomplish much except to forfeit the trust of Christians in his or her own teaching, since the instinct of ordinary believers to trust the Bible is greater than their instinct to trust such a teacher.

Warfield was right to say that one does not need to rush to negative conclusions but ought to wait patiently for the text to reveal itself. Biblical scholars are sometimes tempted to declare, in reaction to the fundamentalists, that the Bible makes mistakes. But wisdom would counsel them to be careful of the way they speak in this regard. It is wiser to delve into the purpose of the text and the reason for the anomaly than to come across in a textually demeaning way. Dogmatism about errancy, as well as about inerrancy, is foolish and immature and creates only problems. Worst of all, it raises suspicions about those very scholars who may in fact have many positive things to contribute.

The way of wisdom is to concentrate on the focused authority of the Bible, which is concerned to bring us the gospel and reconcile us to God, and not allow the marginal difficulties to cause us so much anxiety. We have all come to a vital confidence in Scripture on the basis of the Bible's less-than-perfect present state, and we must never forget this simple fact. It did not require a perfectly errorless Bible to give us certainty in the worth of the salvation narrative conveyed to us by Scripture. This fact ought to lower the pressure many feel and enable us to approach the problem of apparent errors in a calmer and more settled way.

Most biblical interpretation can make satisfactory progress without raising or answering this issue of marginal textual errors. Indeed, it is likely that evangelicals have spent too much time arguing about it, causing them to fall behind in productive scholarship. Not all difficulties have to be resolved for us to advance in our understanding of God's Word. Certainly, because of inspiration, we are right to expect a high degree of ordinary reliability from the Bible. But we are not in a position to know precisely what degree of inerrancy, according to our modern understanding of perfection, God has willed to actualize in the Scriptures. All we can do is trust the Bible and look to see what is there. When we encounter some perplexing detail in the text, we inquire into it to see if it will yield its meaning. If not, we will let it stand, refusing to cover up the difficulty by some scholarly ingenuity. The Bible has never lacked perplexing features, but we can count on it to work effectively in spite of them—as it always has.

In relation to biblical inerrancy, it might be best to adopt an inerrancy expectation as an operational policy. Although the New Testament does not teach a strict doctrine of inerrancy, it might be said to encourage a trusting attitude. Inerrancy is a very flexible term in and of itself. All those who use it qualify it in various ways in response to the perceived phenomena of the text. We are told by inerrantists that the Bible, in order to be inerrant, need not always give numbers exactly or spell everything just right or make precise references to things. It is not an intrinsically narrow term just because some use it that way. Therefore, given the fact that inerrancy expresses a sturdy confidence in the trustworthiness of the Bible in a day when we need it and also, when fairly interpreted, allows latitude in application, we see some wisdom in retaining use of the term. Donald Bloesch is right when he says: "I am not among those who wish to give up inerrancy and infallibility when applied to Scripture, but I believe we need to be much more circumspect in our use of these and related terms. Scripture is without error in a fundamental sense, but we need to explore what this sense is."[36]

Inerrancy, as we would employ the term, simply means that the Bible can be trusted in what it teaches and affirms. The inerrant truth of a parable is, of course, parabolic, and the inerrant truth of a fable is located only within the confines of that literary context. If Matthew gives us some fictional midrash, then it is inerrant according to the demands of this genre. All this means is that inerrancy is relative to the intention of the text. If it could be shown that the chronicler inflates some numbers for his didactic purpose, he would be completely within his rights and not at variance with inerrancy. The term "inerrancy" possesses a combination of strength and flexibility that makes it usable even in relation to biblical difficulties. It also enjoys wide acceptance in our day as symbolizing the trustworthiness of the Bible.

Inerrancy is not, to be quite frank, an ideal term to say what needs to be said. This is chiefly because it connotes for many people a modern, scientific precision that the Bible does not claim or display. The term thus requires a nuanced, flexible definition like Millard Erickson's: "The Bible, when correctly interpreted in the light of the level to which culture and the means of communication had developed at the time it was written, and in view of the purposes for which it was given, is fully truthful in all that it affirms."[37] This definition conveys the strong respect we are seeking as well as the room needed for handling the acknowledged difficulties in the biblical text.

Scripture and Church Authority

The same impulse that led the early church to define the canon of Scripture also led it to other conclusions. Underlying the logic of the Scripture principle is the belief that God will see to it that revealed truth will not perish but be reliably transmitted. This logic requires more than

36. Donald Bloesch, *Future of Evangelical Christianity*, foreword.
37. Millard J. Erickson, *Christian Theology*, 1:233–34.

a Bible because new questions arise and people wonder how the text should be interpreted. This kind of concern led the church corporately to move toward doctrinal definitions in the form of creed and dogma in order to spell out just what the message essentially was. Judaism had done much the same thing in extensive commentaries on the sacred text. Such authoritative commentary was particularly urgent when the church was soon confronted with religious pluralism and theological heresy.

Beyond this, a further safeguard of the truth was located in church authority. Christians began to think in terms of an authoritative institution that would not be subject to human failings and would be able to guarantee right perceptions of the truth year in and year out. Thus, the expectation underlying the Scripture principle itself resulted in other products as well, especially official creeds and a mediating church authority. The Roman Catholic tradition has believed that the truth is best served in this way. How, when the message is complex and the Bible's teaching less than self-evident, can we avoid moving along this logical path? We need more than the Bible to ensure that the saving truth will be passed along in its purity. The development of the church in a catholic direction from very early on is quite understandable.[38]

Protestants like to think they are different in this regard, but they really are not. The Protestant Reformers accepted the creeds of the early church and drew up extensive confessions of their own, as if a canon beyond the canon were needed to clarify what the Bible teaches. There is admittedly less tendency to accept institutional authority in Protestant groups, but even here pious things often are said about God calling together some church assembly and God guiding the wisdom of a particular church declaration. When this happens, the differences between Protestant and Catholic in the area of authority look faint indeed.

Of course, the same process is visible today. In response to the attacks on biblical authority, many conservatives believe that we ought to define the doctrine of Scripture with great precision and then specify the rules of its interpretation and the limits of critical study. Such rules and limits are like hedges around the Torah and are designed to prevent readers of the Bible from getting the wrong ideas. For all our talk about *sola scriptura*, the Bible is seldom left "alone." It is ironic that, in order to remain "evangelical" today, we find it necessary to be more catholic! The fact is that evangelicalism is theologically catholic without knowing it. Why would we refer back to Calvin or Luther or Augustine on the doctrine of Scripture unless we considered church tradition to be important? Today's call for a catholic evangelicalism should not surprise or disturb anyone.

38. Farley (*Ecclesial Reflection*, chap. 4) is clear and informative on this matter.

The logic that sees God providing Scripture to convey his Word and then raising up church leaders to further protect and define the message is good and scriptural. The idea surfaces in the Pastoral Epistles and is well articulated in 1 Timothy 3:15: "the church of the living God, the pillar and bulwark of the truth." Not only in the post-apostolic church, but in the New Testament period itself, false teachers arose and tried to pervert the truth. Action had to be taken against them. Paul warned the elders of Ephesus about the problem of heresy and instructed them to keep a close watch over the flock of God (Acts 20:28–31). He told young Timothy to be sure to pass the message deposit along to faithful persons who could do the same for others (2 Tim. 1:14; 2:2; 4:1–6). The Bible needs the church as its bulwark. How else will the sacred text be preserved, translated, interpreted, and proclaimed in proper ways? How else will its message be protected against attempts to distort it?

There is a link between the authority of the Bible and the work of the Spirit in the faith community. As the Preacher put it long ago: "A threefold cord is not quickly broken" (Eccles. 4:12). The Bible is the church's book and does its work best in the ecclesial context. Since Christian faith has clear content, we are dependent on definitions and delineations for proper understanding of that content. We need to have abbreviated statements of the faith once delivered. We need polemical demarcations of what is and is not Christian when false teachers propose their imaginative novelties. Sometimes it is necessary to define doctrines in the face of a serious challenge.[39] Where, then, is the Protestant any different from the Catholic in this area?

The difference came about through historical necessity. It would have been so much better if the threefold structure of authority had remained intact and the church of Jesus Christ with it. But the regrettable fact is that it could not. The message of salvation became seriously distorted in the tradition and had to be reclaimed. Luther's protest had to be made, even though its effect was traumatic for the unity of the church. Scripture had to be separated from the too-close embrace of the institutional church so that it could be free to reestablish its liberating message. As in Jesus's own day, the tradition that so often serves the Word of God well became a hindrance and had to be corrected. The tragedy was that the correction was resisted and the path of schism taken. Protestantism stands for the freedom of the Word of God to critique church traditions and bring them back into line with the gospel. It means abandoning traditions, if necessary, to get back on track.

Ideally, Scripture would be a norm along with tradition and church; but as it happened, Scripture had to be put over tradition to bring about

---

39. Hans Küng goes into this in *Infallible?* 144–50.

a reformation. What came to light was a keener awareness that, although the Bible is an infallible rule, the tradition is not. We may speak, as Hans Küng does, of the indefectibility of the church, of God's promise not to let it fall irretrievably into error and fail in its whole mission, but we may not speak of its infallibility, of any inability to go wrong and require reformation.[40] The catholic tradition tends to take the logic of God preserving his Word one step further than Protestants do, to the point of declaring the church magisterium itself infallible. Although understandable in terms of logic, it seems to be unwarranted scripturally and in view of historical developments. Tying up the package of authority so tightly in this way binds the Word of God to the creaturely realm more than it ought to be and permits the message to come under too much human control. Luther saw that we must give Scripture the focus of our greatest attention and let it have the primary authority.

All this seems to be implied in the notion of canon itself, which suggests a unique normativity over the developing traditions. Otherwise, the Bible would just melt into human traditions and lose its capacity to bring about change and reform. In opting for the canon, the church chose an external criterion of truth, a text that stood over and, at times, against the church. By accepting the norm of Scripture, the church declared that there was a standard outside itself to which it intended to be subject for all time. Being the Word of God in this special sense, the Bible could measure the other authorities and be the foundation for the Christian hermeneutic. The church can fall into error and needs the Bible to measure itself by. In turn, the church serves the canon by continuing in the truth and faithfully proclaiming the Word of God.[41]

40. Hans Küng, *Church*, section D, part 3, 1–2.
41. Oscar Cullmann, "The Tradition," in *Early Church*, 59–99.

PART 2

In Human Language

4

Incarnation and Accommodation

Thus far we have concentrated on the first duty in regard to the Bible, namely, to treat it as the written Word of God given to the church. Now we want to begin to speak about a second duty, the responsibility of accepting the fact that God gave his Word in human language. If we are going to grasp what God is saying to us through the Bible, we will have to understand these documents as historically and concretely as possible, in all their particularity. We will have to take note of the vocabulary, the literary forms, the character of the propositions, and the cultural background in order to pick up the nuances of teaching in the Scriptures.

The Bible is God's Word in human language. These God-human aspects should not be disassociated. God has willed the human characteristics of the text as much as the poverty of the manger and the hard wood of the cross. In the present chapter, we will consider the humanity of the Bible in general terms. In the next chapter, we will look at a host of textual phenomena that give flesh to this humanity. In chapter 6, we will examine the problems associated with biblical criticism.

Looking at the humanity of the Scriptures need not give us anxiety, because it is part of God's will for the Bible and because the Bible, with all of its humanity, has proven its effectiveness in carrying out its religious purpose in Christian experience. The Bible was given not as an end in itself but as a medium through which one can come to know and love God, just as eyeglasses are purchased not to be an object of examination but to help us see better. Ordinarily, the wearer of glasses is not conscious of having them on. The main thing is that they enable a clearer view of reality. Of course, glasses can be removed and inspected if the wearer wants, and this is what we are doing when we talk about the humanity of Scripture.

Anxiety for the believer ought to arise in this context only when the biblical medium is not functioning well for its intended purpose. If that is the case, the problem lies at a much more basic level than specks on the lens, as it were. No one who has come to know and love God through the good news of the Bible is likely to feel threatened by some supposed flaw on the periphery of the medium through which this knowledge has come (unless, of course, some rationalistic theologian comes along and suggests that he or she ought to!). Such a believer will more likely be puzzled by and curious about it, and want to obtain some information on the matter. We examine the humanity of the text, not because it poses a threat to the divine character of the medium of God's Word, which has already been settled for the Christian, but to facilitate its proper interpretation.

The Human Form of the Text

When we are open to receive the human form of the text, in which God was pleased to give us the Bible, we honor the divine way of wisdom in this matter. God himself has chosen to communicate with us using the resources of human literary composition, which belong to the creaturely realm. Therefore, it is irreverent for us to disregard this divine decision. It would be comparable to despising the bread and the wine in the Lord's Supper or, even worse, to demeaning the true humanity of our Lord Jesus in the interest of exalting his true divinity. This latter tendency in orthodox religion we call Docetism; it is a heresy that crops up also in the doctrine of Scripture, and for the same reason. We are reluctant to face fully the reality of the human in the case of Christ and the Bible for fear of obscuring the divine authority, and even the divine essence, of them both.

One recalls the occasion when Dorothy Sayers's play *The Man Born to Be King* was first performed on the BBC in 1941. Strong protests were heard because of the way she presented Jesus as a man among men. The listeners were unwilling to believe that Christ actually laughed and said "good morning," and they were shocked by her depiction of the crucifixion scene in the eleventh installment. The belief that Jesus is God incarnate tends to cause us to neglect any real sense of his being also truly human.

What is at stake with Christ and the Bible is whether we are prepared to honor the manner in which God has chosen to reveal himself to us.[1]

---

1. G. C. Berkouwer (*Holy Scripture*, chap. 1) is particularly concerned about the possibility that the conservative doctrine of Scripture will take a docetic attitude to the Bible. He feels that this doctrine is motivated by too great a preoccupation with apologetic reasoning.

God's will, evidently, is to reveal himself to us in forms of the creaturely realm in which the human is a fundamental element that cannot be ignored and should not be scorned. It is unbelief to be afraid of the divinely chosen mode of revelation. We should no more take offense at the plain, even vulgar, forms of expression in the Bible than at the humble circumstances of the birth of Jesus. For, in both cases, beneath the unimpressive exterior lies a treasure more valuable than all the world.

God's Word comes to us in human words and thoughts that are not transubstantiated, as it were, into divine words and divine thoughts. Earthly modalities are what have been chosen to convey the freight of divine revelation, and this must suffice. We have looked at the Bible as though from above; it is now time to look at it from below and consider the human dimension. There is no point in trying to save the Bible from its humanity. God chose it to be this way.

There is a very practical reason why we should honor the divine decision to employ the human in revelation. If God has joined content to form in this way, we can only understand the content in relation to the form. "What God hath joined together, let not man put asunder." If we are to rightly explain the word of truth (2 Tim. 2:15), we must pay the closest attention to the way in which the Word has been given. Neglecting the human flavor of the communication is bound to lead to misunderstanding. Only by taking careful notice of the human shape of the text will we be able to pick out its distinctive truth claim and receive God's Word as God intended.

If we were explaining the parable of the Pharisee and the publican, for example, we would need to understand what Pharisees and publicans were like in the first century and how people regarded them, and we would have to guard against reading modern presuppositions about them into the parable. In particular, we would have to remember that the Pharisee was a much-respected member of the community and not the social pariah that the name suggests to us today. If we do not know this, the parable will not register with the force it did when first told. It is very important to let the text speak authentically, and in order for that to happen, we the readers must give attention to the human form and situation.[2]

The texts in the Bible were oriented to another world than ours, and this must be taken into account if we hope to understand them. We will not understand revelation if we refuse to take into account the historical, literary, and cultural dynamics at work in it. Had Paul's letter to the Galatians been received by the Corinthians instead, how hard it would

2. Anthony Thiselton brings this point out forcefully in an essay titled "Understanding God's Word Today," in *Obeying Christ in a Changing World*, ed. J. R. W. Stott, chap. 4.

have been for them to understand it! Texts like Paul's epistles were written to specific communities and exemplify distinctive emphases. The more we can discover about these settings, the better our interpretation of these texts will become. Revelation comes to us embedded in history; therefore, we must attend to both. The human and divine components cannot be separated. As in the incarnation, they dwell together in unity. Both the divine Word and the human form are present in every place, and both call for recognition if we hope to understand rightly.

Let it not be said, then, that the reason we ought to attend to the humanity of Scripture is to win favor with negative critics who like nothing more than to point out how very human the Bible is. On the contrary, we do it in order to understand the Scriptures better. Unless we pay due attention to the form in which God's Word comes to us, we will not be able to grasp what that Word is. Instead, we will tend to twist the text and make it say what our context wants to hear. If we replace the original sense by superimposing upon the text our modern set of assumptions, we will abuse the Bible as surely as if we had denied its authority and declared independence from its rule. It is not only the modernist, after all, who twists the Bible. We all do it whenever we skip over the historical integrity of the text and choose the interpretation that our own situation calls for. If the Bible is our authority, then we must be committed to historical hermeneutics, which means we must view the text in its context and not as if it were floating above history.[3]

This, in turn, means that we will resist a certain tendency in orthodoxy to place the whole Bible on the same level of absolute assertion. Once the church has identified the whole Bible as the Word of God, the temptation is enormous to forget about the original historical situation and to regard every verse as a kind of oracle for us. This is the danger reflected in Augustine's expression "What the Bible says, God says." When we yield to this danger, we no longer hear the precise word spoken to people by the text in the first instance but construe it as universally valid, independent of the original context. Thus, a text may no longer have a merely provincial meaning but must have a universal application. The tendency is to dehistoricize the vehicle of revelation and make each text an immutable and inerrant proposition. Since God (in Hellenistic thinking) does not change in any way at all, neither can God's Word signify anything different for diverse communities existing at varying points in history. Progressive revelation is thus lost sight of and the Bible becomes a rigid, legalistic tool. Even though God, as revealed in the Bible narrative, obviously does command one thing for one group

---

3. David Tracy (*Blessed Rage for Order*, 49–52) articulates the principle that the Christian classic, the Bible, must be interpreted historically.

and something else for another (the Jewish and Christian communities, for example), there is an impetus at work in the doctrine of Scripture to minimize this feature of the text. The Bible must always be valid, even in changing circumstances. The remedy for such precarious deductions is, of course, due attention to the human form of the text.[4]

The Positive Side of Biblical Criticism

The positive value of the scholarly study of the biblical text, often called (wisely or not) "biblical criticism," is the way in which it focuses on the text as a past object and helps us to see it as it really was, not as an image from our own self-projection. Criticism tries to bracket the reader's prejudices and allow Scripture to be heard on its own terms. It asks about the date of the composition, the historical setting of the text, its function in the original receiving community, the type of literature it is, how it relates to similar texts, and so forth. By distancing the text from the reader, criticism allows the Bible to register better its own message and stand over our biases and preconceptions about these matters.

Such criticism's relative inability to tell us how to apply the text to our context does not overshadow or negate its ability to shed light on the original meaning of the text, which is the starting point, if not the end point, of hermeneutics. Biblical criticism has succeeded brilliantly in vastly expanding our knowledge of the historical, cultural, and linguistic backgrounds of the Bible. It has put into much sharper focus the distinctiveness of Israel's faith, the origin of the Synoptic Gospels, the religious environment of Paul's mission and message, and so on. Thus, biblical criticism is a permanent feature of the church's ongoing task of ascertaining the meaning of the Scriptures.[5] It is legitimated by the human character of the Bible, which comes to us not in a supernatural form raised above all human weakness but in the form of language that has to be translated, evaluated, and interpreted.

The subject of biblical criticism is burdened by the fact that, as a result of the fundamentalist-modernist debates of the 1920s, theological conservatives came to distrust biblical criticism, seeing it as a tool of Bible-denying influences. They were so alarmed by the anti-Christian presuppositions that often cropped up in criticism that they refused to see the good fruit that also came from scholarly study of the Bible. Although the suspicion has by no means disappeared, we are in a bet-

4. Edward Farley (*Ecclesial Reflection*, 42–46) calls attention to this tendency.
5. Willard Swartley (*Slavery, Sabbath, War, and Women*, 92–95, 243–45) shows a keen sense of the positive role of criticism in reverent biblical interpretation.

ter position today to appreciate the fruitfulness of criticism, especially when it proceeds unaffected by negative presuppositions. Indeed, we have come to the place where we can insist on the necessity of biblical scholarship as something that the Bible as a human medium requires us to employ.

As George Ladd has put it: "Because it is history, the Bible must be studied critically and historically; but because it is revelatory history, the critical method must make room for this supra-historical dimension of the divine activity in revelation and redemption. A methodology which recognizes both the historical and the revelatory aspects of the Bible is what we mean by an evangelical criticism."[6] Biblical scholarship implies not that we sit in judgment upon the Scriptures but that we take the historical nature of revelation seriously and ask intelligent questions of the text in terms of its history, philology, composition, and the like. The term "criticism" derives from a Greek word that means making judgments, and criticism as an art means asking questions of the text so as to learn more about it. In this sense, anyone who asks these questions is a critic. The opposite approach is to be unthinking in our use of the Bible—and thus disrespectful of it.

In the last analysis, the question is whether we are willing to accept the Bible as it is or demand that it be something else. Curiously enough, in their different ways both liberals and conservatives insist on a Bible different from the one that is given to us. The liberals criticize the Bible when it does not teach what they would like, but the orthodox sometimes want to save the Bible from itself when its humanity is uncomfortably obvious. Coming upon a difficulty or a hard saying, many interpreters resort to some desperate expedient to get around it and not have to face up to the divinely willed or at least permitted form of the text. However we do it, twisting the text to make it more acceptable to our convictions, whether liberal or conservative, is not something we ought to be doing. We are not in any position to prescribe for God how he must give his Word; we may only ask how God has actually given it.

If it appears that God gave the divine Word in some surprisingly human way, we must conclude that it is possible to be done that way. What exists must be possible.[7] Moses felt that he was not the kind of prophet God needed, and we may feel that the Bible is not the kind of text God ought to have given. But, ultimately, we have to defer to God's will in this matter as revealed by the results. After all, we are not fully competent to know what is best for us, so it is risky to prescribe what

6. George E. Ladd, *New Testament and Criticism*, 33.

7. Paul Achtemeier (*Inspiration of Scripture*, 95–99) notices how conservatives try to save the Bible from its own phenomena.

God should do. It lies within the divine freedom for God to do what he wills, and the wise course on our part is to receive gratefully what apparently has been done. We have no right to determine in advance what the biblical text must be like. What we must do is to look and see what actually is.

A Threat to Biblical Authority

We must be cautious, of course, when we stress the importance of the human, not because we fear what God has done, but because in the modern world people will take the human to have swallowed up the divine. In the past, the idea of divine revelation tended, as we have noted, to obscure the processes of human composition. God's initiative was very much brought to the fore. But now it is human work, human traditions, and human responses that are allowed to threaten revelation and inspiration. Revelation is being used to refer to human insight that emerges out of tradition. The Bible sounds as if it is God-given, but, in fact, it is being called a product of the human mind.[8] In place of orthodox Docetism, we have liberal Ebionitism that surrenders the divine authority of the text in favor of the human.

As Helmut Thielicke has pointed out, emphasis on the human dimension can swiftly lead to a radical questioning of the position of Scripture as the norm and rule over us. What may begin as an effort to study the human factor alongside the divine often spreads out to cover the whole territory. The integration of divine and human is lost, now in the opposite way.[9] The authority of the Bible is made relative, and its teachings are viewed in the context of transient human thought and time-bound cultural perspectives. The Bible is seen only as a human response to divine revelation, not as itself revelation or a divinely inspired product of it. As Langdon Gilkey says, the Scriptures are human, not divine, bearing witness to God, but themselves full of errors and mistakes, a means of grace but no true witness in terms of content.[10] In this way, the divine is displaced by the human and we are forced to regard the Bible as fallible human utterance.[11]

The reasoning behind this shift to the solely human sounds plausible. Modern consciousness tells us that any statement will be conditioned by its historical context and will share the biases and limitations of that time. There is no definitive culture. Every community is in continuity

8. John Goldingay, *Approaches to Old Testament Interpretation*, 125–45.
9. Helmut Thielicke, *Evangelical Faith*, 3:103.
10. Langdon Gilkey, *Message and Existence*, 52–53.
11. See, for example, Donald E. Miller, *Case for Liberal Christianity*, 36–37.

with every other one in the flux and change of human development. Every utterance, including those of the Bible, is thought by "postmodern" persons to be part of the time-bound, transient human situation, part of a network of fallible, human meanings. To think that the Bible is one enormous exception to this postmodern perception strains credibility.

Thus, the deepest problem facing biblical authority today is not whether there are errors in the text but whether the text can be viewed as anything more than a reflection of its time and place. How could it have escaped the relativity that hangs over all things human? The Scripture principle seems to violate the assumptions of modern historical consciousness.[12] This would mean, as David Tracy observes, that even "the theistic self-understanding of Christianity may be as time-bound and indeed erroneous as other of its once-cherished beliefs."[13] Even Karl Barth was prepared to admit that the biblical writers were not only capable of making mistakes, but actually did: "The men whom we hear as witnesses speak as fallible, erring men like ourselves." Of course, he turned away at the last minute from the dire implications of this statement for his own theology by appealing to the miracle of religious encounter and by questioning human competence to judge error in any given case.[14] Barth was obviously very close to the precipice.

We need to admit what a serious question this historical relativity raises for any thinking person today. As human, the Bible does exist in a network of history that can be examined. How can it be a divine Word unless it was directly dictated by God (a theory that has always attracted some conservatives because it seems to solve this problem)? How did the work of ancient biblical writers escape the historical relativity that is the human condition? No wonder classical Christians almost instinctively shy away from too close an examination of the human aspects of the Bible. They feel in their bones the danger of the human devouring the divine.

Grant Wacker has pointed out what a powerful effect the modern historical consciousness has had upon contemporary theologians. William N. Clarke, a leading nineteenth-century liberal in North America, started out believing in the inerrancy of the Bible, but because of his increasing awareness of the historicity of all things human, he moved gradually to the view that it is humanly fallible. And more troubling still for an evangelical, the great conservative A. H. Strong was greatly troubled by the same factor. He felt torn between the timeless certainties of the old

12. Farley, *Ecclesial Reflection*, 135–40.
13. Tracy, *Blessed Rage for Order*, 62n58.
14. Karl Barth, *Church Dogmatics*, 1/2:506–14 (quote on 507).

theology and the historical relativity recognized by the new theology. The two dwelled together in his mind and never did become resolved.[15]

To make matters worse for conservative theology, we do not admit the cultural limitations in the Bible very often. Not many of us insist on women wearing veils in church, even though Paul seems to command it (1 Cor. 11:5). Whether this is what Paul meant by "covering" in this passage does not affect the point. Christian women today typically do not refrain from braiding their hair or wearing jewelry and robes, despite Peter's instruction (1 Pet. 3:3). Even though people are often described as being demon-possessed in the Gospels, very seldom today do we resort to this explanation to account for strange behavior when we see it. We seem to have no difficulty transferring to the modern context what Paul said about slaves being obedient—we hold to abolitionism as self-evident. We readily accept references such as Philippians 2:10 as culture-bound, prescientific allusions (e.g., the three-decker universe connoted by "above," "on," and "under"). In other words, almost without thinking about it, we seem to acknowledge the liberal contention that there are culturally conditioned elements in the text that do not carry over authoritatively into the modern world. We seem to practice naturally the kind of "demythologizing" that we denounce when liberals speak openly of it. And we seldom explain what it is we are doing, even to ourselves and our faith communities.[16]

How might we explain it? Because we believe in the humanity of the Bible as the mode of God's revelation to us, we are not opposed to recognizing culturally conditioned aspects of the text, if that is what they are. We gladly admit that, in order to convey the divine Word to the church, God used forms of expression that were culturally authentic and meaningful to the time they are given. But we do not deny the infallibility of the Word that God is conveying, and we do not arbitrarily decide which material is culturally conditioned and which is not. On the contrary, we try to discern the claim that the text is making on us and submit ourselves to it. We search out diligently the intended assertions of the text and commit ourselves to them. In doing so, we keep in mind the covenantal purpose of the Bible, and in difficult cases we compare one Scripture with another. In everything, we seek the mind of the Lord and recall the wisdom of the past.

Admittedly, it is not always clear how we should handle the text. Should we perhaps wash one another's feet as Jesus said that disciples should? Should we not take the possibility of demon possession more

15. Grant Wacker, "The Demise of Biblical Civilization," in *The Bible in America: Essays in Cultural History*, ed. Nathan O. Hatch and Mark A. Noll, 121–38.
16. Robert M. Price ("Crisis of Biblical Authority," chap. 6) puts his finger on this painful feature of unreflective conservative thinking.

seriously than secular culture does? We should never pass by any declaration simply because it offends modern opinion. It is natural for a modern person to judge that, when calling God "Father," the Bible is reflecting the assumptions of a patriarchal age and thus we are free to adopt non-sexist language in place of "Father." But our respect for the reliability particularly of Jesus's usage of the term makes us hesitate to dispense with it. It makes us ask what the difference would be had the Bible spoken of God as "Mother" instead, and whether that difference does not still hold true.[17] But these are not matters in which dogmatism is called for, and they illustrate the careful caution that is appropriate. We strive to be biblical people, but we must not pretend that there are no difficulties in knowing how best to be so.

The real threat comes not from relatively unimportant questions like foot washing and hairstyles; it comes from the attempt to use the presence of culturally conditioned communication to evade and deny what the Scriptures most certainly do teach. Because of his thoroughgoing radicalism, Rudolf Bultmann illustrates what we must oppose. Starting with the assumption that the New Testament is basically a kerygma collection not intended to teach objective truth about God or deliver authoritative information about almost anything, Bultmann labels as mythological practically the whole of the New Testament message. Modern persons cannot believe in the incarnation or the atonement or the parousia or the resurrection or the Holy Spirit or the fall of Adam or miracles or Satan or sacraments! The result is not entirely negative for Bultmann himself, because somehow he exempts God from the list of unacceptable beliefs and sees value in the existential thrust of the New Testament, which is certainly part of its teaching. He supplies by his work an apt illustration of what can happen when the divine authority of the text itself is lost.

The answer to this kind of Bible denial lies in the fact that the New Testament, contrary to Bultmann's assumptions, most certainly does want to teach us truth about God and salvation and is not limited to giving a vague existential address. It is incorrect to say that Paul did not intend to communicate objective truth when he said that Christ died for our sins, or to suggest that the New Testament writers were not interested in the bodily resurrection as such when they proclaimed Jesus Christ risen from the dead. Of course, such assertions have a bearing on human existence; however, they possess relevance because they are true apart from our existence. As Paul puts it, "If Christ has not been raised, then our proclamation has been in vain and your faith has been in vain" (1 Cor. 15:14).

17. See Michael Novak, *Confessions of a Catholic*, 35–41, 49–58.

Before a redemptive fact can be existentially meaningful, it must first be a fact. Before we can safely trust the atonement as taking away our guilt, there must have been the shedding of blood. Biblical writers do use pictorial and analogical language in speaking about God—they had to, as do we. We cannot speak about God literally without falling into idolatry. But they were referring to transcendent realities when they used the imagery. They did mean to tell us truth about what concerns us ultimately. The similarity between what Bultmann does and what Bible-believing Christians do when they seek to discern the meaning of the Bible for today is significantly different. The latter seek to submit themselves to the Bible's teachings once they have determined what these teachings are, whereas Bultmann has no intention of doing so, having determined that the Bible is a fallible human book, not reliable in what it says except in a very limited existential sphere.[18]

What of the larger question of the modern historical consciousness? How could the Bible, even in part, be free of the nexus that seems to exist in all things human and that prevents any human utterance from being considered a Word of God? In the final analysis, this is a question about God and his freedom. The modern scientific approach is atheistic methodologically, as it should be. It is fitted for investigating the mundane creaturely realm. It cannot rule out the possibility of an absolute creator on whom the contingent world depends. Indeed, it seems probable that belief in God is necessary if the world is to be accounted for rationally. Christian theology, in any event, presupposes such a Person and therefore is not beyond its epistemic rights in claiming that God has reliably revealed himself and his will in a set of creaturely modalities. Belief is under no obligation to explain how it could be, because it frankly confesses the mysteriousness of God and his activities.

So long as the God of the gospel is believed in, the Bible itself is no conundrum. It can be God's infallible Word in exactly the way that it claims to be his Word, the product of God's revelational activity. If Jesus Christ was raised from the dead (and the evidence for believing this is strong), then the process of revelation and its products that center on the Christ are vindicated and validated along with him. How can the Bible transcend the causal nexus of the total human situation? It can do so because the nexus is not a closed one but a pattern of causality created by God and fit to be the theater of his self-communication. To deny this is both to lose hold on an infallible Bible and to give up the message of which it is part. Although liberals have chosen such a path,

18. Two fine critiques of Bultmann's theological method are Robert C. Roberts, *Rudolf Bultmann's Theology*, and Barry Smith, "Rudolf Bultmann's Hermeneutical Theory."

and the logical implications of traveling down it are plain, let it not be said that there is no other road to choose.

The Bible does stand over our culture and is the critic of the thoughts and intents of the human heart (Heb. 4:12). We recognize that the culture of today is very different from that of the Near East millennia ago, and we admit that in interpreting the Bible we have to take into account the distance between these two worlds. By no means, however, need we grant that the message of the Bible about the living God who sent the Son to be the Savior of the world is uncommunicable today and lacking in authority. Exactly in the way in which that same message challenged the polytheism and magic of the ancient world, it can today undercut the presuppositions of atheism and pantheism that underlie these objections to biblical authority.[19]

The Accommodation of Revelation

There are at least three categories we can use to bring out the human dimension of the Bible, categories drawn from Scripture itself and appropriate to our subject. The first category is *accommodation*. It is a familiar one from the history of theology. Many of the older theologians, like Origen and Calvin, spoke of God stooping to our human condition and lisping in his speech with us as a parent might lisp in speaking to small children.[20] In order for God to communicate with us, the infinite with the finite, he is compelled to employ the symbols of earthly speech and experience if we are to understand his Word. Perhaps we ought to think of these symbols as created by God in order to make his self-communication possible. Cross-cultural communication on this scale certainly requires God to accommodate his revelation to our creaturely condition so that we might be able to receive it. Selecting analogies from our universe of discourse and framing his message in the cultural forms we understand, God effectively revealed himself to us.[21] Immersed as we are in culture, this was really the only way to proceed.

Revelation comes in the form of a servant like the Lord himself. Because of the humility of God, Jesus was willing to partake of all sorts

19. J. I. Packer (in *Scripture and Truth*, ed. Carson and Woodbridge, 228–32) takes on D. E. Nineham and his contention that the differences between the way the Bible thinks and the way in which we think today are so great that they cannot be overcome.

20. Rogers and McKim (*Authority and Interpretation of the Bible*, chaps. 1–2) give many fine quotations in which the language of accommodation is used by classical theologians in reference to the Scriptures.

21. Charles Kraft (*Christianity in Culture*) goes into the dynamics of God revealing the divine being through culture.

of human weaknesses, and the Bible also bears the marks of its true humanity. In choosing to inspire a literature, God took up a human vehicle and adapted his revelation to the categories of understanding our minds are fitted to employ.[22] For this reason, it is important that we readers take careful note of the communication model of accommodation and make a serious effort to understand what is being conveyed by this means. It will be crucial to learn what the text meant in the cultural world in which it was first given before deciding what it ought to mean in our own. If we do not do this, we will be in danger of imposing on the text the expectations of our cultural circumstances and very likely missing the point.

Speaking of accommodation can make us feel uneasy. If revelation is not above the human and the Bible not unmistakably divine, how far is the text free from human taint, and how far can it be trusted? For this reason, some hesitate to use the category of accommodation at all, particularly because it seems to imply error in details of the text, and this would make God a liar (so it is said).[23] But surely, this is overreaction. Jesus, when he wanted to use an analogy of a seed for the kingdom of God, mentioned the mustard seed as the smallest seed of all. It was not scientifically the smallest seed in existence, but in the Jewish world of the day it was considered the smallest. God gives his Word to us authentically in ways that we understand, in ways that are culturally specific and able to be understood by those who come later.

Revelation comes to us as an earthly event, bearing the marks of humanity, in the forms of a prevailing culture, but without being swallowed up by it. As for those phenomena we call "apparent errors," they have been allowed to exist in the Bible. It may help some to tell themselves that the Bible once was free of these (in the autographs), but they have never seen such a Bible and cannot prove from the Bible's own claims that such a Bible ever existed. What we all have to deal with is a Bible with apparent errors, the exact status of which we cannot precisely know. Whether in his inspiration or providence, God has permitted them to exist. From this we may suppose that flaws such as these are not meant to make us stumble or divide the body and can exist without compromising the integrity of the intended revelation.

The second category is *incarnation*, the prime example of accommodation in revelation. Unlike the God of Judaism and Islam, the God of the gospel does not stay in a safe sphere free of contact with the lowly

---

22. Bernard Ramm, "The Modality of the Divine Condescension," in *Special Revelation and the Word of God*, chap. 2.

23. Wayne Grudem (in *Scripture and Truth*, ed. Carson and Woodbridge, 53–57) is very worried about any use of the term "accommodation" that might imply that inspiration permits the smallest error.

creation; God moves out of heaven and dwells with us in the God-man Jesus Christ. God is prepared to communicate to us, not only in personal, creaturely terms, but actually through a human life not protected against weakness and death. The preexistent Son did not cling to his rights as God, but laid aside his glory and took upon himself the form of a servant (Phil. 2:6–9). In this manner, God could reveal things about himself that could be shown in no other way. All the books in the world, as the evangelist said, could not contain the riches and depth of this disclosure (John 21:25). Paul, too, experienced the weakness that is intrinsic to human life. The body, as he said, is sown in weakness and raised in power (1 Cor. 15:43). The apostle was not ashamed to admit that he felt his human limitations keenly, just as prophets like Moses and Jeremiah had much earlier. He claimed to be no super-apostle, but rather an earthen vessel entering into the sufferings of Jesus. He even boasted in his weaknesses because God could be glorified through them (2 Cor. 12:10).

It is natural to see an analogy between the incarnational character of revelation and the Bible. As the Logos was enfleshed in the life of Jesus, so God's Word is enlettered in the script of the Bible. In both cases, there is some kind of mysterious union of the divine and the human. In each case, both the divine and the human are truly present. The analogy helps us to defend the true humanity of the Bible against Docetism and to defend its divine authority against the Ebionitism of liberal theology.[24]

Two other points should be mentioned in this connection. First, just as Jesus's sonship was both hidden and revealed, so that some people saw it and others did not, so it is with the Scriptures. They look like ordinary writings; they are interpreted in ordinary ways. Although they shine with glory to the eye of faith, they seem quite unspectacular to unbelief. We must take care in our defense of the Scriptures not to give the impression that we can prove their perfection in such a way as to make belief in them inescapable. God's revelation leaves room for our cognitive freedom and does not welcome such apologetics as might try to rip away the veil.

Second, the analogy between Christ and the Scriptures is often used in the following way. Just as Jesus, although human, was free from sin, so the Bible, although human, is free from error. Is this a legitimate argument? Even though the parallel is rhythmic and pleasing, it is not exact since sin and error need not be equated so closely. Jesus himself did not know all things, by his own admission, and therefore sometimes spoke in terms that belonged to the first century. In this he did not sin

24. Paul R. Wells (in *James Barr and the Bible*, 9–33, 340–49) has a lengthy discussion about the use of the christological analogy.

but acted as a man of his times. He claimed truth for what he taught but made no such claims for what he had not received from the Father (Mark 13:32; John 12:49). By analogy, we cannot conclude that the Bible never makes any mistakes, if these do not affect what the Bible was truly teaching. In other words, this issue cannot be settled by appealing to this analogy as a shortcut.

The third category is *human weakness*. As we have just noticed, Jesus was crucified in weakness, and Paul gloried in his weaknesses. "God's weakness is stronger than human strength" (1 Cor. 1:25). Revelation has not come to us in the unmistakable forms of glory but in the midst of human weakness. This is something to exult in rather than shrink from or be ashamed of. Some of our attitudes toward Scripture suggest a reluctance to embrace this truth. Our exaggerated concern about perplexing features in the text strongly suggests that we fear that people will not believe in Christ unless we remove all trace of weakness from the record. We should say with Peter, "Lord, to whom can we go? You have the words of eternal life" (John 6:68). We must not take offense at the Bible because it partakes of human weakness any more than we would at Jesus or Paul. Is not the quest for an errorless Bible, which presumably once was but is no longer, an indication of disordered priorities? The preaching of Paul and the message of the Bible bring human beings to Christ, despite their being weak—is that not enough for us?

In what way does the Bible show marks of this weakness? There are many details we can mention. For one thing, propositions fall short of expressing exactly what a speaker would wish. There seems always to be a gap between what is said and what was intended, and this leads to misunderstanding and the need for further clarification. Words possess a range of meaning and, even with the best intentions, one cannot prevent potential misunderstandings. Difficulties increase when the meaning has to be carried from one language to another. Some of the nuances cannot be expressed well in the receiving tongue. Furthermore, language is in constant motion, the language of both text and reader. Sentences can change their meaning in a new situation and become quite unintelligible. When we ignore such factors, texts can become weapons of our own ideology as we make them serve our private ends. Moreover, the Bible is a literature that no one would claim always excels in rhetoric and grammar. Its linguistic forms were not perfected but used in their ordinary human ways. There is often a strangeness in the Bible's manner and mode of expression.

We desire not to malign the Bible but simply to point out that God, in giving us a literary vehicle of his Word, accepted a definite limitation upon himself. God shows himself willing to speak to us within the limits of human language and to accept the risks that belong to this decision. Karl Barth was right to speak about a distance between the Word of God and the text of the Bible.[25] While the medium is limited in various ways, the message given through it overcomes these restrictions and triumphs gloriously. Language, although imperfect, is nonetheless a marvelous instrument of communication, so that, in spite of all the background noise that is present, the truth about God's saving plan is effectively stated. This has been our Christian experience, and it is the promise of God to keep his church in the truth.

In reaction to the Roman Catholic claim of infallibility and out of fear of modern secularism, many Protestants have exaggerated the perfection of the Bible and made it appear as though God literally were the real author, with the human writers merely passive writing instruments. We have tended to shy away from any thought of human weakness attaching to the sacred text. The slightest flaw, we have said, would have to be charged to the Spirit and would bring the authority of the Bible crashing down. It is time that we stopped denying the humanity of Scripture in this way. The Bible does not claim to be free of all deviations from a modern standard of truth, and a close study of the text proves that it is not so free.

Mark says that David entered the house of God and ate the loaves of offering under the high priest Abiathar, whereas 1 Samuel says it was under Ahimelech (Mark 2:26; 1 Sam. 21:1–6). In Matthew, the fulfillment of a prophecy from Zechariah is reported as coming from Jeremiah (Matt. 27:9–10; Zech. 11:12–13). Of course, explanations can be devised to make such examples fit with strict perfection, but it is not necessary or proper to seek them. The Bible does not attempt to give the impression that it is flawless in historical or scientific ways. God uses writers with weaknesses and still teaches the truth of revelation through them. It is irresponsible to claim that in doing so God makes a mistake. What God aims to do through inspiration is to stir up faith in the gospel through the word of Scripture, which remains a human text beset by normal weaknesses. Thus, God achieves his ends without doing violence to the human through a complete avoidance of weakness and historicity. As Hans Küng says, "Through all human fragility and the whole historical relativity and limitation of the biblical authors, who are often able to speak only stammeringly and with inadequate conceptual means, it happens that God's call as it finally sounded out in Jesus is truthfully heard, believed, and realized."[26]

The Bible is not, like the Qur'an (which is claimed by Islam to consist of nothing but perfectly infallible propositions), a book that should not be

25. See Bernard Ramm, *After Fundamentalism*, 89–95.
26. Hans Küng, *Infallible?* 215–16.

translated or commented upon for fear of corrupting the incorruptible. The Bible did not fall from heaven. We do not need to wash our hands before picking it up. Inspiration did not make the writers superhuman. It did not cancel out their historicity and weaknesses but guaranteed that through them the true testimony to Jesus Christ should come that would have lasting normativity and authority in the church. We place our trust ultimately in Jesus Christ, not in the Bible. He alone is the foundation and ground of our faith. What the Scriptures do is present a sound and reliable testimony to who Jesus is and what God has done for us in him. The marvel of it is that God has communicated, not through angels, but through ordinary human beings with all their limitations.

The Interplay between Human and Divine

A great mystery is involved whenever the divine and the human come into some kind of union. In the case of the Bible, it is natural to ask how the inspiration of God caused the human writing of the Scriptures. This is a speculative question with practical implications. Were we to think of God dictating the Bible, we would certainly fall into the docetic error of denying its true humanity; if we put all the emphasis on the literary freedom of human authorship, we might end up denying inspiration entirely, except in a nominal sense.

The traditional doctrine of biblical inspiration has certainly employed images that suggest total divine control of the process. The Fathers were fond of the image of musical instruments, thinking of God playing out a tune upon a flute. In plainer terms, they thought of God as the author of the text and the human writers as his instruments. The recognition of these biblical writers as truly authors themselves surfaces only occasionally (in Jerome, for example), and then only sporadically and inconsistently. In Scholastic theology, the Aristotelian category of efficient causality was brought into use. God effects his goal of an inspired Scripture by employing human beings as one might use a piece of chalk. The human agents were manipulated by the divine Author to realize his aim. It is easy to see how unsatisfactory this would sound to one who cared about free human authorship.[27] In the modern period, most conservatives wish to avoid giving the impression that God dictated the text word for word, but they still want to hold on to the ideal results of such a dictation. Whether God speaks "directly to people, through the lips of his spokesmen, or through written words, He is viewed as

27. For the patristic and medieval images of inspiration, see Bruce Vawter, *Biblical Inspiration*, chaps. 2–3.

the sovereign Lord of human language who is able to use it however he wills to accomplish his purposes."[28]

A text that is word for word what God wanted in the first place might as well have been dictated, for it leaves no real room for human agency. This is the kind of thinking behind the militant inerrancy position. God is taken to be the author of the Bible in such a way that he controlled the writers and every detail of what they wrote. Were we to allow that they made any kind of slip in the smallest detail, this would have to be attributed to God himself, which is impossible. Therefore, any appearance of such slips must be judged unreal, and an explanation must be sought that will prove that no slip occurred. Inerrancy thinking is deductive, rooted in the assumption of total divine control. Needless to say, it has a wide appeal for ordinary believers who have not looked closely at the human dimension of the text and who see it as a simple way of preventing denials of the Bible. Unfortunately, it also gets one into great difficulties with the actual phenomena of the text and places the entire truth of Christianity on not finding any slips in the whole Bible.[29]

In short, although it is true that few modern conservatives would admit to believing in the mechanical dictation of the Bible, they often talk as if they did. They believe in it materially, but not formally. To hold that God predestined and controlled every detail of the text makes nonsense of human authorship and is tantamount to saying that God dictated the text. Denying this conclusion is merely quibbling over words.[30]

The willingness of many modern conservatives to think in terms of total divine control, thus inviting the charge that they believe in dictation, stems from the Calvinistic orthodoxy underlying so much of the current evangelical movement. The theology of a B. B. Warfield or a J. I. Packer, which posits a firm divine control over everything that happens in the world, is well suited to affirm a verbally inspired Bible. The words of the Scriptures are thought to be predestined in God's immutable decrees and cannot be other than what they are. As the Westminster Confession puts it, "God from all eternity did, by the most wise and holy counsel of his own will, freely and unchangeably ordain whatsoever comes to pass" (chap. 3). The divine initiative in such a theology is so powerful and irresistible that it can determine the human response. Human beings can be said to choose, but what they choose was never in any doubt and

28. Grudem in *Scripture and Truth*, ed. Carson and Woodbridge, 54.

29. Gleason Archer thinks along these lines and has the ingenuity and the scholarship to make it seem to work. If he is to succeed, he will need to expand his *Encyclopedia of Bible Difficulties* to several additional volumes. On the other hand, the first one may be sufficient to convince many not to approach things this way.

30. William J. Abraham is getting at this point in *Divine Inspiration of Holy Scripture*, chap. 1.

cannot be other than what God predestined. Applied to inspiration, this means that the biblical text, down to the smallest detail, is what God ordained it to be and nothing else. It was easy for Warfield to say that God could make Paul write exactly what he did write just as a builder could get rose-colored light in his church by installing rose-colored panes of glass. People can be manipulated, according to this mentality, just as tools and materials can.[31] It is sometimes called "divine monergism," which means that God's actions are the only ones that really count.

Two qualifications are in order. First, there are some in the Reformed theological tradition who, like Barth and Berkouwer, would not endorse the high Calvinism we have just described. Still holding to divine sovereignty, they would not use it to deny human freedom, as rationality would invite one to do, but leave the two in tension and unresolved. Similarly, there are many who do not think systematically and limit their Calvinism to this one subject. After all, victorious divine sovereignty that is able to secure a perfect Bible has strong appeal to a broad conservative constituency that has little taste for other implications of predestinarian thinking. These groups think opportunistically. They want to be able to appeal to strong divine causality when it suits them (e.g., to secure a perfect Bible), but not when it does not (e.g., when a madman blows up an airplane). But one can only be permitted to do this if one admits that thinking consistently is not very important.

For a great many Christians, the idea of God being in total control of all things in general and of the Scriptures in particular is disturbing. If God really is in total control, then he must have willed all the tragedies and atrocities that have happened throughout history. He must have wanted them to happen to serve some higher purpose. Repeating the disclaimer that predestination does not make God the author of evil cannot change the fact that it surely does. God is the one responsible for everything that happens if he willed it so completely, and he must take the blame. This is the kind of theology that makes atheists. The only way around it is to posit a degree of creaturely autonomy and divine self-limitation.

There is a dimension of creaturely freedom alongside divine sovereignty that accounts for the events that go contrary to God's will. God brought a significant universe into existence outside himself and established a dynamic interaction between himself and the creation that Calvinism cannot satisfactorily account for. In terms of our subject, biblical inspiration, it is not logical to say that God is in total control of the Bible's composition and also that there was genuine human author-

---

31. "If God wished to give his people a series of letters like Paul's, he prepared a Paul to write them, and the Paul he brought to the task was a Paul who spontaneously would write just such letters" (Warfield, *Inspiration and Authority of the Bible*, 155). We are inclined to call this "Calvinistic theism."

ship. Such lack of logic leads directly to Docetism, which reduces the human aspect to a merely nominal one.

What is the alternative to such a lack of logic? How can God achieve his will in the world and with the Bible if his sovereignty is not all-victorious? Surely, inspiration means that these humanly chosen words are also divinely willed. If they were not, would the Bible not be a mixture of truth and error? How can one see it other than in a Calvinistic way? These are common and important questions.

At the level of worldview, we ought to conceive of God's will as including all things within its scope, but not as determining all things. As Paul says, "We know that all things work together for good for those who love God" (Rom. 8:28). It is not that God predestines everything to happen just as it does, but that he is able to overrule negative factors that come against his will and to bring about a good result. God is not yet in full control of a world in rebellion against him (we pray, "Thy kingdom come"), but God neither intends nor is forced to let that frustrate his purpose to save the world. God permits many things that displease and even anger him, but God is wise enough and powerful enough to weave them into the tapestry of his unfolding plan.

One might think of the master chess player who does not have to control his opponents to win a victory. He wins it through simple skill. Or, to use a more positive illustration (since humanity is not God's opponent in a game but the object of his love), God is like the bridegroom able to make the marriage work, or like a wise parent able to raise children in the way they should go. The point is that God is not manipulating puppets on a string but dealing with personal agents whom he created to resemble himself. God does not take away freedom from the creature in order to force his will and gain his ends. On the contrary, God is everywhere at work in the creation, upholding the structures of created causality, not working to undo them.

In relation to Scripture, we want to avoid both the idea that the Bible is the product of mere human genius and the idea that it came about through mechanical dictation. The via media lies in the direction of a dynamic personal model that upholds both the divine initiative and the human response. We want to allow for a human element in the composition of Scripture and also a strong role for the Spirit to ensure that the truth is not distorted by the human receptors. God is active in overseeing and directing the process of inspiration, and human beings are active and alive in responding to divine initiative. The prophet feels a fire in his bones and has to declare the divine message. The writer of wisdom and narrative feels no such action of the Spirit but proceeds to work under a quieter influence of the Spirit. The writers work "in many and various ways" (Heb. 1:1).

Variety and multiplicity characterize the results. One biblical writer will come across as intellectual, and another as emotional. One will patiently carry forward the tradition, another practice literary artistry. Some are nonconformists; others speak for the people. In all these dynamically different ways, the Spirit is active, inciting, superintending, and drawing out the work. God is present, not normally in the mode of control, but in the way of stimulation and guidance. The writers really are what they seem, truly human beings expressing themselves. God did not negate the gift of freedom when he inspired the Bible, but worked alongside human beings in order to achieve by wisdom and patience the goal of a Bible that expresses his will for our salvation.

If we were after a perfectly errorless Bible, this model of inspiration would not be enough. Such a text would have to be more strongly determined. The whole mental activity of the writers would have to be overruled in order to produce a text that was a divine utterance in each and every detail. But this is not what the Bible claims to be. Instead, it presents itself as an adequate and sufficient testimony to God's saving revelation, which culminated in Christ. A higher degree of perfection would no doubt require a Calvinistic cosmology and a material dictation, but this is not something the Bible aspires to. The authority of the Bible in faith and practice does not rule out the possibility of an occasionally uncertain text, differences in details (as between two of the Gospels), a lack of precision in the chronology of events recorded in the books of Kings and Chronicles, a prescientific description of the world, and the like.[32]

The Bible claims to be God-given Scripture, but not to be inerrantly dictated. Therefore, we are free to go back and check what is actually there in the text. Although expecting only truth, we can be open to diversity, various genres, perplexing features, and intents of different kinds, all the while keeping our eyes on the basic thrust the Scriptures were given to deliver. We will not have to panic when we meet some intractable difficulty. The Bible will seem reliable enough in terms of its soteric purpose, and the perplexing features on its margins will not strike fear into our hearts and minds. In the end, this is what the mass of evangelical believers need—not the rationalistic ideal of a perfect book that once was but is no more, but the trustworthiness of a Bible with truth where it counts, truth that is not so easily threatened by scholarly problems.

Classical Christians need not be much affected by the observation that the Bible's humanity makes it impossible to regard it as divinely authoritative as well. If God made the world for his own self-communication,

---

32. Richard J. Coleman brings this out in *Issues of Theological Conflict*, 163–65.

then it should not be too difficult to believe that it is the kind of world in which revelation must be possible. What we have, in effect, is a struggle between two kinds of Monophysites: conservatives who think of revelation as entirely divine, handed down from heaven, virtually unmediated, and liberals who think of revelation in very human terms, historically relative and open to continual change. In this debate, it is clear that we must be willing to grant the human reality of revelation ungrudgingly. Revelation does not simply come to us from above; in fact, it is mediated through the human. Were we to admit this fact, we would be less defensive in facing up to the sometimes perplexing phenomena actually found in the biblical text.

Biblical inspiration should be seen as a dynamic work of God. In this process, God does not decide every word that is used, one by one; rather, God works in the writers in such a way that they make full use of their own skills and vocabulary while giving expression to the divinely inspired message being communicated to them and through them.

The Human Dimension

Thus far we have considered the human aspect of the Bible in a general way. The moment has come to examine some of the specifics that fill in the category. We want to ask exactly what God has done in accommodating his Word to human language. What is involved in confessing the humanity of the Scriptures?

As in Christology, it is important to approach biblical revelation both from above and from below. We need to look at the Bible from the standpoint of its claims to be the canonical Scripture of the church and from the standpoint afforded by the phenomena of the texts themselves. The claims give us a framework in which to operate, whereas the phenomena add specificity to our understanding. The two factors are dialectically linked, and we need to travel back and forth between them. To ignore the claims leaves us without any overall perspective, and to bypass the textual phenomena leaves the doctrine of Scripture empty of detail and in danger of distortion by the observer who will add his or her own expectations derived from modernity.

Our respect for the Bible as the Word of God means at the outset that we will be open to allowing the text to declare itself, and will resist seeking to change the literary vehicle to suit our own expectations. We will not try to be more biblical than the Bible. It would not be a good witness if we are found tampering with the text in order to deal with some awkward detail. The Bible must be allowed its distance, and this means not trying to overcome its strangeness by dubious means. There should be a willingness to face up to the facts, whatever they are. Belief in biblical inspiration commits us to respecting the concrete forms in which God gave us his Word.

When we inquire into the difficulties of the text, we are touching on a pastoral and apologetic issue. Christians can be disturbed by what they read in the Bible, and it is part of our care of souls to try to relieve their minds. But non-Christians can see difficulties as a barrier to faith and demand answers. Sometimes these two obligations can pull us in opposite directions. In order to assure believers, we may be tempted to offer answers of a strict and safe kind, whereas for outsiders, we may try creative solutions to make it easier for them to believe. But the two needs are not really at odds. Believers deserve the same kind of solid and honest answers that unbelievers demand. Ministry to the former includes ministry to their minds, and the answers for the latter must go beyond the merely intellectual to the challenge to decide about God's offer of salvation. Dealing with Bible difficulties is an aspect of our ministry of the Word of God.[1] Modern readers of the Bible will find difficulties in the material being read, and we are required to face up to the reader's problem.

Before beginning to categorize these textual problems, we should remember that, to a large extent, difficulties exist in the eyes of the beholder. For example, a person with a modern scientific worldview might take exception to premodern Hebraic expressions in the Bible and find them difficult. A person of Catholic or Calvinist persuasion will run into some text that will sound problematic in his or her ears. Someone who expects absolute perfection of detail will stumble at the smallest slip, whereas another will take such minutiae in stride. It is important, therefore, to consider whether a given difficulty exists in the Bible itself or is created by a reader who balks at something in the text. After all, the Calvinist's proof texts are difficulties for Wesleyan readers, and the other way around.

Human Modes of Thought and Expression

At the level of minimum difficulty, the biblical writers employ the linguistic resources available to them. They have to make use of their

---

1. Gleason L. Archer's *Encyclopedia of Bible Difficulties*, apart from its alarmist stance and overcautious approach to possible solutions, is in many ways a helpful contribution to this literary genre.

vocabulary stocks, semantic ranges of meaning, peculiar forms of expression, conventions, even styles of thinking and of argument. In all of this, they are not lifted off the earth or out of culture but function in their own contexts.[2] The language of the New Testament, for example, is Koine Greek, which differs in grammar and vocabulary from classical Greek. Thanks to archaeology and the discovery of first-century papyri, we understand much better the New Testament writings. Along with the language, we have to pay attention to the style of teaching and argument employed. Using Semitic hyperbole, Jesus can speak of cutting off a hand, and in a rabbinic manner, Paul can write about Mount Sinai and Hagar in an allegorical way (Matt. 5:30; Gal. 4:21–31). In the various books, the personalities of the writers also shine through, giving us a vivid impression of what Jeremiah or Amos must have been like. Evidently, the Spirit did not dominate these writers in such a way as to obliterate their individualities. Paul was a real man, beset by deep concerns and a universal vision, who spoke to specific situations in a directly relevant manner.

We should pay close attention to the language that is used if we hope to discover the precious truth embedded in the Bible. Even translation is a tricky business. Words change their meanings over time, as an Old Testament writer reminds us: "The one who is now called a prophet was formerly called a seer" (1 Sam. 9:9). A word can broaden or narrow its scope, or shift to what was once only a marginal nuance of its meaning. It can be frustrating to look for the best equivalents to the biblical phrases in our modern languages. The writer of Ecclesiasticus understood this when he remarked, "You are invited therefore to read it with goodwill and attention, and to be indulgent in cases where, despite our diligent labor in translating, we may seem to have rendered some phrases imperfectly. For what was originally expressed in Hebrew does not have exactly the same sense when translated into another language. Not only this book, but even the Law itself, the Prophecies, and the rest of the books differ not a little when read in the original" (prologue). In order to get at what was originally intended by the Bible, we have to look very closely at the tools and media of communication and also stay modest in judging the efforts of others in interpretation, seeing how difficult the task can be.

A slightly greater problem is the cultural assumptions of the biblical writers, which can create difficulties for readers of other times and places. For example, the Bible measures time not by atomic clocks but by the monthly cycles of the moon and the yearly turn of the seasons. When it wants to make psychological remarks, the Bible will refer to the heart, the bowels, or the liver. When it wishes to describe the physical

---

2. George B. Caird, *Language and Imagery of the Bible*.

universe, it will do so in ways that correspond to Hebrew beliefs. The New Testament writer may refer to the Septuagint, the pre-Christian Greek translation of the Old Testament, to make a theological point, even though this may make some nervous (Heb. 11:21). In other ways, the sacred writers are much less concerned than we are about precision when they quote texts and report events. Even more striking is the way they freely make use of beliefs that were traditional but not necessarily asserted by the writer. For example, the writer of Job, as well as other writers in the Old Testament, refers to the great serpent Leviathan that God defeated at the dawn of creation (Job 3:8; Ps. 74:14; Isa. 27:1). Baal defeats him in the texts from Ugarit, and he appears in the Bible as Satan the great serpent. In a different example, Jude refers to the apocryphal book of 1 Enoch in his epistle, probably because it was a respected source among his own readers and expressed a valid insight on the point at issue (Jude 14–15).

In cases such as these, the difficulties can be resolved by observing that the detail in question enters into the formulation of the text but does not constitute the burden of its teaching. In themselves, these difficult passages are certainly not transculturally inerrant in an abstract sense. They belong and remain part of the furniture of the vehicle bearing the freight of revelation to us, but they do not constitute the revelation itself. They illustrate how God elects to speak to people in the ways in which they are accustomed. It would be wrong to denounce these expressions as errors but also to defend them as not culturally bound. They are merely the means by which God gave us his truth.

The question, obviously, is how we distinguish between what is normative in the text and what is only cultural. There is no simple rule of thumb. We have to learn to discern what a text is asserting through experience in interpreting texts. It is a skill that comes with experience, and one not limited to reading the Bible. Bernard Ramm makes a wise comment:

> In reading Plato, Aristotle, Augustine, and Aquinas, we frequently find items that are purely of the culture of the time. But this does not prevent us from laying bare the essential metaphysics of Plato or Aquinas; nor do these purely local, temporal, cultural items disqualify the basic metaphysics of these great thinkers. By taking as our guide those clear transcultural statements of Greek and Medieval authors, and adding to this a knowledge of the culture of their times, we can readily thread our way through their writings to determine what is essential metaphysics and what is not. There is no clear and precise rule for the classicist to tell what is cultural and what is transcultural. That is an art, and a skill developed from his learning.[3]

3. Bernard Ramm, *Christian View of Science and Scripture*, 54.

The truth can still shine through in spite of some difficulty in getting hold of it. The rule would be to go after the intended teaching of the passage in question, noting what is incidental to that meaning and considering the matter in the light of the purpose of the Bible as a whole. Accommodation is risky, but it is the price of good communication.

The risk becomes concrete when we encounter religious liberals who desire to eliminate some feature of a text. For example, they may wish to deny that Paul taught a substitutionary atonement, and try to support the denial by saying that the belief in blood atonement was a cultural assumption and not meant to be carried over into modern theology. Or they might claim that so-called holy war or Jesus's remarks concerning hell belong to the incidental and the culturally conditioned aspects of the text and should therefore be passed by. The question must always be, Is this truly incidental to the text or simply objectionable to the reader? We have no right to exaggerate the quantity of what is cultural merely to accommodate our own hermeneutical difficulties. Such difficulties are not really in the Bible but only in our own minds. We must resist misusing the principle of cultural relatedness as a cloak to evade what the Scriptures really want to teach.

Of greatest difficulty in the area of human thought and expression are those theological and ethical assumptions that are linked to language and culture. To what extent do such beliefs affect biblical teaching? Were the destruction of the Canaanites, the practice of polygamy, and the institution of slavery Israel's way of thinking, not God's commandment, even though represented as God's will in the Bible? These difficulties are much more sensitive because they enter into what the Bible does want to teach and thus cannot easily be labeled incidental to it. If matters in the actual teaching content of the Scriptures are understood as fallible, that is the end of the Scripture principle. Does it not place a question mark over the Bible's competence and authority to be our guide? Would it not land us in the dilemma posed by James: "If you judge the law, you are not a doer of the law but a judge" (James 4:11)?

Everyone would grant that God took a people for his name and service where he found them. He did not insist that they be perfect; nor did God make them perfect all at once. Israel may have been delivered from Egypt but was not yet completely delivered from sin. The Old Testament makes no attempt to gloss over the sins of even its main figures—Noah, Abraham, Jacob, David. They all behaved disgracefully on occasion. We are not meant to imitate them but to learn lessons of another kind.[4]

It is also clear that God engaged Israel in a process of education that was meant to take them from a lower to a higher plane of religion and

4. John W. Wenham, *Goodness of God*, chap. 7.

morality. It is very important in interpreting the Bible to recognize the principle of progressive revelation. God's truth is not given all at once. The light begins dimly and grows brighter. Seeds are planted early that grow into mature trees. Revelation takes human beings where it finds them and does with them what it can. The old covenant was replaced by a new covenant. The promise was met with fulfillment. Values relating to power and wealth expressed in the Old Testament were sharpened and deepened in the New Testament. Jesus introduced changes in Old Testament Sabbath law, and Paul declared circumcision not to be binding upon Christians. In the soil of Old Testament texts, God sowed principles that later would flower into a more perfect disclosure of his will.[5]

Let us not skirt the crucial question: Does progressive revelation go from false to true, from fallibility to infallibility? Certain difficulties in the Bible tempt us to think so, but the implications for the Scripture principle would be very serious. Fortunately, Jesus speaks to this kind of issue in his pronouncements on divorce and provides us with a model for proceeding. Having been asked about the Mosaic statute that gave limited permission to the male to divorce his wife, Jesus replied: "For your hardness of heart Moses allowed you to divorce your wives, but from the beginning it was not so" (Matt. 19:8 RSV).

In this reply of Jesus, we are given several valuable principles to use in thinking about progressive revelation. First of all, Jesus clarified that God really did grant such permission to Moses in that time and for that dispensation, so there is no question of it being a mistake or merely a human idea of Israel's. It is very important when reading the Bible to ask whether a given command is meant for us and, if it is, whether in the same form or in some other. God gave many commandments to Israel; some of them do not apply to us at all, and others apply to us differently. We have to take our stand within the circle of messianic revelation, as Christ did, to find out what now applies and how. Second, Jesus identified this commandment as less than ideal, given for the hardness of their hearts. It was not God's highest and best command but the one demanded by their moral and spiritual condition. It even fell short, as Jesus pointed out, of the creational purpose of God. Jesus saw the command, not as a mistake, but as a culturally-directed and less-than-ideal value that had validity when it was given, although now it was being transcended in the gospel. Evidently, there are texts in the Bible that are not as relevant and adequate as others for Christian purposes, and we need to be alert in reading them. In a certain sense, there is a canon within the canon, insofar as the Bible itself indicates a certain weighting of the material by

5. James Orr, *Revelation and Inspiration*, 175–77; and Richard J. Coleman, *Issues of Theological Conflict*, 166–69.

messianically directed revelation. In the most obvious case, the New Testament must be taken as the key for interpreting the Old Testament.[6]

To see if this paradigm will work, let us apply it to a few of the greatest difficulties, those in which the severity of God is shown. Paul refers to "the kindness and the severity of God" as two facets of the divine action in the world (Rom. 11:22). Although it is easy for us to credit a revelation of God's grace and salvation, it is harder to credit examples of God's wrath and judgment. If, however, we wish to approach the Bible as Jesus did, in line with the Scripture principle, it will be necessary to search out the truth and wisdom even in these passages and avoid rushing to negative judgment that probably would be based on our own prejudices. Where the Bible differs from our modern attitudes may be precisely the place where we need to listen most carefully to it. We must not regard our own opinions as absolute when we read the Bible, for it is wiser than any of us.

Many Bible readers have great difficulty with God's command to Israel to slay the Canaanites and spare no one. In terms of holy war, they were expected to devote the whole population and its goods to the Lord by means of complete destruction. It would be bad enough if it were Israel's idea, but the text presents it as God's command through his servants (Josh. 10:40). What a temptation to put this down to human sinfulness and deny the teaching of the Bible at this point!

Three comments are in order. First, this command should be viewed in its context. It was directed to the destruction of an exceedingly wicked people. It did not become the policy of Israel in later centuries. At a later date, the prophets often counseled surrender rather than all-out warfare. We have to see the command to exterminate the Canaanites in relation to their own sinfulness and the threat they posed to Israel's relationship with God in those early days of covenant life. Texts from Ugarit have revealed some details of Canaanite religion and culture (child sacrifice, religious prostitution) that suggest that these people were ripe for destruction, as the Scriptures say (Gen. 15:16). The Lord is a holy God and does not indefinitely tolerate human abominations.

Second, history is the record of the destruction of civilizations, which have fallen because of their corruptions. What bothers us here is that Israel was used as God's instrument of judgment. Indeed, this is the only time God used his people in this way. The fact is that, through the providence of God, nations come and go in every age. Although it is not pleasant to be the executioner or to view the process in action, God's command is certainly just, and even merciful, when viewed in the larger context.

6. Edward J. Carnell, *Case for Orthodox Theology*, chap. 4.

Third, Jesus more than anyone else warned of a divine judgment to come that would be more universal and terrible than any before it, so it is difficult to make the case that New Testament revelation judges holy war in the Old Testament to have been morally illicit. If anything, the severity of God is brought out more strongly in the gospel than in the law. It may be that we have to ask ourselves whose assumptions need correcting, the Old Testament's or our own.[7]

The so-called imprecatory psalms, along with divine curses that are pronounced upon the wicked, are additional examples of this divine severity that grate upon our modern minds. We may recall that C. S. Lewis felt it necessary to judge such sentiments unacceptable to the Christian mind. How can we sympathetically understand a writer who wants babies to be dashed against a rock? Even when we allow for an example of human frustration in the face of gross evil, how can we countenance such sentiments? Again, we have to be receptive and view the issue in the broader biblical context. Blessings and curses are a basic part of God's covenant with Israel. God blesses those who love and obey him and curses those who disobey his commandments (Deut. 27–28). The prophets bring out very plainly God's intention to curse those who do abominable things. Ezekiel and Jeremiah are full of oracles of divine judgment, which is the proper response to wickedness.

These difficult texts belong to a larger doctrine of divine justice and should not be viewed in isolation. Things do not alter when we enter the New Testament. Jesus himself declares to some, "Depart from me into the eternal fire" (Matt. 25:41). He speaks of whole communities being destroyed on the day of judgment (Matt. 11:24). His own death on the cross is interpreted as a curse upon him in his capacity as the sin bearer (Gal. 3:13). And the saints of the Revelation cry out, "O Sovereign Lord, holy and true, how long before thou wilt judge and avenge our blood on those who dwell upon the earth?" (Rev. 6:10 RSV). We simply cannot dismiss texts of cursing without asking about the broader picture the whole Bible gives us of the justice of God. The biblical writers and poets are crying out to God to vindicate his holy name and bring deserved judgment upon the wicked. Perhaps if we had faced a Stalin or a Hitler we would have found it easier to read these texts. True, God does not delight in punishment but desires to save sinners (Ezek. 33:11). Nevertheless, the Bible is very plain in saying that in the end God will judge them. There can be no question here of revelation progressing from false to true. Judgment is part of revelation from beginning to end.

To take another example, in Old Testament law the death penalty is invoked for a number of crimes, including murder, adultery, homosexual-

---

7. Wenham treats this problem well in *Goodness of God*, chap. 8.

ity, witchcraft, and incorrigibility. Did God really command such things, or did Israel misread his will? Notice that we are not asking whether we should adopt this practice in modern society (that is a separate issue) but whether God expected Israel to adopt it in theirs. Does the Word of God fail us at this point, or is there some other explanation?

Here we come up against a real difference between the Old Testament and many modern ideas. In our society, sentiment for abolishing the death penalty has been widespread. We have considered it more just and humane to put a murderer away for twenty-five years without hope of parole (in Canada) rather than put him or her to death. In the Bible, on the other hand, God says the murderer ought to die. Have we merely adopted humanist ideals rather than biblical ones in this case? Do we find ourselves in a situation where the Bible's solution seems increasingly more just than our own? Whose morality is defective at this point, the Bible's or ours?

What we have to do in these cases is consider the wisdom to be found in the ancient statutes, however peculiar they seem to us. Witches were to be executed in ancient Israel because they represented a threat to the divine plan for God's people. Homosexuals were threatened with death because their lifestyle was a gross contradiction of God's created order of sexuality and destructive of family and, ultimately, the nation. We do not know how often, if ever, such sanctions were put into effect, but they stand as a warning against theological and moral corruption in Israel.

By contrast, in our permissive society with its high rate of family breakups, it is hard for us to take seriously the Old Testament when it prescribes death for adultery. Maybe our values need correcting. Is it not ironic and savage that our law punishes a person harshly for stealing money or goods but is very lenient toward a person who robs father or mother and ruins family and home? In terms of harm and misery, adultery is far worse than the theft of material resources. We had better be cautious before we point out the mote in the Bible's eye, considering the beams in our own.

Even in the case of the incorrigible youth who is to be put to death for stubborn rebellion, we can see the divine wisdom (Deut. 21:18–21). This becomes clear as soon as we ask what our own supposedly superior policy is. Do not our rebellious youth die in car crashes or spend their lives in prisons and asylums or go on destroying their own lives and the lives of others? Having this kind of sanction to back it up, the ancient Israelites had means of persuasion and hope of true reformation that we lack. Even in the hardest cases, we ought not to be hasty in judging the Bible, which has a tendency to prove wiser than all its critics.

To conclude, we are not in a position superior to the Bible. God's Word comes to us in human language, and there are features in it incidental to its teaching purposes; but, in "all things necessary" in relation to what the Bible wishes to teach us, it is true and coherent and possesses the wisdom of God.

Human Modes of Literary and Historical Composition

At the basic level of minimum difficulty, we have to put aside modern inhibitions and alien expectations and permit Scripture to employ whatever forms of literary composition it chooses. It is a simple question of the sovereignty of God and the freedom of the text to determine its own thrust and form. Although it is natural for readers to expect those forms familiar to them, we must be open to surprises when the text employs literary forms no longer in use. To some extent, the problem is eased by the great influence the Bible has exercised in Western culture, so that forms such as proverb, parable, and lament are familiar to us already. Nevertheless, we must remain open to fresh examples that may come out of the ongoing scholarly study of the text. It is not our right to sit in judgment on the text and measure it by our standards of appropriateness.

Divine inspiration can make use of all forms of literature employed by humans and make them into media of the Word of God. Note this: "We affirm that the text of Scripture is to be interpreted by grammatico-historical exegesis, taking account of its literary forms and devices, and that Scripture is to interpret Scripture."[8] The reason exegesis is important is to enable us to understand the text better. Unless we grasp the language scheme that is being played out in the text, we may not be able to comprehend what is being communicated in it. Valid interpretation requires that we pay attention to such factors as literary form.

The modern reader is able to take a large number of these literary forms in stride. We have become accustomed to Jesus using hyperbole (hating father and mother, Luke 14:26) and picturesque speech ("the kingdom of heaven is like a mustard seed," Matt. 13:31). These were ways of communicating the truth vividly in first-century Palestine, and they can still be effective when people are open to them. In his use of the Old Testament, Jesus saw parallels between himself and figures and events in the sacred narrative. His own impending death was typified in Moses's raising up the serpent in the wilderness (John 3:14). He under-

---

8. Typical of the *Chicago Statement*, the next sentence reads: "We deny the legitimacy of any treatment of the text or quest for sources lying behind it that leads to relativizing, dehistoricizing, or discounting its teaching, or rejecting its claims to authorship" (article 18). One feels a certain reluctance to accept certain literary forms even if the text suggests them.

stood the Old Testament to prefigure what was going on in his own day. Occasionally, even allegory is used, as when Jesus spoke of himself as a vine (John 15), and when Paul spoke in detail of the Christian's armor (Eph. 6).

Every language has its pithy sayings and proverbs. Because of their brevity, they often express only one side of a complex truth and will be balanced out in the collection by a seemingly contradictory proverb, inviting the reader to think about the issue and decide what course to follow. Besides prophecy and proverbs, there is apocalyptic, whose interpretation is made difficult by the extraordinary imagery used in representing events present and future. It is common for this genre to suffer misuse by those who refuse to study the original setting and this distinctive form of discourse. Hebrew poetry is familiar to us because of the psalms, with their imagery and parallelism. The book of Job is a literary composition in the form of a long, dramatic poem that grapples with the problem of evil in human existence. It has always been apparent that Matthew arranged his genealogy of Christ deliberately so as to create three groups of fourteen names, even though it meant dropping out some of the links given in the Old Testament. Obviously, he was following the literary conventions of Jewish historians of his day and made good use of the possibilities they afforded. Examples such as these create no real difficulty for most current readers of the Bible because they do not grate harshly on their own literary presuppositions.

However, it is not always clear sailing. Conservatives are very touchy about the historicity of the fall of Adam because of its importance to their soteriology and theodicy, and, therefore, about the status of the Genesis narratives on that event (Gen. 2–3). They are reluctant to admit that the literary genre in this case is likely figurative rather than strictly literal, even though the hints are very strong that it is symbolic: Adam (which means "Mankind") marries Eve (which means "Life"), and their son Cain ("Forger") becomes a wanderer in the land of Nod ("Wandering")! Pentateuchal criticism is often associated in our minds with evolutionary theories of Israel's religion and is held suspect by biblical conservatives. Nevertheless, the literary characteristics that underlie the theory are there and must be accounted for. They include the use of divine names in certain large blocks of material, the duplication and even triplication of the same story, breaks in sequence, differences in vocabulary and syntax, and the like. These are literary facts, not liberal theories, and call for some explanation.

Serious differences in the numbers in parallel accounts in Samuel, Kings, and Chronicles have been noted for centuries. How many men, chariots, and horsemen were there, anyhow? It would seem not only possible but even likely that some of these discrepancies may be explained by assuming that the inspired writer(s) or editor(s) took the figures as found in the official records and copied them for their own purposes. It was enough for the chronicler, let us say, to acquaint the returning captives with their heritage by publishing this material just as it was, and not necessary for the Spirit to rectify any mistakes in it. Inspiration can make use of ordinary channels of information without raising them to a standard of complete perfection.

Chiefly out of a concern to defend belief in the miraculous, conservatives have been strong defenders of the historical genre of the book of Jonah. It reads like a historical account and is used by Jesus in relation to his own historical victory over death. But there are also indications that the book might be didactic fiction serving a prophetic function. After all, Jonah does seem to die, according to 2:2, not merely suffer extreme privation in the belly of the fish. Could it not be a storylike narrative pointing forward to Jesus Christ? And then there is the book of Daniel. Although it seems to be made up of some prophecies given to a man named Daniel in the sixth century BC, there are also good indications that it is somehow tied in with events in the second century and the Maccabean revolt (Dan. 10–12). From this, many would conclude that the book stems from that later period. There is the possibility that the book was attributed to Daniel out of godly, not evil, motives. In the case of Ecclesiastes, at least, it is almost universally granted that the writer was not Solomon, even though that is the impression one would get from the first verse and from allusions later on in the text. The actual writer had a good reason for putting the piece in the mouth of Solomon.

To take a few examples from the New Testament, when we read the Synoptic Gospels, it is obvious that someone is copying from someone else. It is also apparent that the evangelists feel free to reword the sayings of Jesus and place them in new settings. Robert Gundry has proposed that we understand the literary form of Matthew as midrash, and that we should not regard every detail in it to be historical in nature.[9] Luke did not hear Stephen's speech, so we assume that he must have reconstructed it himself from reports available to him (Acts 7). There are unusual features in the Pastoral Epistles that lead one to wonder if they might not have been written by a disciple of Paul's rather than by Paul himself. Jude appears to refer to a legendary incident in the life of Moses to make a point (Jude 9).

The point we are making is this: the Scriptures have the right to choose what literary forms they will use, and we must be open to what they decide. This is not to say that we have to accept whatever speculation biblical critics advance or that we have to deny a traditional interpretation

9. Robert H. Gundry, *Matthew*, 623–40.

just because it is traditional. It is simply a question of our willingness to respect the liberty of the biblical writers to choose their forms of literary composition, even if it shocks us and contravenes our standards of writing. Once we grant Jesus the right to use fictional stories called parables to make a point, we are on the right track. He did not use parables to deceive people about historical facts. He simply decided that this was a good way to teach the people at that time. Therefore, we must not be suspicious of the biblical scholars who try to inform us about these matters, but give them a fair hearing because their expertise is precisely to determine unfamiliar literary practices and to help us understand the Word of God better. We have our literary ideals in the Western world and must take care not to impose them on the Bible, which has its own.

Many of our difficulties with the Bible arise from its way of writing history and from its manner of using details. We in the West are schooled to look for exact information and factual accuracy, so when we read the Bible, we expect the same thing. We automatically suppose that a detail is recorded because it corresponds to factual reality and is not fictional. If it is not true in this scientific sense, we do not look kindly on it. When we read the creation story, we think immediately about evolutionary biology, not about those issues that concerned the ancient writer. We simply tend to assume that apparently descriptive narrative is necessarily what it appears. Because we impose such expectations on the text, we create for ourselves a large number of difficult problems.[10]

We must not yield on the principle that the Bible has a right to report history the way it chooses; it does not have to answer to us. Despite history being crucial to the biblical message, we have to grant the Bible its freedom to employ the styles of historical writing it wants to. The *Chicago Statement* was correct in making this generous concession: "We deny that it is proper to evaluate Scripture according to standards of truth and error that are alien to its usage or purpose. We further deny that inerrancy is negated by phenomena such as a lack of modern technical precision, irregularities of grammar or spelling, observational descriptions of nature, the reporting of falsehoods, the use of hyperbole and round numbers, the topical arrangement of material, variant selection of material in parallel accounts, or the use of free citations."[11]

In essence, the problem is that the Bible was written long before a clear line was drawn between strictly historical and storylike narrative. Whereas we are eager to distinguish the factual from the nonfactual, the same cannot be said of the biblical writers, and we worry about the

10. This is a point made repeatedly by Northrop Frye in his book *Great Code*.
11. Article 13. This comment is so generous, in fact, that some strict inerrantists will live to regret it simply because it allows a large degree of critical freedom. It is difficult to think of a liberal critical opinion that could not be worded to fit into this specification.

imprecision they permit in their work. We are even tempted to improve their work by making definite what they left indefinite.[12] The price we pay is a large number of biblical difficulties that exist not so much in the text as in our own enculturated minds. A few illustrations will bring this into focus.

Starting with some Old Testament examples, indications of the special character of the Bible's historical writing crop up again and again. At the very beginning, we are confronted with a six-day creation and begin to wonder how the world could have been created in so short a time. When we look for other explanations, we soon notice the internal parallelism of the days (days one to three describe spheres, and four to six point to the inhabitants of those spheres) and contextual factors (the need of the Jews to correct the theology of the Babylonian creation myths). The problem seems to be a misunderstanding of the literary genre. In the narrative of the fall of Adam, there are numerous symbolic features (God molding humans from dirt, the talking snake, God molding woman from Adam's rib, symbolic trees, four major rivers from one garden, etc.). It is natural to ask whether this is not a meaningful narration that addresses more than factual matters. Then there is the long life span of the antediluvian patriarchs, who are said to have lived an average of 857 years according to Genesis 5. Are these not, perhaps, an imitation of the epic traditions of Sumer, whose kings lived many times longer still? Conservatives sometimes are bothered by the figures, with some of them suggesting a different meaning for "year" (without any evidence).

In Genesis 10 there are figures named Egypt, Canaan, and Sidon, supposed ancestors of those later entities. It is like reading about Mr. Canada and Miss France. The Great Flood of Genesis 6–9 is presented as if it engulfed the whole world in water, but we have to wonder if the purpose of that description was to have us seriously investigate the archaeological evidence for such a remarkable catastrophe. The genealogy in Exodus 6 allows for only four generations between Levi and Moses, a period of 430 years, an obvious abbreviation of the actual time span. In the chronology of the judges and Samuel, periods of twenty, forty, and eighty years are continually assigned to the various leaders of Israel. Elsewhere, it is said that Moses, Eli, Saul, David, and Solomon all reigned for forty years. It is suggested that the figure 480 years in 1 Kings 6:1 is really an aggregate number made up on the basis of twelve generations of forty years each. It is rather clear that the Old Testament does not use such numbers in the way we do today. As is well known, the numbers in the versions of the census recorded in Numbers are both confused

12. Hans Frei has called our attention to this fact in his important work *Eclipse of Biblical Narrative*.

and abnormally large. According to Numbers 1:45–46, the number of able-bodied men in the exodus wandering was 603,550, which means, if you count women and children, that the number of people must have neared three million. This number can hardly be taken literally when one considers that the Canaanites were said to be more numerous and that Israel herself was chosen even though she was "the fewest of all peoples" (Deut. 7:1, 7).

Efforts have been made to have the term "thousand" mean many fewer, but these do not work out smoothly and look like a dodge. It is probably best to admit that we do not know what these numbers mean and consider them part of the epic style intended to magnify the majesty and miracle of the deliverance from Egypt. This may also be the best explanation of the chronicler's numbers. Although his are not always higher than those of the parallel accounts, he spoke of the million men who fought against Asa, and it seems that his purpose is not to give the plain facts but to adorn the victory by exaggeration (2 Chron. 14). Our point is not that there are no solutions to these difficulties that bring them closer to factual truth, but simply that the overall impression is of a style of historical narration different from ours and not to be twisted against its will into conformity with ours. We may be creating problems for ourselves because of our unwillingness to let the text be itself.

The same phenomena are found in the New Testament, although on a smaller scale. When we study the Gospels, we find different wordings of the same sayings of Jesus, placed in different settings. In one story Jesus will say something that someone else says in the parallel account. Many questions occur to us: How often did Jesus go up to Jerusalem? On what day was he put to death? What exactly was written on the sign above his head? How often did the cock crow? How interesting it is to compare the catechetical plan of Matthew's arrangement with Luke's order and his unique account of Jesus's journey from Galilee to Jerusalem. In cases such as these, rather than force the material into an unnatural harmony, we should admit that these texts were not written to satisfy modern historians or to conform to our current standards of historiography. They were written to lead people to know and love God and were designed on historiographical principles native to the ancient world. Neither should we charge the Bible with error or struggle to eliminate what we should just accept. If we would stop objecting to the form of the Bible for our own apologetic reasons and let the phenomena be what they are, we could be more relaxed with the Bible and do less violence to the text and ourselves. So many of our difficulties are not in the Bible at all, but in our own heads.

The stakes are highest when we raise the question of whether there is legend in the Bible. Although perfectly natural in the sense that legend is a universally known literary form, it is highly controversial. To admit legend is to touch two sensitive nerves at once: the factuality of biblical history and the reality of the miraculous. If we admit legend in the Bible, would we not be opening the door to a program of demythologizing that would reduce the gospel to anthropology? What on the surface seems to be a simple question of literary form suddenly becomes a theological hot potato. Once you admit that Lot's wife may not have literally turned into salt, where can you stop in turning the biblically narrated mighty acts of God into fables? Is the history of salvation only a way to present existential truth and not important as divine action in time and space? Surely not! Scripture does care about historical facts that prove the power of the Lord. Their existential significance arises out of their objective reality, and complements it. To demythologize and existentially reinterpret them would be to falsify the claim that is being made. Even so, minds should not be closed to varying literary types and readings appropriate to them.

Legend as a biblical literary type is a modern problem as much as a biblical one. It is problematic, not so much in itself, but in our eyes and for modern reasons. On the one hand, we cannot rule legend out a priori. It is, after all, a perfectly valid literary form, and we have to admit that it turns up in the Bible on occasion. We noted already Job's reference to Leviathan and can mention also Jotham's fable (Judg. 9:7–15). There the prophet speaks of the trees going forth to anoint a king over them. Obviously, he is teaching a truth in the form of a nonhistorical tale. Jesus's parables present something of the same form. There is no good reason why we should deny the possibility of legends in the Bible, apart from our own anxieties about how far it might lead.

It is unfortunate that Scripture is not more precise about this point. It does not label anything "legend," nor does it rule out legend in a categorical statement. The Bible comes from a time when it was not necessary to draw a clear line between the objectively factual and the storylike features of narrative. Today, however, we see a need to make a sharp distinction. We are worried that, once something is admitted to be legend, there will be no stopping people from calling things legend that certainly are not; thus, we want to close the door firmly on the whole category. But we cannot do this methodologically, because we are committed to facing squarely the humanity of the Bible and are not free to twist the evidence to suit our own contemporary agendas. Legends are possible in theory—there are apparent legends in the Bible, but we fear actually naming them as such lest we seem to deny the miraculous.

It would be helpful if there were clear criteria for identifying legends, but there are not. What makes something seem to be legendary is its abnormality. People do not turn into salt; they do not come out of hot furnaces unburned; they do not live a thousand years. When we read of such things outside the Bible we do not hesitate to regard them as legend, because we prefer to think in terms of ordinary causation rather than special divine action (even though we would not rule that out in principle). We believe that God can do anything. But if "there is nothing too difficult for God," how can we ever know that a given case of the improbable is or is not a legend? If we believe that God is active in a decisive way in the sphere of history narrated in the Bible, how can we ever come to the conclusion that something is a legend there? We cannot go beyond saying that there are legendlike features in parts of the Bible, because the story of redemption itself is an enchanted tale (God's spell), as Tolkien reminds us, and opens up to us a realm deep in wonder and mystery. If we do not make room for the miraculous here, we may miss everything, even the whole point of the story itself.[13]

We think it best to approach this difficult subject in the following way. Revelation, according to the Bible, is much more than a set of eternal truths or a plain historical record. It is the disclosure of a mystery that can be understood up to a point but also goes beyond full understanding. To convey this mystery, the Bible uses a wealth of literary forms. In addition to historical records, theological meditations, and poetic outpourings, there is imagery that grips and challenges us. Some aspects of the Bible's idiom offend us as modern people. We tend to think of things like myth and legend as primitive and outmoded, as practically devoid of value for teaching truth—even an impediment to the scientific mind. Therefore, in our apologetics we often leave no room for such a category and try to sweep it under the carpet. We worry that if we were to allow it in Christianity, we would introduce fiction and error. Being arbitrarily restrictive in this way, however, we not only narrow down the scope of revelation but close our minds to aspects of the Bible itself.

When we look at the Bible, it is clear that it is not radically mythical. The influence of myth is there in the Old Testament. The stories of creation and fall, of flood and the tower of Babel, are in pagan texts and are worked over in Genesis from the angle of Israel's knowledge of God, but the biblical framework is no longer mythical. God is described as sovereign over history and every power, breaking down the presuppositions of myth. What we find, however, are "broken myths," allusions to ancient myths now translated into different terms. They occur in the Bible as symbols of the realm of transcendence and no longer as events and literal references.[14] But the mythical traces are still there and need not

13. Royce G. Gruenler (*New Approaches to Jesus and the Gospels*, chap. 10) has a fine discussion on Tolkien's liberating perspective on the good magic of the godspell.
14. Brevard S. Childs, *Myth and Reality in the Old Testament* (London: SCM, 1962).

be denied. In Psalm 74 it is stated quite plainly that Yahweh fought with the sea-monster: "You broke the heads of the dragons in the waters. You crushed the heads of Leviathan" (vv. 13–14). In Psalm 29:1 it is plain that the writer does not deny the existence of multiple "heavenly beings" but only insists that Yahweh rules over them, whatever they are. The fact is, "the LORD is a great God, and a great King above all gods" (Ps. 95:3).

Frequently in the biblical text we read of things like night hags (Isa. 34:14) and a rock that followed Moses in the wilderness (1 Cor. 10:4). We read of a coin turning up in a fish's mouth (Matt. 17:27) and of the origin of the different languages of humankind (Gen. 11). We hear about the magnificent exploits of Samson and Elisha. We even see evidence of the duplication of miracle stories in the gospels. If we read any of these things in another book, we would surely identify them as legends.[15] Perhaps there is an explanation for the sun going backward (Isa. 38:8) and the day being lengthened (Josh. 10:13), but maybe not. The category of legend would explain them all.[16] Karl Barth has suggested that we speak of "saga" in these cases, a kind of writing that is neither myth nor exact description but a storylike expansion of God's intervention in history, an expansion not accessible to historical investigation as such.

What we really want to avoid is what has happened in New Testament criticism over the past century. Operating out of a rationalist framework, men like David Strauss argued that the entire gospel was a mythical message embodying in a primitive form the philosophical idea of God-manhood. Soon after, scholars of the history of religions school contended that the New Testament message was decisively influenced by the Hellenistic mystery religions. The mythical mystery god simply acquired a new name—Jesus of Nazareth. In the twentieth century, Rudolf Bultmann maintained that the gospel is given in mythical terms in the New Testament and needs to be demythologized and existentially reinterpreted. This mythology stands in the way of modern people believing the good news and must be eliminated. In Bultmann's positivist world, every aspect of the paranormal is labeled myth and legend and then discarded. Even the resurrection of Jesus is viewed as likely a myth because the dead do not rise and any such historical happenings, if they ever did happen, are not the central point of the gospel message anyway.

Our point is that being receptive to legend as a possible literary form does not open the door to the improbable and destructive thesis of Bultmann. There is no mythology to speak of in the New Testament. At most, there are fragments and suggestions of myth: for example, the strange

15. Caird, "The Language of Myth," in *Language and Imagery of the Bible*, chap. 13.
16. Ramm (*Christian View of Science and Scripture*) supplies some ingenious explanations for phenomena that at that time he was unwilling to identify as legends.

allusion to the bodies of the saints being raised on Good Friday (Matt. 27:52) and the sick being healed through contact with pieces of cloth that had touched Paul's body (Acts 19:11–12). But these are not typical of the New Testament story. In it we find the emphasis on the bodily resurrection of Jesus as the factual occurrence that grounds the message of salvation (1 Cor. 15:14). No wonder several passages in the New Testament denounce even the category of myth, so far is the gospel message from that hazy world of discourse (1 Tim. 1:4; 4:7; 2 Tim. 4:4; Titus 1:14). As Peter emphatically states, "For we did not follow cleverly devised myths when we made known to you the power and coming of our Lord Jesus Christ, but we had been eyewitnesses of his majesty" (2 Pet. 1:16). The gospel is simply not a mythical message and should not be treated as if it were. Only distortion can result from doing so. At the same time, we are free to inquire about any individual detail, whether it is intended as simple fact or is a legendary embellishment.

The important thing is to note carefully what the text says and implies. Matthew and Luke both present the miraculous conception of Jesus, although they differ in what they relate in almost every other respect. This makes it difficult for us to appeal to this miracle as an apologetic proof, but its location in the context of the great miracle of the incarnation that so excites the entire New Testament ought to discipline us against considering it a legend. The temptation of Jesus sounds mythical in picturing Jesus being interviewed by Satan in the desert and standing with him on a mountain from which they could see all the kingdoms of the earth. It is likely that this is the mode of presentation only, the point having to do with Jesus defining his own messianic mission in relation to dark alternatives.

Satan is much more than a furtive figure one might bump into on a trip through a desert. In Capernaum, Jesus was opposed by a man with an unclean spirit and overcame him. It was certainly important to Mark that the demon was real and that it knew the true identity of Jesus (Mark 1:21–28). For ourselves, we are able to admit to the reality of the demonic, too, but are usually unsure how to define and locate it. We would usually consider it part of the incomprehensible mystery of evil and not be able to say much more. But there is no reason for us to deny the demonic supernatural any more than the divine. It is enough to know that Jesus has the authority to overcome the powers of darkness and to deliver us from them.

There are cases in which the possibility of legend seems quite real, such as the account of the coin in the fish's mouth (Matt. 17:24–27). The miracle is almost incidental to the pericope. It supplies the actual coin with which to pay the tax but is not necessary to the teaching, which concerns our obligation toward taxation. The event is recorded only by

Matthew and has the feel of a legendary feature. From the book of Acts, in addition to the strange miracles mentioned earlier, there is Paul's escape from poisoning in Malta (Acts 28:1–6). Prior to this, Paul had a number of narrow escapes from danger. God is seeing to it that his journey to Rome will be successful. It is entirely possible that God delivered Paul in precisely this manner; it is also possible that this reference forms part of a hero narrative and is not an expression of literal fact.[17]

On this matter, current believers have become unnecessarily polarized. Some liberals have insisted on the nonfactual character of biblical history in favor of its existential nature, with the result that conservatives have felt it essential to defend the factual to the last detail. But historicity and existential significance are not in opposition to each other, and there is no reason to create the chasm between them that we have. History and theology are closely intertwined; little is gained from trying to pull them apart. One unfortunate result has been to make it difficult for conservatives to be relaxed in the face of the Bible where history is concerned. Our respect for the Bible should compel us to grant that the text has the sovereign right to employ the literary and historical modes of writing that it decides to use.

Conclusion

First, it must be stressed that the literary vehicle, Scripture itself, has the right to determine its own forms, not the reader. The Bible does not attempt to hide the marks of its humanity. In inspiring the Scriptures, God made full use of human intermediaries operating out of specific cultural contexts. His Word comes to us through a variety of literary forms, and all of them deserve our close attention. It is inevitable that a modern reader will have difficulties with the text at numerous points, and assistance should be offered. But seeking to skirt issues or engaging in ingenious attempts at harmonization are not wise because they dishonor the Bible and discredit its supposed defenders.

Simple honesty is essential. It is not edifying to see liberals or conservatives tampering with the text to avoid something in tension with their own presuppositions. The distance of the text, its integrity apart from us, must be maintained if it is to be our norm. We must be willing to face the facts, whatever they are. Because religion touches the deepest emotions, believers easily become inconsistent when their whole worldview seems to be threatened. We can be tempted by clever epistemological tricks that offer to ease the pain of religious doubt. But our love for the

17. Bruce Kaye, *Supernatural in the New Testament*.

God of all truth must be great enough for us to refuse such seduction. What lies in mystery should be allowed to so lie.

Second, the kind and number of difficulties in the Bible definitely vary with the expectations brought to the text by the reader. The Calvinist will want the Bible to be Reformed, the Wesleyan will want it to be Wesleyan. A scientific person may want it to be technically accurate, whereas a literary person may glory in the symbols and the imagery. The difficulties arise when the Bible does not meet these expectations. In a sense, we create the difficulties for ourselves. None of them are "in" the Bible per se. They are self-imposed burdens that we bring as modern readers.

Among classical Christians, including ourselves, there is the conviction that one ought to expect the Bible to be reliable and true because it claims to be God's written Word and carries the message of salvation to the world. That is to say, the burden of expecting the Bible to prove reliable ought to be accepted as part of the revelation package of authentic Christianity. It should be gladly borne; it is the Scripture principle. Part 1 of this book has already explained the basis for making this assumption. But there is a debate within the ranks of conservative Christians concerning how the Bible is reliable and true and to what extent it is perfect. The debate arises from the natural desire to believe the Bible without reservation.

Conservatives feel instinctively that their faith rests on the authoritative information and instruction the Bible yields, and that the Bible must therefore be totally trustworthy down to the smallest detail. God's own reputation is often thought to be at stake. Therefore, there are a large number of evangelicals in North America defending the "total inerrancy" of the Bible. The language they use seems absolute and uncompromising: "The authority of Scripture is inescapably impaired if this total divine inerrancy is in any way limited or disregarded, or made relative to a view of truth contrary to the Bible's own" (*Chicago Statement*, preamble). It sounds as if the slightest slip or flaw would bring down the whole house of authority; we ought to defend the errorlessness of the Bible down to the last jot and tittle in order for it to be a viable religious authority. As critics like James Barr point out, attempting to bring off this errorless stance involves a good deal of strained reasoning.[18] Even worse, it has set brother against evangelical brother and created an atmosphere of destructive suspicion. How one addresses this tragic circumstance becomes more important than the other great issues in theology. How can we move beyond this impasse?

18. Much of James Barr's book *Fundamentalism* is devoted to making this point painfully clear.

Recalling what was said in chapter 2 about the Bible's claim to be the reliable covenant document of the church, let us compare our emphasis with the claimed inerrancy of the Scriptures. The Bible itself claims to be able to bring us to know and love God in Jesus Christ and to nurture us in that saving relationship. Nothing is said about vowel points in the Hebrew text of the Old Testament. Nothing is laid down about grammar or literary conventions or proper historiography. We hear nothing about original autographs and how perfect they were, as distinct from our present copies. The New Testament writers do not seem embarrassed to cite the Old Testament text freely or even creatively. The complexities we debate today simply are not discussed, and we do each other wrong when we make too much of them. Let us not try to be more evangelical than the New Testament by drawing up a rigidly orthodox belief at this point and using it to shut people out. We could not do this if 2 Timothy 3:15–17 were our guide rather than a scholastic conception awkwardly deduced from it.

In saying this, we have no desire to pick and choose in the Scriptures on the basis of this larger purpose we have identified. We cannot decide which of the assertions of the text we would deem worthy to stand in the privileged circle of revealed salvational truth! Such a procedure would surely put the reader in a position to gain control over the Scriptures, eliminating texts displeasing in their thrust. For example, one might not follow Paul in his teaching on homosexuality, saying it does not matter because it does not constitute salvational truth. But it is up to the writer and text to decide that. If the Bible asserts it, it must be part of its purpose or else it would have been omitted. The situation is rather more like this: We know well what the Bible was given to do—to be our reliable teacher for salvation and sanctification and to testify to God's undeserved grace for sinners. We trust it to be able to carry off its great purpose, in part because it has achieved its goal in our own case. We have, in fact, come to love and serve God because of the Bible. So its reliability in the fundamental sense has been established for us. After all, the Bible is the medium of the gospel, and we have come to know God by reading and hearing the gospel in and through it. This is by far the most important thing.

Therefore, when we encounter difficulties in the biblical text, we face them calmly and consider what they are and how they fit in. If we have come to know God in the Bible, they will appear to be relatively unimportant and we may have to leave the questions they raise unanswered. We should not be stampeded into specious logic but approach the difficult texts in a spirit of calmness and hope. Just as precritical Christians found it possible not to worry about perplexing features because God still speaks effectively to them through the text, so postcritical believers who know more about the difficulties can also tolerate them, even when they are not solved, because they know where the real authority lies and can turn a wise hand to the difficulties themselves. We think that the real problem is the Christian who otherwise lacks assurance about the living God and fears losing all security if a single difficulty appears unsolved in the Bible. We doubt that any number of clever solutions will be able to put that mind at rest.

Are we saying that no difficulty could successfully shake the Christian's confidence in the Bible because it is grounded in religious experience and not in these empirical matters? No, we are not. Could nothing falsify one's confidence in the reliability of the Bible? Yes, something could, but not such things as whether Methuselah lived 969 years or whether the bowels have a psychological function. Phenomena on this order cannot bring the house of authority down. Only something that could falsify the gospel and Christianity could truly falsify the Bible, such as a difficulty that radically called into question the truth of Jesus and his message of good news. A point of chronology in Matthew that could not be reconciled with a parallel in Luke would certainly not be such a difficulty. Let us never put the church in a position where difficulties on this tiny scale loom so large as to threaten its fundamental confidence in the message the Bible exists to declare.

The Bible makes a strong claim to be true in a particular way. We have no basis for being dogmatic when we encounter perplexing features in the text. We cannot say that an apparent error will be solved sooner or later by our scholarly efforts; nor can we confidently say that this is a flaw for which there can never be a solution. We have to take the evidence as it comes, not rush to judgment, and rest in the marvelous gospel of Christ that shines clearly through the divinely revealed biblical text.

6

Biblical Criticism

The more conservative a Christian, the more negative the view he or she is likely to have of biblical criticism. The etymology of the term "criticism" itself suggests standing in judgment over a text, in this case something that ought to stand in judgment over us. Historically, biblical criticism has been a principal tool in the critique of classical theology by forces of the Enlightenment. By subjecting the Bible to humanistic presuppositions and treating it as a merely human text under the control of our supposedly superior techniques, we have seen the gospel message relativized and debunked time and again. "Criticism" is hardly the natural term for classical Christians to use when describing the careful study of the Bible. When criticism comes in, very often faith goes out. It is all too easy to slide from the critical methodology to the critical theology of religious liberalism.[1]

Nevertheless, in spite of the dangers, biblical criticism has come to signify many things and many methods, not all of them hostile to the interests of faith. Under this heading a great deal of careful, reverent, scholarly study of the text goes on that builds up the church. Just as there is a reading of the Bible for the purpose of dissecting and discrediting it, there is also a reading of it for the purpose of penetrating and grasping better its authoritative message. One can define criticism to mean analysis and discerning study of the phenomena of Scripture. As George E. Ladd says, "Biblical criticism properly defined is not an enemy of

1. Robert M. Price ("Crisis of Biblical Authority," 41–42) gives testimonies by Harry Fosdick, Robert Alley, and A. J. Mattill to this effect.

evangelical faith, but a necessary method of studying God's Word, which has been given to us in and through history."[2] Such criticism involves asking nonprejudicial questions of the text while remaining open to its revelational function. It is the kind of criticism represented so well by F. F. Bruce and G. E. Ladd, the kind that strives to make plain the meaning of Scripture and has supplied the church with magnificent new tools in the form of commentaries, dictionaries, and monographs of every kind. It is a reasoned approach to the text that uncovers vast stores of historical, linguistic, and literary insight and information that in turn shed light on the text and God's enduring intention through it.

Thanks to biblical research over the past century, we understand the biblical message more clearly and are enabled to appropriate it more adequately. The more we know about first-century Judaism, the better we can grasp what Paul was teaching on the doctrine of justification by faith; everything stands out more sharply. Such scholarly study, often called biblical criticism, can assist the text to stand on its own and speak in its own way to us. True, we have to go beyond scholarship and receive the Word of God in faith. Nevertheless, scholarly analysis can help us to do so intelligently. God has communicated to us in history, and it is essential for us to attend to the historicity of the text in order to respond to it properly. This is what godly criticism can help us to do.

Biblical criticism in the modern world, then, has two faces. It can denote positive operations in the analysis of the text of the Bible, with a view to the obedience of faith. But it can be something very different. We need to have our faculties trained to distinguish good criticism from bad (Heb. 5:14).[3] Although we should not in any way minimize the real benefits that accrue from careful biblical scholarship, we must not fool ourselves into thinking that there is nothing for us to fear. The time for innocence in this matter is long past. A hearty suspicion is entirely in order.

In essence, we must be aware that criticism has been the chief means by which the Scripture principle has been overturned for many people, and with it the pattern of orthodox doctrine. As Peter Hodgson and Robert King note, "No single factor has been more important in the reconception of theology in the modern period than the collapse of authority and the emergence of the historical-critical method."[4] Why is this? Quite simply, it is because criticism is a child of the Enlightenment, as Troeltsch pointed out. It secularizes the Scriptures by treating them just like ordinary sources and, from the start, closing itself to the possibility

2. George E. Ladd, *New Testament and Criticism*, 53.
3. Carl F. H. Henry (*God, Revelation, and Authority*, vol. 4, chap. 17) speaks of the uses and abuses of historical criticism.
4. Hodgson and King, *Christian Theology*, ix.

of revelation and miracle.[5] With a single stroke, the entire assumption lying behind the creation of the Bible in the Jewish and Christian communities—namely, that the Scriptures are God-given—was swept away and an entirely new way of reading the Bible was begun.

Instead of the reader standing underneath the Scriptures to hear God's Word, the Bible in Enlightenment hands was made to stand before the critics as a defendant must stand before a judge, critics who were not of a mind to consent to the Bible's central message. The text was seen as an ordinary product of human culture to be judged by the presuppositions of modernity. Enlightenment criticism works out of a worldview that simply does not allow for the possibilities that the Bible itself announces.[6] In this framework, the Bible cannot possibly be a truth-guaranteeing vehicle of revelation. The content of the Bible is placed within the sphere of a naturalistic approach to reality that, if permitted to, will explode the system of classical theology based on supernaturalist assumptions.[7] Such criticism is plainly incompatible with historic Christian belief and leads to a new theology at odds with it. Scripture can no longer function as it once did in orthodoxy as a means of establishing truth, but will be made subject to human autonomy.

If only more critics were as honest as Julius Wellhausen. When he saw what his work was doing to students preparing for ministry, he withdrew from the faculty of theology and took up a post in Semitic languages so as not to be a stumbling block to any. It is more common, unfortunately, for critics to remain in theology while holding that the Bible is only the word of some leading Christians and not the infallible Word of God.[8] Therefore, it is appropriate to sound the alarm. Gerhard Ebeling is naive when he advocates that we let everything burn that will burn in the work of criticism.[9] If we employ criticism that denies the Bible and is essentially atheistic, everything will burn, including whatever vestiges of classic Christianity a neo-liberal like Ebeling wishes to preserve.

There is a common misconception that only conservatives have any trouble with biblical criticism. To see this, one need only ask what aspect of the text the more liberal person holds on to and then observe that this, too, can be critically undermined by the same methodology. Suppose that Jesus believed in violence and the Gospel writers covered this up with

5. Edgar Krentz, *Historical-Critical Method*, 55.

6. Edward Farley, *Ecclesial Reflection*, 135–40.

7. Gerhard Hasel, *New Testament Theology*, 18–28, 209–11.

8. Wellhausen knew that the manner in which he was studying the Bible would not lead anyone to hear God's Word from it. See Leon Morris, *I Believe in Revelation*, 101. For James Barr (*Bible in the Modern World*, 120), the Bible is a human product only. The problem is that this was not Jesus's view of it or the Bible's view of itself.

9. Gerhard Ebeling, *Word and Faith*, 51.

a pacifist overlay, something that has been argued by S. G. F. Brandon and others. Suppose that he did not consistently trust in God but lost his faith in the face of the crucifixion, or that we have not understood Paul's doctrine of justification and that the apostle had something quite different in mind. All of these convictions are subject to the same critical analysis and debunking that the traditional views sometimes suffer. There is no part of the biblical treasure that cannot be placed in doubt by the consistent application of negative criticism.

Every Christian will encounter criticism's hostile face at some point. Nevertheless, it is true that criticism poses less threat to religious liberals, for the simple reason that they have already surrendered so much biblical ground and retreated to more minimal positions that seem less vulnerable.

Faith and Reason

In the conflict between Enlightenment criticism and Christian faith we have a prominent example of faith presuppositions colliding with supposedly rational requirements. The critics insist that it is simply a question of the facts and whether Christians will be willing to face them. Such Bible scholars approach the text as neutral scientists (so they think) and expose the errors and fallacies they seem to find there. This method thinks of itself as relatively value-free, that is, free of presuppositions. If it does not find room for categories like revelation and incarnation, that is because the method is oriented to this-worldly sources, causes, and effects. It is thought unfortunate that the approach tends to lead to a dissolution of the Scripture principle and the undermining of classical beliefs. Critics cannot be blamed for pursuing the truth in their disinterested way. They are committed to the morality of truth.

However, Christians should not accept these pretensions. This supposedly neutral way of reading the Bible is totally out of keeping with the nature and claims of the text. The Bible calls for faith in God, and to treat it from the beginning as just a piece of literature is to say "no" to that claim. This value-free approach is an illusion, an inappropriate and unfruitful way of coming to the text. It reminds us of Jesus's denunciation of the lawyers: "You have taken away the key of knowledge; you did not enter yourselves, and you hindered those who were entering" (Luke 11:52).

To be sure, there are a number of ways one can approach an object. A flower may be approached by a bee to find nectar in it, or by a butterfly to rest on it, or by a botanist to determine its classification, or by an artist to paint it, or by a chemist to analyze it. Certainly, the Bible can be studied as literature and as history as well as divine communication. But we must take into account how the Bible wishes us to approach it and for what purpose. It obviously wants us to come to know God in Jesus Christ. Therefore, we are within our epistemic rights as Christians when we insist on approaching the Bible in the spirit of faith. Further, we suspect that those who refuse to do so have really decided to reject the Bible's central claim and are out of harmony with the essence of the text they pretend to study. The secular, academic approach to the Bible is already predisposed to reject the Bible's message. It is not neutral, scientific investigation at all but has a built-in debunking character. The whole spirit of the enterprise breathes the human autonomy that wishes to be free of God and not subject to his Word.[10]

The common critical pretension to being a value-free point of view is an illusion, in spite of the protest to the contrary. One might say that the reason the question of God and faith is bracketed is not necessarily because one is closed to it, but because scientific methodology, even when used by believers, brackets it as a matter of course. Scientific method is self-consciously oriented to mundane reality and does not bring God into problems that need solving. It is a closed approach methodologically, metaphysically, and theologically. Only by being closed, it assumes, can it serve to get rid of the kind of supposed superstition that plagued humanity before the rise of a truly scientific method.

However, there is a major bias here, even if some critics refuse to admit it. It makes a very big difference whether a Bible reader believes or does not believe in the God of the biblical story. For the one who does not believe, the entire Bible tends to become implausible and irrelevant. What is called methodological bracketing might as well be a metaphysical blockade because the result is the same. The Bible makes it clear that, in order to understand its message, one must be personally involved with the God of the gospel. The issue cannot be effectively bracketed. Not to decide is to decide. On the ultimate question, one cannot really abstain. A value-free orientation to the Bible predisposes a person to reject its message.[11]

Behind this whole discussion lurks the modern question, Why should one seriously consider God when reading the Bible, or in life generally? Surely we cannot expect scholars to view things theistically, at least not as scientists. It may be that on this rock the spade is turned, as Ludwig Wittgenstein said. Belief in God is a basic belief, like belief in color or causation or the existence of other minds. It is properly basic and does

10. Walter Wink makes this point in what James Barr (*Holy Scripture*, 107) calls his "wild, thoughtless, and journalistic work" titled *The Bible in Human Transformation*.
11. Royce Gruenler (*New Approaches to Jesus and the Gospels*, chap. 8) makes effective use of Polanyi's postcritical hermeneutic.

not need to rest upon something more ultimate. There is no way to verify belief in God, a belief that inevitably affects profoundly the question of how to approach the Scriptures. One simply must decide to believe or not. It is within one's epistemic rights to believe without having to give reasons. For ourselves, to demand an answer to the modern question rings hollow. For the person who asks why he or she should believe in God, we should try to do more than repeat the demand for faith. What can he or she think except that bracketing God in criticism was probably the right thing to do after all?

To our way of thinking, one ought to approach the Bible, and reality as a whole, in the spirit of faith in God. Through the eyes of believers, this is the only way to make sense of all that is. As Karl Rahner and Wolfhart Pannenberg have effectively argued, we as human beings are oriented to a horizon that encompasses and transcends us. We are driven inescapably to decide in relation to the mystery of our existence. The question of God is the question of our own life and its meaning. The universe outside us also calls for some explanation. How did it come to exist, especially in its intricate forms of design? The story of the Bible itself, and the claim that it makes to be the historical revelation of the otherwise unnamed mystery of existence, carries its own ring of authenticity. Where else shall we encounter a person like Jesus of Nazareth, and how else shall we explain what happened to him?

Most important for us individually is the experience of salvation through Jesus Christ, by which we have entered into a personal relationship with God that now colors everything we see and do. Ultimately, it is a question of whether or not to trust in God. In considering how to answer, the mind is by no means passive and uninvolved. The presupposition that the Bible invites us to embrace is more deeply rational in the broad sense than the modern attempt at being neutral—which is to be basically atheistic. In any event, the question of faith cannot be sidestepped in the matter of biblical criticism.[12]

Even if we grant the basic point about reading the Bible sympathetically in faith and in line with its own claims, what difference does that make? How can that tell us anything specific about critical questions? In the last analysis, one still has to sift the facts and decide what they mean. Indeed, is it not important that criticism not be controlled by dogmatic presuppositions but be free to follow the truth where it leads? Surely we want to know what the Bible says and not have it filtered through liberal unbelief or dogmatic presuppositions, as it often has been across the centuries of church history. How we analyze the composition of Genesis,

12. The approach to the philosophy of religion that we espouse is sketched out in Clark Pinnock's *Reason Enough*.

for example, has little to do with presuppositions, one might argue, and a lot to do with literary characteristics that anyone can see.[13]

Granted, at the micro-exegetical level there is no place for corrupting exegesis by feeding traditional conclusions into the operation. As we have been arguing, we must face honestly the actual phenomena of the text. Not being careful with the evidence is hardly worthy of those who profess to love the truth.[14] Nevertheless, there is a gospel manner of approaching the Bible that inclines one to be open, positive, and receptive to what it has to say. As we have shown, to read the Bible as the reliable Word of God is to read it the way the Bible itself asks us to. It is not an arbitrary assumption introduced into the discussion from our tradition or culture but one that arose in the first place from the text itself. It is obviously a conviction that will affect everything in a general way. It means that we do not assume we are superior to the text and in a position to rewrite it according to our way of thinking, but that we will be open and receptive to the Bible in a way critical theories often are not. How differently the Gospels will appear to the one who accepts the New Testament claim of incarnation. Is it not obvious that Gospel studies divide between those who radically suspect the text as propaganda and those who listen to it with open and accepting ears? Differences on this scale cannot easily be accounted for on the basis of empirical study; they seem definitively rooted in a prior decision about the Bible as reliable testimony.

Now, this does not mean, in our thinking, that our confidence in the Bible cannot be shaken and that it is impervious to empirical data. Many have once held to the historic Scripture principle and then, for one reason or another, abandoned it. This can certainly happen. To use an illustration, we trust in a particular dentist to be well-meaning and competent. This confidence is founded on evidence of various kinds, including direct experience. Should something change and we could no longer trust, we would change dentists. The Scripture principle could be overturned for us, as it has been for others, if it were contradicted by the facts, broadly speaking. In particular, if its central message should prove to be unreliable and incredible and fail to mediate to us the presence of the absolute Savior, we sadly would have to abandon confidence in the Bible. As Paul said, if we come to the place where we no longer believe that Christ was raised, then our faith is surely vain and empty (1 Cor. 15:14), and such should be admitted.

13. Both in his *Holy Scripture* and *Fundamentalism*, James Barr is very concerned to defend critical freedom against a resurgence of dogmatic Bible reading.

14. William J. Abraham (*Divine Inspiration of Holy Scripture*, chap. 1) is critical of those conservatives who appear to do so. Insofar as he himself expects the Bible to tell the truth, though, he is not completely free from the same dilemma.

Our approach to the Bible is not unfalsifiable in principle or in fact. Nor, for that matter, is the approach of unbelief. It is perfectly possible (and this also happens, praise God!) that a nonbeliever can find the Word of God to be living and powerful, bringing conversion to a saving relationship with the Lord who speaks to us out of the text of the Bible. This has happened countless times.

Positive Criticism

Since biblical criticism in the modern situation has two faces, it is necessary to sift out and discern what is positive and edifying for the church and what is negative and destructive of her life and mission. If we approach the Bible as the Scripture of the church in a believing way, how shall we pursue scholarly biblical analysis? It cannot be merely a question of British reasonableness, as when John A. T. Robinson suggests that we eschew a foolish cynicism that takes the Bible to be fictional and a fearful fundamentalism that is afraid to ask hard questions, proposing instead his own committed conservatism, which somehow avoids both extremes. It is not a golden mean we wish to honor here, but the divine origin and function of the Bible as God's written Word.[15]

Positive biblical scholarship, let it be said, is a very useful thing for the church. It is a valued aspect of a sound ministry of God's Word and serves the gospel by shedding light on the meaning of Scripture, preventing its distortion. As Martin Hengel says, "Theological exegesis which thinks that it can interpret the New Testament without the application of the relevant historical methods is not only deaf to the question of truth but is also in danger of distorting what the texts say and falling victim to docetic speculation."[16] Confidence in the Bible as God's Word underlines the crucial importance of getting back to the original form of the text and to its authentic meaning. The scholarly efforts to do this show genuine appreciation for the text. Because God gave his Word in a historically situated way, it is essential that we use historical methods to ascertain what the biblical statements are and what they signify.

To deny the church the tools of biblical scholarship would be like denying a person a knife and fork to eat with—it would impede the appropriation and assimilation of the truth. We must not bind the hands of biblical scholars. Church people need the results of their labors in order to make important judgments about the meaning and significance of the text. Protestants, who first placed the Bible in the hands of the

15. J. A. T. Robinson, *Can We Trust the New Testament?* chap. 8.
16. Martin Hengel, *Acts and the History of Earliest Christianity*, 134–35.

people, should not now take it away. Of course, we are well aware that historical criticism is often skeptical toward biblical claims and alienated from a faith commitment, but we must also realize that such prejudices are not intrinsic to biblical scholarship but regrettable accretions that can be cut away.[17]

A positive scholarly approach to the Bible, according to the Scripture principle, views these texts as authorizing and authoritative for believers. They have the established right of standing in judgment over us. As Martin Luther saw, the Bible is our adversary, the merciless critic of our lives and traditions, able to pierce through our best defenses and lay us open before God. Such scholars would not be critics at all but would voluntarily criticize themselves. Their approach to Scripture would not be secular or neutral but would identify the text as normative, inspired Scripture—trustworthy, coherent, and deserving of respect. Their scholarship would be ministerial in service of the text and of the community whose Scripture it is, and their goal would be to elucidate its claims.

Such scholars read Paul on the resurrection or salvation, not merely in order to discover where Paul got the ideas, but to face up to God's truth for us. Of course, they may have to ask in the process where such ideas fit into the development of Paul's own thoughts. Even so, the goal is always to attain and obey God's Word in the text. These scholars read each text in the canonical context as the basic horizon and concentrate on the teaching and implications of the final text. This already relativizes the importance of much critical work. The speeches of Jesus in the Fourth Gospel stand there whatever critics conclude about their originality, and they will be heard as Jesus's words. Whether or not there ever were sources such as Q or D does not change the fact that the text lies before us to be heeded. While research into the backdrop of the text may have something to contribute to an understanding of the canonical Bible, its results are far from assured and cannot assume greater importance than the final product of inspiration. As a preparatory study, research may shed light on the text. The real work, however, remains the exposition of the text God gave.

The attitude of positive criticism is one of openness and faith, marked by the willingness to hear the text even when it is alien and strange. It employs a hermeneutics of consent that stands open to God's work of salvation in history and to God's Word of life in the Bible. The approach is reverent in the presence of the God who speaks, humble and believing before him, ready at all times to trust and obey. This disposition to believe the Bible does not determine in advance the answer to every critical question, but it does indicate the stance that ought to be taken.

17. Raymond E. Brown, *Critical Meaning of the Bible*, 25.

Obviously, theories that cast doubt on the text's credibility will be refused. This does not lock us into traditional opinions in matters that do not have the status of God's Word but leaves entirely open such questions as whether J was a source used in the composition of the Penteteuch or John was the last Gospel to be written or Solomon was the author of the Song of Songs. What it excludes are theories that prevent the Bible from functioning as the truth-telling Scriptures of the church.

Since faith is the proper attitude in positive scholarship, it follows that the church is the proper context for its exercise, not the secular university. The latter is precisely where the claims of Scripture will tend to be resisted. Because of the humanistic presuppositions dominant in the modern university, the Bible as Scripture cannot expect to get a real hearing. Far from receiving an objective treatment, the Bible usually is wrenched from its natural context of the worshiping and confessing community and forced onto the procrustean bed of alien assumptions. Rather than being rescued for objective study, the Bible is examined under the control of new and alien presuppositions and effectively silenced as the Word of God.

The positive approach to the Bible as Scripture, pursued in the spirit of faith, entails certain behaviors. The goal, never novelty for its own sake, would always be the hearing of God's Word. There would be a spirit that anticipates coherence in the teaching and truth in the concepts, a patient spirit that waits for the text to disclose itself and does not rush to negative judgment. Respectful of the literary wholeness of the canon, it is not inclined to cut the text up into atomistic units. This approach tends to be cautious in what it proposes, preferring the text itself to speculative fancies that are anything but assured. It respects "those who are weak in faith" and does not burden them with "quarreling over opinions" (Rom. 14:1). It knows that critical knowledge puffs up, but love builds up (1 Cor. 8:1).

This attitude, rather than a set of specific opinions about biblical problems, characterizes positive scholarship in the Christian context. Although it would be easier if we could just employ a checklist of approved opinions regarding Daniel or the Pastorals to determine whether or not the criticism is positive, doing so would only show whether it is traditional, not whether it is respectful of God's Word. How one dates John or Isaiah is not a reliable test for the spirit of faith. We look, rather, for integrity in the total operation. Such scholars may not even advertise or reflect consciously on their commitment to inspiration, but the way they carry out the work will tell decisively where they stand. Biblical studies need to be reformed on the basis of this principle and attitude and learn again how to be active in theologically responsible ways.

In calling for a reformation of biblical scholarship, we have no basis for smugness. Often, because of our confidence in the Bible, we have not bothered to investigate it seriously, on the supposition that we already had in hand all that was necessary for full understanding. It took critics, with their principle of doubt, to shake the branches and see some new leaves float down out of the tree of Scripture. Has not our attitude of trustful faith sometimes led us to complacency, so that we became known for reprinting older commentaries rather than being the source of powerful new readings of the Word for today?

Styles of Positive Criticism

We now will list specific examples of the kind of positive work that can be done within the framework of evangelical convictions. We want it to be plain that there is considerable freedom to move with the evidence and still remain within this framework. Positive work can be done in all the familiar fields. Results can be obtained that serve the text and the church and do not denigrate the Word of God.

Form criticism is the study of the different forms of literature in which the witness to Jesus was passed down in the oral tradition. Although often allied to skepticism regarding the historicity of the material and to a naturalistic worldview, there is value in form criticism as a literary tool that can distinguish and help to elucidate the genres of the New Testament. It is not necessary to accept the notion that the early church freely created sayings of Jesus or invented the course of his career. Bracketing such assumptions, the conservative is left with an exegetical tool for understanding the development, style, and meaning of the New Testament.

Redaction criticism is the study of the purposes and perspectives of the various Gospel writers as they combined their sources into the final work as a coherent and meaningful whole. It tries to detect in the small changes made in the common material shared by the four Gospels, for example, the motives and concerns lying behind them. By studying the composition of each Gospel in turn, one can learn more about the specific nature of the evangelist's theology and gain a deeper understanding of his message. The uniqueness of each writer comes to the surface in this way. Often, in practice, redaction critics are skeptical about the historical basis for the redactional distinctives, but putting that aside, using redactional techniques, the evangelical scholar can probe more deeply into why and to whom the evangelist wrote. This technique sees each writer with a distinctive contribution to make and emphases all his own that ought to be noticed. Instead of merging the Gospels together, redactional studies have revived our interest in comparisons between them. Of course, conservative work in this field will not push too hard on incidental clues, or presuppose a nonhistorical motive as a general rule, or set the writers against each other, as if their respective theologies were incompatible.

Textual criticism is concerned with recovering the original text of the Bible. Mistakes are bound to creep in when a document is copied by hand over generations, and it is the task of the text critic to spot these errors and determine the best reading. By studying various manuscripts and scribal techniques, a science of textual criticism has evolved that can aid in attaining the original text and therefore the original meaning of its author. Conservatives often favor this field of study because it seems to be most objective and relatively free of non-Christian presuppositions.

Literary or *source criticism* can also aid the biblical interpreter, even though it is a difficult undertaking. Several biblical writers, like Luke and the chronicler, admit to using sources, and in the case of books like Kings that cover hundreds of years, it is apparent that sources must have come into play. There is also indication that the Synoptic Gospels consulted one another and probably also made use of common sources. However, caution is always required because, unless we know sources are being combined in a passage, it is hard to be certain about it. If we cannot be sure of such matters in many contemporary books, how can we have much confidence when scholars announce the sources used by ancient authors? Therefore, literary criticism must admit to a high degree of speculation and not claim too much for its findings—unless we happen to have a part of the source as well as the later document that makes use of it.

Even greater caution is in order in *tradition criticism*, which tries to penetrate behind the sources and come up with the history of the tradition before it was committed to writing. Conclusions in this area are very hard to confirm. Yet this discipline is important in the case of the Gospels because these texts were composed after the resurrection of Jesus and introduced certain alterations to the received material, as can be observed in the Synoptics' variants. Jesus is, after all, both a figure of the past and the living Lord of the churches from which the Gospels came.

Historical criticism considers the historical setting of a document, the time and place in which it was written, and the nature of the events that it describes. It would ask concerning the exodus from Egypt about the nature of the literary sources and the support, archaeological and otherwise, for the event in question. Again, certainty is in short supply in these areas, and speculation abounds. Furthermore, in the case of the exodus, there are radical theories that allege that the Old Testament picture is quite different from what really happened. In this and many similar cases, conservative scholars will find themselves in opposition to theories that deny the validity of the Bible. Rather than abandoning the field, however, they need to stay with it and help the faith of the church attain understanding.

There also is value in newer fields of study called *structural* and *rhetorical criticism*. Structuralism, as the name implies, attends to the structures of language to which the particular linguistic expressions in Scripture belong and tries to explain how, at this deep level, the language functions. It does not probe behind the text historically, as many kinds of criticism do, but concentrates on the text itself as a literary phenomenon. It is interested in the mental structures of human thinking that express themselves in these texts and symbols. Although structuralists tend to assume that material apparently historical is actually mythical, thus denigrating the historical foundations of the Bible, it is not necessary to follow them in this. There is value in this emphasis on the text itself and the attention given to the total context in which words are found. Rhetorical criticism is a supplement to form criticism. It looks for those devices of speech that reveal the personal character of a writer's thought. Again, there is a concentration on the message of the text itself and the rhetorical processes by which it is propounded. It allows the text to speak and inform us of the intention of the writer and the expected impact on the original readers.

In the area of literary composition, it is certainly possible for the conservative to ponder the problems with considerable liberty. There are some reasons for dating 2 Peter after the death of the apostle Peter, including its appeal to Paul's letters as Scripture, its extensive use of Jude, and the kind of heresies it confronts. The conservative is not free to conclude that the letter is a forgery passed off in the name of Peter and meant to deceive the readers. But that does not shut off the possibility that a writer other than Peter himself embodied Peter's teaching and had no intention of deceiving anyone. Posthumous publication in Peter's name does not deny its Petrine character and does not advance any deception. In the accepted conventions of the time, Peter's name could fairly be claimed for such a work.

Something similar arises in the case of Ephesians. Though it is likely that this epistle is the quintessence of Paul's theology and his final masterpiece, there are some features in it that suggest some shifts and further developments of Paul's thought. The tensions between Jew and Gentile seem to have been overcome, and terms are employed in slightly new senses. Were a conservative to be convinced by such factors, he or she would not be compelled to label the epistle a forgery but could see it as the work of a disciple and colleague like Luke, who faithfully represented his teacher's thought and adapted his teaching to a situation in such a way that it could be fairly said to be Paul's. The reason we suggest Luke is that a large proportion of the words unique to Ephesians among the Pauline letters occur in Luke-Acts.

The same sort of question comes up in connection with the Pastoral Epistles, which use a style and language somewhat different from Paul's and treat church polity more fully than Paul did. It is also hard to fit their composition into the chronology of Paul's life as we know it from Acts. But if we suppose that the Pastorals were written by an assistant of Paul's, all of these features would be accounted for. We are not arguing for the truth of these proposals; we simply seek to show the freedom that there is for positive biblical scholarship to operate within a high doctrine of the Bible. In our reaction against truly negative criticism, we must not deny ourselves fruitful avenues of research that can hold promise for a better understanding of the biblical text.

Now, one might say in objection to our manifesto for evangelical liberty in biblical criticism that the approach we are taking allows for a dressing up of most critical theories in acceptably pious clothing, enabling the scholar to remain a conservative and still practice biblical criticism like everyone else. What negative view, given a little ingenuity, cannot be framed in orthodox terminology? The simple answer is, no theory can be so framed that has the effect of denying what the text intentionally asserts. Admittedly, this question of assertion is key, and we have no human authority who can answer infallibly in each case. We have to do our best exegesis in the good company of other scholars, always open to the Spirit's wise working in the process. The defenses against deceitful and unscrupulous persons are not impregnable. Even so, we cannot surrender the liberty in interpretation we treasure and must continue to hope that those hypotheses that truly exalt the truthfulness of the Scriptures will persist and those that denigrate it will become apparent to all. Meanwhile, it is imperative that we not deny to our biblical scholars the freedom that is their right, which, in the end, will serve the people of God through the new insights that come out of untrammeled investigation.

Classical Christians might well ask themselves whether even what they call positive criticism has not changed the Bible for them from what it was in precritical orthodoxy. Have not we, too, become accustomed to ask if this is Jesus or Luke we are reading? Was this Paul, or the work of a disciple? Should Hebrews be canonical? Even when we are most conservative, has not criticism lowered the certainty quotient? Can we return home to the innocence of the simple faith we now have abandoned? If the certainty referred to was really a kind of rational certainty based upon equating the words of the Bible and the words of God and not allowing for the human dimension, there is no going home. But if our certainty rests instead where it ought to, for simple as well as for educated believers, in the effectiveness of the Bible to mediate to us salvation in Christ, then positive criticism poses no threat. Instead, it offers clarification and new light on the Word of the Lord.

Negative Criticism

There is a kind of biblical criticism that is inconsistently Christian at best and operates within a naturalistic circularity. Such criticism has played a disastrous role in the lives of many believers and carried some to ruin. What kind of Bible study is negative criticism?

A negative critical approach comes to the text as if it were merely human literature, not the Scripture of the church—thus denying its own claim and historical reality. This approach sees the Bible chiefly as the literary sediment of human traditions, as an expression of the religious identity of an ancient people, not as the oracles of God. It looks to the Bible to discover what people have thought, not what God is saying. This type of study is divorced from belief in biblical inspiration and from orthodox traditions in general. Therefore, it does not expect the Bible to be true or coherent or relevant and is not bound to sit beneath the Bible's normative authority. Seeing the Bible as a library of disparate documents collected apart from any underlying divine plan, it is not inclined to treat the documents as a literary whole, and certainly not as a canonical whole. It grinds the text up into little pieces that have no meaning within a broader context.

In essence, negative criticism seizes the prerogative to subject Scripture to independent rational critique just like any other book. It is magisterial, not ministerial, in relation to the text, and raises the serpent's question, "Did God say?" (Gen. 3:1). Instead of bringing the Bible closer to the reader, it has a distancing effect and makes the Bible appear to be a strange, antique object to be dissected rather than a Word to be heard and obeyed. The result of such criticism is to render the Bible less known and respected today than before. Although it is true that the Scriptures have a historical aspect that can and should be carefully analyzed in a historical way, it is also possible to dominate them by means of criticism and in effect bypass them as authority. Criticism itself can seize the normative position and demote the Bible to a lower status.

The spirit of negative criticism is marked by mistrust rather than by faith and employs a hermeneutics of suspicion rather than consent. Instead of sitting under the text, it is prepared to place judgment on the text. Reason is employed, not in the service of faith or in the context of the church, but in the service of a humanist worldview and in the context of the academy. Very often negative criticism has functioned on the basis of positivist presuppositions that go against the special character of biblical theology and history. Supposing that reason could readily come up with true hypotheses about complex ancient texts, it has repeatedly claimed assured results of a negative kind (that have troubled the people of God) and almost delighted in coming up with theories that debunk the ones that went before. Pastorally, this criticism has had harmful effects in seeming to overturn the truth base of faith and in replacing a devotional knowledge of the Bible with an arid, academic study of it that is sterile when it comes to worship and Christian living.

We hear much about the value of biblical criticism against the danger of Docetism, but not enough about the danger of the havoc criticism can wreak when its results collide with the Scriptures and destroy faith's foundations. There is need for spiritual discernment here. Much criticism goes contrary to God's Word and is issued in an appealing form that only the experts are able to evaluate. Church leaders and conservative scholars have an obligation, therefore, to watch out for the faith of Christ's little ones. According to Galatians 5:13, "You were called to freedom, brothers and sisters; only do not use your freedom as an opportunity for self-indulgence, but through love become slaves to one another." Critical freedom, like any other form of Christian liberty, ought to build up the community, not cause honest believers to stumble. If it tears down the church and causes weak believers to lose their footing, it will come under the judgment of God. Of course, there always will be believers who are threatened by any questioning of traditional belief as they were taught it. Responsible scholarship cannot stop because of their possible reactions; however, it should proceed gently and respectfully.

Form criticism is beset by a historically skeptical and antisupernaturalist attitude leading to minimal conclusions often unusable by the church. Redaction criticism often displays a condemning attitude that questions the value of what a biblical book says—for example, alleged anti-Semitism in Matthew or John. Even textual criticism can be the basis for arguing that the textual shape of the canonical Scriptures is hopeless, making slightly absurd any claim to belief in the "Bible" (what is it?). Literary and source criticism can be the sphere of endless wrangling and nit-picking about hypothetical sources, leaving the content of the text ripped apart and the text itself in tatters. Getting behind the text in tradition criticism is more speculative still and often poses direct challenges to the validity of biblical teaching. In each field of study, it is possible to develop negative theories that bring God's Word into disrepute.

Criticism of the theological content and historical substance of the Bible is where the negative approach hurts most. Consistent with the denial of inspiration, critics now often do not assume a unity in biblical teaching. Disunity has become a principle of New Testament criticism. The writers are understood in such a way that their several theologies cannot be systematized into dogmatic theology, and one is compelled to choose among their differing teachings. The result is that the basis of orthodoxy is destroyed and one is free to take any direction one likes in theology and ethics. Let us consider a few leading examples.

It sometimes is held that Jesus taught a quite different message from the one preached by the early churches after his death. Supposedly he taught the coming of God's kingdom in his own day, but then the early church had to gloss over this fact because of its delay. The spread of Christianity to Hellenistic settings also required new theologies at odds with the original faith of Palestinian Jewish disciples. Jesus began to be thought of as God, and church order began to become more hierarchical. One passage sees the state as God's instrument, while another views it as Antichrist. The New Testament contains half a dozen different doctrines of Christ, and these cannot and should not be harmonized. Even internally, an author may prove inconsistent in his views (Paul on the resurrection) and mistaken from our standpoint (Paul on women). The list could go on of examples of critical theories incompatible with belief in the full authority of the Bible. They must be deemed negative and unacceptable to the church.

A result that flows from this view of the Bible as a network of contradictions is that one is forced either to select those themes one finds appealing (a theology reflecting one's own culture and prejudices) or, more consistently, to select none at all, since none of the viewpoints in the Bible is necessarily truer or more valid than any other. Why should a theology critically deemed to be earlier be more authoritative than one thought to be later? One may as well believe that there is no possibility of establishing a normative position now. One might as well strike out on one's own and exercise one's own creativity, just as the New Testament writers presumably did long ago. We will have to find categories in our world to express what is ultimate and beyond us. The New Testament can offer us suggestions and stimulation, but little more. Certainly it cannot provide the basis for any orthodoxy or any unified Christian theology that Christians could agree on. A person or church can no longer claim to have a unified theology based on the Bible. Everyone is free to do and think what seems right in his or her own eyes.

How should Bible believers respond to this pattern of denial? We must be forthright and admit that contradiction is not something that we can consistently allow since it overthrows the Scripture principle, falsifying a central theological assumption and shaking the foundations of our faith. But we should hasten to add that no such situation exists at present, despite these bold claims. Criticism has the distinct tendency to look for and find differences where there are none and contradictions where there are only differences. Scholars have delighted to set James against Paul, Matthew against Mark, J against E, when it is unnecessary. Of course, one can see the contrasts, but in every case there would follow a different result if similarities rather than differences were stressed. The believer expects to find unity, not contradiction, and in practice it is not difficult to do so. It takes effort to see why the various Christologies of the New Testament cannot participate in a unified, whole model of Christ. Our task here is not to answer objections in detail, but rather to indicate what negative criticism is according to sound evangelical principles and how it should be handled.

In historical matters, the negative critic is not committed to upholding the truth of the biblical record. This hurts most in the career of Jesus, where the Christian message is rooted and assumes its most supernatural form. In a painful dilemma, one wants to investigate the life of Jesus using historical methods but finds these methods unsuited to deal with this phenomenon and sometimes producing conclusions that overturn the very core of Christian faith. In fact, the portrait of Christ in the Gospels is at the same time both the presentation of a thoroughly human life and the portrayal of an episode in the life of God, hence its profound supernaturalism. God the Son dwelled among human beings in the life of Jesus of Nazareth—what can historical study make of this remarkable claim? Is it the work of mythical imagination, or did such a person actually walk the earth? Ironically, it is our traditional theology that gets us into this historical problem. We cannot assent to the high claims of church Christology if these claims have no historical basis in the real life and teachings of Jesus.

Much of the difficulty here arises from the naturalistic worldview that dominates academic and intellectual life at this stage in Western history. Although there are many signs, such as a belief in the paranormal, that may indicate that we are moving out of it, at present Christians do face serious opposition to their basic truth claims. The secular mentality will not grant room for such events as miracles within scientifically intelligible reality. The pressure has caused religious liberals to redefine miracle as a religiously significant event that does not transcend the alphabet of nature's ordinary potential. Jesus cannot have walked upon the water, because such a challenge to the law of gravity (even by the creator of gravity!) cannot be permitted. It must be a mythological picture designed to express for believers an existential truth about Jesus.

Unfortunately, the Christian faith rests on such events as the bodily resurrection of Jesus, so the challenge of unbelief has to be faced rather than evaded. We have to insist that the world did not come to be through chance, and we do not know that reality is a closed system of material cause and effect. It is unfair to the Bible and to natural intelligence to declare dogmatically that miracles cannot happen before one has even looked into the evidence to see if some apparently have occurred. Christians are not materialists and should not treat the Bible as if they shared naturalistic presuppositions. Of course, as Western people we have assumptions that predispose us against miracles at first, but as Christians we must deal with this cultural reality as we would in any other case. The Word of God stands over our prejudices and judges them. We must not suppose that our beliefs constitute absolute perspectives over all reality and that they permit us to judge negatively a central feature of the biblical message.

The main point is that the historical method, although properly oriented to mundane reality, need not and should not be imprisoned within a naturalistic worldview. Reality is not perfectly homogeneous; although we look for similarities in history, we must be open for dissimilarities as well. There is no reason for us to accept the dogma of modernity that holds that the world is closed to God and the miraculous. If we believe that God created the world, then we already believe in a miracle that dwarfs all others. It is inconsistent to believe in creation and then draw back from the other mighty acts of the Lord. Likewise, it is inconsistent to believe in human freedom and also hold to a closed causal nexus. It is truly a mystery how Bultmann can deny miracles on the basis of a closed scientific world and then champion existential freedom, as if freedom somehow escapes from scientific determinism.

Having said that, we should not react too severely to the threat of a naturalistic bias. Bultmann's outright denial of the miraculous is certainly an extreme position, but it is not necessarily typical of everyone who has a concern in this area. Our openness to the supernatural certainly should not make us gullible and allergic to any analysis at all. After all, there were prescientific views in the air in the first century, and these may have found their way into the biblical formulations and narratives. This possibility cannot be ruled out. To do so would be as anti-empirical as ruling out miracles themselves. We do not need to assume that every time a paranormal event is referred to, the biblical understanding of it is the only possible one. Without denying the demonic, we should allow that Mark's descriptions of such possessions are not the only way to render what happened, but only his way of interpreting it. It is no denial of miracles to ask whether the feeding of the four thousand is a variant of the more famous feeding of the five thousand, and whether other cases of miracle duplication may have occurred. The question is not whether God can affect the physical world, but when and how God has done so in each given case. Should it be true that Matthew tells the birth story in a midrashlike way, this has nothing to do with being anti-supernaturalistic. One can be both metaphysically open and historically tough minded.

The point is that what looks like a miracle at first sight may not in fact be one. Just because we are open to it does not mean that we should uncritically accept appearances at face value. Using the ordinary rules of empirical observation, some have asked: What kind of star was shining over Bethlehem? What might have caused the series of plagues that God's judgment sent upon the land of Egypt? How universal was the Great Flood? It is only natural to ask these questions, and we have no right to be hard on religious liberals who do so.[18] Being open to God's actions in history does not mean that we suppress inquiry into the nature of them.

The limitation often employed by this method of biblical criticism is that it inhibits us from seeing what transcends the normal and the regular. If we heard of a man who turned into a banana, we would hardly accept the report at face value because, like Sarah of old, such things do not happen in our experience. Sarah laughed at God's promise of a son, not because she ruled out the possibility absolutely, but because her experience worked so much against it. She was thinking by way of analogy with the other things that had happened in her life and had trouble getting her faith around this fresh promise. Perhaps she should not have "waver[ed] concerning the promise of God" (Rom. 4:20), but her uncertainty was understandable and did not turn God away from his plan for her. Criticism is negative when it closes itself to the wonderful deeds of God, but not when it asks in a reasonable way about the specifics of the claims to which it is fundamentally sympathetic.

Conclusion

The Bible is the Scripture of the church that lives on the basis of the nourishment of God's Word, while serving to defend the Word against misuse and abuse. There is great promise in the fact that there are large numbers of people today who are experts in biblical scholarship and who can serve the Word of God in ways that edify the church. We would be badly mistaken, however, if we did not recognize the perils as well as the benefits of such study. Unbelieving elements have become mixed with the procedures and methods and pose great danger to the faith community and its house of authority. Often denied are the reality of God, God's revelatory intervention in history, and the validity of miracle and

---

18. Barr (*Fundamentalism*, chap. 8) points to the common inconsistency of conservatives in this regard.

prophecy. The authority of the apostles is frequently bypassed, and the historical truth of the text is made light of. Such developments have to be opposed, not only as contradictory to the overall claim of Christianity based on the Bible, but also as devoid of good scholarly basis and alien to proper principles of historical method.

Biblical criticism is a major unsolved problem in the church. This is particularly delicate because it touches faith's foundation so directly. Biblical scholars need to be sensitive to the high stakes that theologians and church leaders perceive in this area and not pursue their work in ignorance or disrespect of them. In return for such awareness, the scholars themselves would receive less nervous attention and be more able to continue their work in the freedom they have a right to.

Christians who are not particularly conservative and who participate fully in critical research would do well to listen to our warning. They often seem to ignore the truly destructive effects that criticism has had and can have on the basis of authority in the church. They pride themselves on having graduated out of fundamentalism and having learned to appreciate the fruits of biblical scholarship, while at the same time wanting to appeal to Scripture as the definitive witness and source of truth for the church. They must decide whether or not to dwell in the house of scriptural authority. Is the Bible the infallible norm in matters of faith and practice, or not? If we believe it is, we must take a stand against the kind of criticism that denies it.

There are great areas of freedom for the Christian scholar and large possibilities for the use of critical skill for the good of the church. But let the scholar also remember to obey the apostles and prophets and be submissive to the Scriptures that God has given us. Let the Scripture scholar maintain the dignity of God's Word and explain it so that it continues to be a source of truth and strength to pastors and people. Let the scholar pursue scholarship, not as an end in itself, but for the purpose of grasping more perfectly the sense God intended through the inspired writers, showing how it contributes to a clearer understanding of revelation and, if necessary, to the refutation of error.

Is it consistent for us, on the one hand, to call for an open, inductive investigation of the biblical claims and, on the other hand, to maintain that we should oppose all biblical criticism that is predisposed against the inherent integrity of the biblical text? We have insisted that the Bible is in part human and must be allowed to reveal its humanity. We are urging Christians to believe that the Bible is God's Word and to look at it in the light of their belief. Their doctrine of inspiration provides an interpretive framework when they approach the problems of criticism. The situation is in flux today. A few decades ago, one could be sure that a conservative would reject criticism, whereas a liberal would embrace and practice it. Now it is common to find conservatives deeply involved in criticism and liberals sounding a warning against doing so uncritically. This augurs well for cooperation and understanding.[19]

Modern biblical scholarship is often oriented to a technical mastery of the text and to the secular knowledge of everything that concerns the text. Although the discoveries that are made can be very helpful to understanding the text as originally given, our fundamental orientation ought to be rather different. It is friendship with God that we ought to be pursuing in the study of the Bible. Our desire is to dwell with God and be in communication with him. Like Saint Bernard, we want to taste and see that the Lord is good, and this is the direction in which our study ought to be oriented. Secularist criticism simply does not address the religious dimension of the texts and therefore fails us badly. We seek an approach that takes the Bible to be a text of integrity and deserving of respect. Fortunately, some of the more recent literary approaches attend to the meaning of the text as a whole and engage its message personally.

We rejoice that the debate over criticism seems to be easing. It is common now to hear liberals warning against the abuses of criticism and conservatives advocating a more scholarly study of the Bible. There is a shared perception that presuppositions have something to do with how criticism operates and that there has been altogether too much scissors-and-paste criticism done with questionable theological and literary integrity. We seem to be closer to one another now than previously, and the days of severe polarization may be in the past.

All in all, we have to be open to the results of inspiration that God has been pleased to allow. Certainly the Bible is true, but we must be ready to admit how complex the category of truth is. A fact may be reported approximately, whereas a command can be neither true nor false. Jesus was in the habit of telling "true" stories called parables that were in fact fictional. Therefore, when we look for the Bible to prove true, we must open ourselves to the kind of truth it chooses to deliver and not try to limit its freedom. We have to let the phenomena of the text guide us, even when they disappoint our expectations or surprise us. It is enough for us to expect the Bible to be entirely trustworthy for the purposes God had in inspiring it. We only get into trouble when we impose further requirements of a deductive nature on the text. Let us rather be guided by the proverb well applied to the Bible text: "If something exists, it must be possible."[20]

19. Richard J. Coleman, *Issues of Theological Conflict*, 144–50.
20. I. Howard Marshall (*Biblical Inspiration*, chap. 3) has an excellent discussion about being open to the actual data of the text.

PART 3

Sword of the Spirit

Word and Spirit

Introducing the Spirit of God into our subject may have radical implications in a number of ways. For one thing, it seems that the Spirit is missing from both sides of the liberal-conservative debate. Each is strongly wedded to the Enlightenment mentality that places most of the emphasis on academic understanding and minimizes the role of the Spirit in recognizing and interpreting God's Word. Rationalistic assumptions lie behind the familiar liberal rejection of the Scripture principle, whereas the conservatives, in reaction, want to prove the Bible is the Word of God by adducing arguments a liberal might be able to accept. Neither says much about the role of the Spirit in stimulating faith in and understanding of the Scriptures. If we were to do justice to the Spirit in relation to the Word, we might find the whole hermeneutical operation loosened up and made exciting and more productive.

As was pointed out in chapter 1, revelation is bipolar. What has been revealed to writers long ago must come to readers today. We have so far concentrated almost entirely on the objective side of revelation and now wish to move to the complementary subjective side. Revelation has to be received and become meaningful to those whom it addresses. The external letter must become an inner Word through the work of the Spirit. We have to avoid both a false objectivity in which revelation is independent of God's present activity and a false subjectivity in which revelation is swallowed up by human experience and cannot be normative for it. We must lose neither the content of the divine disclosure nor the reality of God speaking to us today. The two aspects belong together, even though there are those who want to suppress the objective in favor of the subjective and vice versa. We need to get beyond the polarization in which the conservative downplays the subjective because revisionists make too much of it.[1]

In one sense, of course, the Bible is a past text. In another sense, it is an instrument of the Spirit peering into our current lives and questioning us. The Word of God is "at work" in believers and not merely something they have control over (1 Thess. 2:13). The text can become the occasion for God to speak to us today. What was given can become fresh and new in our hearing, a fire in the bones, like honey to the taste. Although we interpret the Bible, in a sense it also interprets us if we are open to it. "The word of God is not chained" (2 Tim. 2:9). The Bible is no mere ancient text resting on the mantle like some dusty antique or museum piece. It claims that the Spirit is accustomed to rendering the text effective as the Word of God in our hearts. God himself meets us in his Word and makes the truth live. This is the ministry of the Spirit.

It is not that the living Word is different from the objective biblical text; rather, through the Spirit, the text comes alive and becomes contemporary to us. The texts become more than they would be to the unbeliever, who only understands their historical meaning. They take on the character of personal address. The Scriptures become "living and active, sharper than any two-edged sword, piercing until it divides soul from spirit, joints from marrow; it is able to judge the thoughts and intentions of the heart" (Heb. 4:12). In this way, the Bible leaps over the centuries and becomes present and meaningful for us today. The Spirit sees to it that the relevance of the ancient Word is seen and ensures that the Scriptures always function as the medium of the Word of God for the church. The real authority of the Bible is not the scholarly exegesis of the text, open only to the elite scholar, but the Word that issues forth when the Spirit takes the text and renders it the living voice of the Lord. Therefore, it is not a text we can master through techniques but a text that wants to master us.

Not without cause, conservative Christians have been a little fearful to give much room to the subjective and the existential. They have seen what can be done when the Word is subordinated to human subjectivity. Neglecting the subjective side, however, cannot be the answer. It can too easily result in Pharisaic legalism that handles the text in a cold, harsh way and never asks what our Lord is saying to us through it now. It can make us afraid for the fate of the Bible, so that we feel that we have to

---

1. J. I. Packer (in *Scripture and Truth*, ed. Carson and Woodbridge, 347–48) sees the need for evangelicals to say more about the work of the Spirit when they discuss the inspiration and authority of the Bible. Millard Erickson (*Evangelical Left*, 79) properly observes that a key aim of this present work is "not to propound a Barthian view of revelation, but to revitalize the evangelical doctrine of illumination of Scripture by the Holy Spirit."

defend it down to the last jot and tittle lest it prove untrue according to some rational standard. It can make us spiritless ourselves and ineffective in reaching those today who are longing for subjective immediacy in faith. Often in fundamentalism there has been a false concentration on the letter and an insensitivity to the illuminating work of the Spirit.[2] Surely, the Spirit is the key to the proper functioning of biblical authority. It is not enough for people to have their heads filled with biblical data if they are not at the same time appropriating the truth subjectively under immediate divine guidance.

The great concern for the Bible in our day is a wonderful thing. We want to get back to apostolic foundations and recover the evangelical message. Renewal in the church is always marked by a new love for the Scriptures. But our concentration on the Bible can also be the mark of desperation, the reflection of insecurity about God. It can be a desperate attempt to recover something solid when the reality of old-time religion has faded, or an effort to bolster orthodoxy rather than a result of tasting new wine. We ought to be clear that a mere doctrine of Scripture cannot guarantee soundness of life in the church unless faith in the working of God's Spirit is present also. The danger that causes Helmut Thielicke to postpone his discussion of Scripture to the end of his dogmatics, so as not to fall into this rationalistic trap, is very real.[3]

The Danger of Subjectivity

Although there is a danger of conservatives overreacting to the shift to the subjective pole of revelation and buying into a false objectivity without the Spirit, we must recognize that the danger of a false subjectivism is also very real. Modern theology is marked by a shift to the functional and the existential. It places tremendous stress on the subjective pole, not to complement, but almost to replace the objective content of the Word of God. We want to avoid falling into either subjective irrationalism or objective rationalism.

There is a threat in the prevalent tendency to downplay the authoritative text and pretend to go with the Spirit, who is in reality equated with the spirit of the times. In this way, the objective requirements of the Scriptures can be twisted and whittled down to suit our own specifications. The effect is to restrict the ability of the Bible to discipline the inner light of human experience and to prevent it from exercising

2. Bernard Ramm, *Witness of the Spirit*, 123–27. This approach leads easily to a "rationalist propositionalism" that is critiqued effectively by Henry H. Knight III, *Future for Truth*, 90–93.

3. Helmut Thielicke, *Evangelical Faith*, 3:103–98.

substantial control over how we think. The usual rhetoric refers to conceiving the biblical text as transformative of the believer in some vague way but not believing it to be informative in regard to specific doctrines and statutes. This leaves revelation without much by way of intelligible content and makes it into an existential event that happens to us. It then becomes possible for the reader to construe the text in personal ways, with the text having lost its true normativity. The shift is very agreeable to those who desire to be free of biblical teaching while still appearing to respect the Bible. One can be both pious and in rebellion against the doctrines of the apostles and prophets.[4]

One possible indication of the beginning of this trend came in the Radical Reformation, when an extremist, Thomas Muntzer, stressed the importance of the inner word, even to the point of denying the authority of the biblical text. The "spiritual" Anabaptists related the Spirit to the Word in such a way that the Bible tended to mirror religious experience rather than be normative for it. For them, revelation was what happens in the heart of the believer rather than objectively in history and in the text.[5]

The concentration on the subjective began in earnest with Friedrich Schleiermacher and the religious liberals in the nineteenth century. Doctrines do not have their origin in divine revelation, they said, but in the religious self-consciousness.[6] They are humanity's way of expressing affections and emotions and not statements of objective truth. To treat them as such would be to misconceive their nature and function. To confess God as creator, for example, is not a factual claim against an evolutionist but an expression of one's sense of absolute dependence. The Bible's authority, therefore, is not to teach us infallible concepts but to shape our God-consciousness. Christianity, rather than consisting of the rule of a content-full revelation and unalterable creed, is a continuity of spirit over time. The context of faith itself will vary according to the worldview of any given epoch. Religious experience is primary, not the forms in which it is expressed.[7]

The early Karl Barth shows signs of the same sort of preference for the subjective over the objective. Although he is known for writing

---

4. Carl F. H. Henry (*God, Revelation, and Authority*, 4:470–75) subjects Kelsey's doctrine of functional authority to critical analysis.

5. Bernard M. G. Reardon, *Religious Thought in the Reformation*, 223–30.

6. Friedrich Schleiermacher, *Christian Faith*, 78. More recently, Joel B. Green (in *Reading the Bible in Wesleyan Ways*, ed. Barry L. Callen and Richard P. Thompson, 134) has announced that it is now time "to loosen our grips on the tradition of modern biblical scholarship and to loosen its grip on us, in order that we might participate in forms of biblical study that take with utmost seriousness our location within the church."

7. Jan Walgrave, *Unfolding Revelation*, 226–29.

dogmatic theology and pays close attention to the content of the Bible, one would not guess it from what is called his "actualism." According to his theory, which stands even in the *Church Dogmatics*, Barth sees the Bible as a fallible human word that gets transformed into an existential Word by a divine miracle.[8] In this way he hopes to preserve the freedom of God in relation even to the Bible. Revelation is seen as a contemporary event, an encounter with God not involving a system of truth. Fortunately, from a classical standpoint, Barth disregards his own theory when he proceeds to do theology and operates on the basis of what amounts to an orthodox doctrine of Scripture that assumes that the content stands beyond the reach of criticism. This would be true also of many who are drawn to Barth's theory but, like him, do not use it in practice. If they did, no such theology as Barth's could be imagined.[9]

Rudolf Bultmann, of course, illustrates well the danger we are addressing. On the basis of a number of dubious assumptions about the New Testament as mythical and existential in nature, Bultmann proposes to interpret it as the seedbed for possibilities of authentic living in the world. We come with our existential questions to a text presupposed to be primarily interested in such questions, and out of the encounter with Scripture there can come an encounter with God. Bultmann respects the New Testament and takes it to be unique and irreplaceable, but for him it is not a teacher of normative truth. Its purpose is to issue a call for decision and to put us existentially in touch with God. It does not matter that the Bible is full of mistakes and contradictions, so long as this existential miracle occurs through it. Its authority does not lie in its content but in its proclamation of the kerygma of God's saving action for us in Christ. The New Testament never intended to give us a mythical picture of the world; it aimed to issue a living word of salvation that can transform human existence.[10]

One finds this kind of teaching on every hand in modern theology. It is our knowledge of ourselves and a relationship with God that matter, says Rosemary Ruether, not revealed doctrines and miraculous events. The truth of faith is the truth found in encounter, not in objective judgments. When it gets expressed in symbols, as it must, these are relative to the historical occasion when they arose and not universally valid.[11] For Claude Geffré, revelation does not consist of truths about God but of what happened to the early Christians when they encountered God.

8. Karl Barth, *Church Dogmatics*, 1/2:528–30.
9. Klaas Runia, *Karl Barth's Doctrine of Holy Scripture*; and Paul Helm, *Divine Revelation*, 40–47.
10. Walter Schmithals, *Introduction to the Theology of Rudolf Bultmann*.
11. Rosemary Ruether, *Church against Itself*, 119–20.

What we want to do is to make that experience contemporary.[12] Paul Hanson believes that the Bible does not want us to think the way it thinks but wants to draw us into a liberating relationship with God. This relationship must not be permitted to fossilize into a concern for facts and doctrines.[13]

Even contemporary evangelicals, because of the pietist character of their movement, can be attracted to a version of the functional authority of the Bible. After all, is not changing lives what the Bible is about? Therefore, it is tempting to consider locating its authority in the existential realm and sidestep a lot of awkward intellectual questions. This is, of course, exactly what attracted pietists like Schleiermacher in the first place. One naturally becomes suspicious when Herman Dooyeweerd tells us that the authority of the Bible is assigned to the pistic level in the scheme of thirteen modalities, and when G. C. Berkouwer wants to correlate the Bible with the faith of the church, seeming to deny its objective truthfulness. People have even wondered if Jack Rogers and Donald McKim had anything like this in mind when they suggested that we limit infallibility to the soteric realm. It is unlikely that they intended anything like Bultmann's demythologizing. Nevertheless, the temptation is there.

What we are dealing with here is a determined effort to reconceive revelation in non-informative terms. The reason for this is apologetic. Modern people find it difficult to believe the Bible intellectually, so they choose to appreciate it in an existential way. Theologians oblige by dropping the demand to believe the content of the creed and by withdrawing to a much weaker stance. By asking only for some vague relationship with the Bible, they hope to make the gospel less vulnerable to critical attack. The new idea is to think of the Bible as less a source of objective truths and much more an instrument that can function in the transformation of persons. It is a clever move, in that changing lives is most certainly part of the Bible's purpose; it is perverse in that it wholly misconceives how such change comes about.[14]

It has been common since Adolf Harnack to maintain that it was a mistake to draw dogmas out of revelation. Christianity began, it is claimed, as a charismatic movement that unfortunately hardened into the confessionalism we call orthodoxy. This, however, is not true. The early church fathers who looked to the Bible for doctrinal information were entirely right to do so. The gospel has content, which can be drawn out and developed. Indeed, that is what the New Testament calls on us

12. Claude Geffré, *New Age in Theology*, 64.

13. Paul D. Hanson, *Diversity of Scripture*, xvii, 1–2, 16, 83, etc.

14. In their volume *Christian Theology*, chap. 2, Hodgson and King present this revolution in theology.

to do. It is obvious that Luke, Paul, and John cared about how Christians understood the basics of the faith in history and in doctrine and instructed them to hold it fast. The idea that the New Testament does not mean to teach us objective truth is an invention of modern theologians. It is more honest to be an atheist and turn completely away from the Bible than to profess respect for it and then refuse to submit to its actual teaching. Of course, the biblical writers cared about the existential significance of what they set forth and its appropriation, but not in opposition to belief in their teaching. It is because these facts happened and these truths were given that the transformation can take place through faith.

Christians are expected to build upon the foundation of the apostles and prophets and be "obedient from the heart to the form of teaching to which you were entrusted" (Rom. 6:17). We have been given a deposit of truth by the Spirit, and we are expected to treasure and guard it (2 Tim. 1:13–14). Obviously, the New Testament cares very much about truth and fact and sees them as crucially important in a person's salvation. It knows nothing of Bultmann's contentless kerygma and gives no support to this modern shift away from the objective. Such a major shift represents an artificial and arbitrary restriction of the meaning of the Bible to a certain set of existential questions we have decided we want it to answer. It is a denial of the true authority of Scripture in the guise of affirmation.

Word and Spirit

Revelation is two-sided: divine and human, objective and subjective. There is an initiative from God and a reception by human beings. There must be a mutuality of the divine Spirit and the human spirit for revelation to become effective in our lives. As Paul says, the Spirit bears witness with our spirit in all these matters of salvation (Rom. 8:16). God works in a double way, making himself present to us and opening our eyes to help us receive revelation. As John Calvin put it, "God sent down the same Spirit by whose power he had dispensed the Word, to complete his work by the efficacious confirmation of the Word" (*Institutes* 1.9). First, God gave us the Scriptures by inspiration, filling them with revelational potential for all generations. Second, God continues to give us the Scriptures in order to activate and actualize this potential in our hearts and minds. The Bible is a content-full deposit that we should receive as from God; it is also the living Word when it functions as the sword of the Spirit. Let us consider the general relationship of the Word and the Spirit.

Because the Old Testament sees the work of the Spirit in a fairly narrow way, working among a restricted company of believers, it does not speak directly to this matter of the testimony of the Spirit, as Protestants call it.[15] It does speak indirectly, as indeed do many texts in the New Testament. When the Old Testament speaks of dry bones coming to life by the Word of God (Ezek. 37:7–10) or asks God to open our eyes so that we may behold wondrous things in his law (Ps. 119:18), it is talking about God doing a work in human beings to place them in vital contact with revelation personally. Jesus refers to this God-given ability to understand when he says to Peter, "For flesh and blood has not revealed this to you, but my Father in heaven" (Matt. 16:17). Not all texts that refer to this matter talk specifically in terms of the Spirit, but they build up the same general impression.

God himself is at work to make a knowledge of himself possible. He gives an inward revelation of the truth and a certainty that cannot be obtained merely from human understanding. According to Paul and Luke, the coming of the Spirit at Pentecost was an event comparable in its importance to the incarnation itself. Having sent his Son into the world, God also sent his Spirit to make the former action historically and existentially effective (Gal. 4:4–6). The apostle refers often to the Spirit as bearing witness in our hearts (Rom. 8:16), confirming the truth of the gospel (1 Thess. 1:5), enabling people to see that his message is the Word of God (1 Thess. 2:13), and giving us inward light and removing the veil and the darkness (2 Cor. 3:16–4:6).

Paul speaks of the Spirit of revelation who operates in the believing heart to give a personal appreciation of all God has revealed and given (Eph. 1:17). How this works can be seen in the case of Lydia as she was listening to Paul's preaching: "The Lord opened her heart to listen eagerly to what was said by Paul" (Acts 16:14). The God who caused light to shine out of darkness is able to send shafts of spiritual light into our hearts to disclose the glory of God in the face of Jesus Christ. Here is a subjectivity we must not turn away from. The saving knowledge of God depends upon it.

The apostle John rivals Paul in the emphasis he gives to this role of the Spirit. Believers, like sheep, will be able to follow Jesus because they will hear and recognize Jesus's voice (John 10:4). The Spirit, when given, will teach them and bring to their remembrance what Jesus said (14:16–17, 26). He will bear witness to Christ and enable us to bear witness in the world (15:26–27). He will lead us into all truth and will take the things of Christ and declare them to us (16:13–15). Believers enjoy an anointing that teaches them what they need to know (1 John

---

15. Ramm, *Witness of the Spirit*.

2:27). Finally, John says that the Spirit is the witness to Christ, the true witness (1 John 5:6). There is a mutuality and a balance between the Word given through Jesus in history and in the Scriptures, and the contemporary witness of the Spirit enabling us to appreciate and penetrate what was given in our own lives. The Spirit does not erase the Word of the gospel but renders it effective and relevant. The Spirit provides the link of continuity between Jesus and the later faith community. John points to a fine balance between faithfulness to the tradition and creativity in interpreting it, probably thinking of his own Gospel as an example of how to render the original Word in a new setting and time.[16]

This truth of the Spirit's crucial work has not fared well in the history of the church. For a long time it was neglected, and then groups like the Quakers sometimes seemed to derive from the Spirit some content alien to the Bible. Especially in religious liberalism, experience became the source rather than the medium of revelation. Theologians like Schleiermacher thought they should and could derive the content of the Christian faith from religious consciousness. This is against both Scripture and common sense. The truth of the gospel was given in history and cannot be rederived from experience. As even Paul Tillich said, "Experience is not the source from which the contents of systematic theology are taken but the medium through which they are existentially received."[17] The Spirit was given, not to take away from the finality of Christ, but to render an effective witness to him, whether in the Bible or in everyday conversation.

The God who gave the Bible still gives it. He helps us receive it as the Word of God and understand what it means for our time. God activates the information so that it becomes effective divine communication. Therefore, the interpretation of the Bible cannot be left to the experts. We need to encounter God in and through the text and discern what God is saying to us now. The possibilities of meaning are not limited to the original intent of the text, although that is always the anchor of interpretation. Fresh insights can arise from the interaction of the Spirit and the Word. We read the text and in it seek the will of the Lord for today.

Revelation has not ceased. A phase of it has ceased, the phase that provided the gospel and its scriptural witness, but not revelation in every sense. If it had, we could not know Christ as Lord because we would be left to our own cognitive powers. We have in us the Spirit of revelation who causes the letter of the Bible to be charged with life and

16. James D. G. Dunn, *Jesus and the Spirit*, 350–57.
17. Paul Tillich, *Systematic Theology*, 1:42.

to become the living voice of God to us. The Spirit did not withdraw from the church after the canon was completed but remains in the church speaking through the Scriptures, revealing Christ to us afresh. Indeed, indications are that the Spirit continues to address us through one another and through special gifts. In the church at Antioch, there were teachers who communicated the faith once delivered and prophets who responded to the word of the Lord in their spirits (Acts 13:1). Paul indicates that prophecy is an important gift to congregations because it builds us up (1 Cor. 14:3). We should not despise prophecy just because we rightly fear false prophecy. The secret is to be critical of prophetic claims and discern what is authentic (1 Thess. 5:19–22). Paul even suggests safeguards, such as employing apostolic teaching as a norm and exercising communal discernment (1 Cor. 14:27, 29). The point is simply that we should not suppress the Spirit's revealing work. We should be docile and receptive in the Spirit's presence.[18]

We have access to the message of salvation through the Scriptures that God has given to bear witness to Christ, and these words become alive and effective in us through the work of the Spirit. Thus, the Bible is an instrument or tool of the Spirit to teach and shape us. The Bible is like a pair of glasses through which we can see the truth of God. Without both the Word and the Spirit we cannot do sound, nourishing theology. Scripture is a means of grace by which God's Word continues to come to us. The Bible is not so much a static collection of timeless oracles as it is the place to stand when one wants to be in God's presence and learn of him. Through the Bible we can orient ourselves to the objective revelation that has been given and, through the Spirit, enter into it personally and dynamically.

Donald Bloesch has suggested that we think of the Bible as a sacrament, as the outward and visible sign of an inward and spiritual grace, a vehicle by which the Spirit preaches Christ to us. Without in any way denying cognitive revelation, this proposal does justice to the freedom of the Word and gets us away from thinking of the Bible in purely intellectual terms.[19] When we consider how the Bible has actually functioned in the church over the centuries as a means of grace and a constant companion, it is a wonder that it did not become incorporated into the sacramental thinking of the church. The way the early theologians like Tertullian spoke of and used the Scriptures is certainly sacramental. As Jaroslav Pelikan says, "The attention to the sacraments in dogmatic theology has failed to do justice to the place of the doctrine of the Word of God, proclaimed but also written,

18. Bruce Yocum, *Prophecy*.
19. Donald G. Bloesch, *Essentials of Evangelical Theology*, 2:269–75.

within the total doctrine of the means of grace during the second and third centuries."[20]

Indeed, if modern evangelicals would reflect on our essentially sacramental use of the Bible ("quiet time" being our daily office), we might understand Roman Catholic theology more sympathetically. When we read the Bible in faith, we are ushered into the presence of God. Like the bread and the wine, the words of this Book communicate the gospel and create communion with God. By the Spirit, the Scriptures occasion fresh events of revelation that are more than just the analyzing of propositions. Of course, textual elements of this sacrament are more than merely fallible human words. A miracle takes place when a person meets the Lord and hears God's Word through the Bible.

Because of the Spirit, the Bible can be a channel of the grace and speech of God to us. The Spirit constitutes the privileged circle in which to stand when wanting to hear God's Word and discern God's will. There is a mystery in the way in which the Bible operates in the life of the church. The Word can be stale and dry for long periods and then spring to life and power. The truth can lie hidden and then come alive and break forth. Jesus and Paul met Jews who cared greatly for the biblical text but could not grasp what God was saying to them in it. The message was hidden from their eyes. In the same way, the church can languish in ignorance of the liberating message of the Bible and then rediscover the grace and goodness of God. This is the mystery of the Spirit and the Word.

Richard Lovelace has concluded that the proper balance of the Spirit and the Word is the key to living orthodoxy. In order to preach Christ effectively, we must, on the one hand, depend on a true knowledge of the incarnate Word through the written Word. On the other hand, we must depend on the risen Lord and his outpoured Spirit to bring to life the information given and focus it existentially on our hearts. Spiritually energized biblical truth is the instrument through which God transforms human personalities.[21] No choice needs to be made between the content of the Bible and our appropriation of it. The Bible is like a telescope that fastens our vision on the Lord. God may not be giving foundational Scripture anymore—this has been done—but he is still engaged in communicating himself and filling our lives with his loving presence and wisdom. God has not and never will finish illuminating the minds of believers with the truth by which they can learn to know and love God better.

20. Jaroslav Pelikan, *Christian Tradition*, 1:162; Geoffrey Wainwright, *Doxology*, 149–50.

21. Richard F. Lovelace, *Dynamics of Spiritual Life*, 279.

Three Specific Operations of Word and Spirit

How does this duality and mutuality of the Word and the Spirit work out in specific ways? What difference does it really make in reading the Bible whether or not one has the Spirit? We will look at three specific ways that the Spirit works in relation to the Scriptures and note a pattern in each case, one of spiritual understanding being built.

Recognizing the Word

Let us consider first how we come to recognize the Scriptures, or the gospel itself for that matter, as the Word of God. In a real sense, how faith comes about is a mystery hidden in the depths of the human spirit. It is hard to be certain how it comes about in one's own life. Nevertheless, there is a level of ordinary understanding involved. Many kinds of evidence have convinced people through the ages of the objective truth of the Bible's message. John Calvin spoke of the good and sufficient evidences that were at hand to establish the credibility of the Scriptures, having in mind such indicators as fulfilled prophecy, miracles, profundity, antiquity, coherence, and the like (*Institutes* 1.8). Although he would never have claimed to be able by rational argument to bring a person all the way to saving faith, Calvin did insist that one could think intelligently about faith. We are not left in the dark in the realm of religion. The truth of the Christian faith has good credentials. It would be very peculiar and tragic if a message addressed to all people could not make good its claim in the public realm, if there were no way the believer could explain to another person in what ways faith in God makes good sense.[22]

In thinking about reasons for faith in the gospel and the Bible, we can distinguish internal and external reasons. Internal evidence includes the way in which the Bible has again and again proved itself true in human lives by supplying the understanding crucial to addressing the questions of meaning, suffering, and forgiveness. The text has a ring of truth about it and can trigger an inner response. In speaking to the deepest questions of human existence, the Bible presents itself as a credible candidate for revelation. A text that makes deep sense, and has been able to grip the best minds of the past few millennia, obviously possesses marks of truth. The claims it makes to be a revelation from God seem to be confirmed in ordinary experience.

External evidence is more objective, such as God's workmanship in the universe and God's action in the history of the world. John Locke maintained, along with a host of other Christian apologists over the

22. David Tracy, *Analogical Imagination*, 62.

centuries, that the revelation God gave was accompanied by outward signs that authenticated the revelation. In this way, Locke believed, revelation was nonarbitrary because it possessed credentials that interested persons could examine for themselves. Although it is not possible to conclude that revelation can be infallibly established by such arguments, it can be maintained that belief in the truth of the Bible and the gospel is rationally preferred over unbelief, because it explains well some important data.[23]

One can, of course, go too far in this direction. There is a personal certainty only the Spirit can give us that must not be lost sight of. In our desire to prove the Bible true, we can easily locate the basis of faith in human wisdom rather than in the power of God. We can become more at home defending the Bible than in proclaiming its message with power. Our supposed expertise can get in the way of actually encountering the truth of the text.[24] The greater certainty sought by scholars can easily damage the faith of the ordinary Christian, so that the whole apologetic operation can backfire. For reasons like these, the Protestant Reformers blew hot and cold about the place of philosophy in theology. They knew that revelation has good credentials, and they referred to them, but they did not want to lose sight of the work of the Spirit in establishing certainty. Can we have it both ways? Yes, we can, but only if we maintain a careful balance and proper perspective.

There is nothing to prevent us from thinking in terms of both rational evidence for the truth of the Bible and the work of God's Spirit that goes beyond such evidence. The evidence can give us an appreciation of the Bible and incline us to crediting its claims, but it cannot give the kind of personal certitude that faith implies and that results from a decision to trust God and believe his Word. It is not that the Spirit turns poor evidence into good evidence or a bad argument into a good one, but that God helps us to have the right perspective and to attend better to the evidence that is there. The resulting conviction is personal and internal, but the basis on which it was made remains public. Personal knowledge builds on the data of ordinary understanding but goes beyond it. It is not irrational, but trans-rational. It is a confidence that commitment brings and that God gives.

The apostle Paul often emphasized that the power of his preaching owed little or nothing to his skill at rhetoric or argument. The gospel came to the Thessalonians with power because of the Spirit's work (1 Thess. 1:5). It was not so much that Paul impressed them as that they had

23. Helm, *Divine Revelation*, 71–88.
24. Paul Holmer (in *Evangelicals*, ed. David F. Wells and John D. Woodbridge, 68–95) seems to worry about this happening in conservative theology.

been gripped by God himself in what was preached. The Word was not experienced as a human message from without but as a divine energy within (1 Thess. 2:13). Similarly, the Corinthians were not convinced by Paul's rhetorical abilities but by a "demonstration of the Spirit and power" (1 Cor. 2:4). Although this phrase was used in Greek to denote a compelling argument, Paul turns it around so that it has nothing to do with argument and proofs. The Corinthians were so conscious of the power of God when Paul spoke that they were not so much intellectually persuaded as spiritually converted. There is a personal certainty that the Spirit gives that cannot be obtained by reasons and evidence. The Spirit enables us to hear the Word and receive it, takes away the veil, rings the bell of truth, and enables us to live with various kinds of uncertainty.[25]

Interpreting the Word

Second, in our look at the Spirit and Scripture, let us consider the interpretation of Scripture. Here, too, there is an ordinary level of comprehension. Anyone can investigate fruitfully the meaning of a text. It should be possible for Christians and others to agree on the historical meaning of the text. This is the validity in interpretation for which E. D. Hirsch pleads.[26] One does not have to rejoice in the truth of John 3:16 to understand basically what it is saying. We should not think of God as giving to believers private information about the original meaning of a text and denying it to others. If he did that, the locus of revelation would shift to subjective experience and away from its connection with the Bible. Intuition would then reign supreme. If the meaning of the text cannot be determined by ordinary understanding, then it must be free-floating and subject to all manner of distortion. Surely the plain sense of the text must be the anchor of all true interpretation. Otherwise, the authority of the Bible will drift off into human subjectivity. Paul's command still stands: "Do your best to present yourself to God as one approved by him, a worker who has no need to be ashamed, rightly explaining the word of truth" (2 Tim. 2:15).[27]

Even so, there is still a crucial role for the Spirit in the interpretation of the Bible. Who has not had the awful experience of reading a scholarly commentary on the meaning of the text, only to be so bored by technical detail and a lack of spiritual discernment about what the Bible is saying that there is no incentive to open the Bible and take it

25. Dunn, *Jesus and the Spirit*, 226–27.

26. E. D. Hirsch, *Validity in Interpretation*.

27. Walter Kaiser (*Toward an Exegetical Theology*) presses this necessity home at every opportunity.

seriously? Obviously, the truth of the text is not secured merely by possessing historical and linguistic tools. What marked commentaries before the rise of criticism was an orientation to want to know God better and grow in his friendship. They did not try to master the text as critics now do but placed themselves under its discipline and tasted the goodness of the Lord. They were, in fact, in agreement with the biblical writers themselves as to what was important and therefore in a better position to grasp what these writers were saying.

The simple fact is that involvement with a text like the Bible and an open receptivity to its message put one in a position to understand it better. Every Bible reader knows of times when study is dry and fruitless, but also times when there is a creative breakthrough in understanding, when lights go on and things fall into place. The testimony of William Lane in his commentary on the Gospel of Mark is worth recording:

> Only gradually did I come to understand that my primary task as a commentator was to listen to the text, and to the discussion it has prompted over the course of centuries, as a child who needed to be made wise. The responsibility to discern truth from error has been onerous at times. When a critical or theological decision has been demanded by the text before I was prepared to commit myself, I have adopted the practice of the Puritan commentators in laying the material before the Lord and asking for his guidance. This has made the preparation of the commentary a spiritual as well as an intellectual pilgrimage through the text of the Gospel. In learning to be sensitive to all that the evangelist was pleased to share with me, I have been immeasurably enriched by the discipline of responsible listening.[28]

This is by no means a call to forsake serious study of the text, but rather a summons to link the mind and the Spirit, study and prayer, in the work of interpretation. As William Cowper put it in his hymn: "The Spirit breathes upon the Word and brings the truth to sight." There is a level of understanding that only comes through involvement with the text and a walk with the Lord. When Jesus referred to children as an example for us, he meant their attitude of openness and trust. The non-expert, reading in a spirit of receptivity, may understand the text better than the expert with all the scholarly tools. This is the only way for the Bible to become a living and transforming book.

Where the Spirit is active, truths become precious that once were avoided, and insights stand out that once were hidden. Coming to the text with the proper faith orientation enables the reader to penetrate more deeply and pick up what the Bible really has to say. If we were to

28. William L. Lane, *Commentary on the Gospel of Mark*, xii.

read Paul, for example, merely as a figure in the history of religions, we would likely be unable to grasp the insight God gave him into the divine mysteries. What is needed is the balance that Paul himself urged upon Timothy when he said, "Think over what I say, for the Lord will give you understanding in all things" (2 Tim. 2:7). Thinking about the meaning of the text and prayerfully considering the purpose of God in the text go hand in hand in interpretation.[29] Although we are often warned about the naïveté of the layperson reading the Bible, we ought to be just as cautious about the scholarly techniques used by experts that miss the meaning because they are not open and receptive to the text. As C. S. Lewis said, "The true reader reads every work seriously in the sense that he reads it whole-heartedly, makes himself as receptive as he can."[30]

There is more involved than just engagement with the text and a prayerful spirit. Of course, the plain meaning of a book like Romans can lie ungrasped for years, only to be seized upon in a time of renewal and released to transform the church. But there is more to it than that. As we will argue in chapter 8, the meaning of a text cannot be equated only with its original meaning. After all, it now stands in a collection with other books and, most importantly, in a messianically structured canon of old and new covenants. Thus, the meaning of the text is far richer than just the first sense it had. There is a surplus of meaning over and above the original. It is fitted to answer questions we pose at many levels.

What did this text mean to Israelites then? What does it mean for Christians now? What does it mean in the light of this text over here? How does it relate spiritually to my life? How is Christ preached in it? Although we decry the multiple levels of meaning in much of medieval exegesis, we have ourselves fallen into a sterile condition and limited ourselves to the precise meaning of the original author. Instead of seeking a rich testimony from God in the text, we have impoverished ourselves and sold the Scriptures short. To see that, one only has to compare volumes from the International Critical Commentary series with those of John Calvin or Matthew Henry.

If the Spirit helps the church with its interpretation, how is it that we do not agree more than we do about the meaning of the Bible? Even those who approach the Bible as the authoritative Word of God often disagree about its message. Tradition must be part of the answer. We read the text with certain beliefs already in our minds, whether cultural or theological, and these certainly affect how we evaluate what we find. Add to that the complexity of the text itself. On the various issues on which

29. Anthony Thiselton, *The Two Horizons*, 85–92.
30. In his *New Approaches to Jesus and the Gospels*, chap. 6, Gruenler examines C. S. Lewis's hermeneutic.

we differ, the Bible sends out mixed signals that are hard to reduce to demonstrable dogma. What does the Bible as a whole say about peace and war or about Sunday worship or about relations between male and female? Great debates revolve around such questions. Our confusion can sometimes be a reflection of the lack of clarity already in the text. What we have to do is work hard at interpretation and be open to changing our minds. We should strive to grasp the ruling principles of Scripture in each matter and make full use of the accumulated wisdom of the community of the faithful. In this way, perhaps we shall grow into a greater unity of faith in the Son of God (Eph. 4:14–15).

Applying the Word

Third, let us consider the application of the Bible. Although there is a certain flexibility in interpretation, there is a great deal more when it comes to application. Here the Spirit has a broad area to work in, and we must be sensitive to the Spirit's leading. Of course, there is the ordinary level of understanding here also. We have to take the commandments, the doctrines, the narratives, and the exhortations seriously in the form in which God gave them. We have been appointed not to revise the Scriptures but to heed them. The Bible sets up parameters to guide our paths. Very often the application is clear in the text. We ought to love one another; we ought to praise God; we ought to believe God's promises; and so forth. The original meaning establishes an unchanging direction for us that ought to be heeded.

But having said that, there is also a large role for the Spirit, in that we need God's guidance in knowing how to put the Scriptures into effect in our situation today. Over and above what the Bible says, we need the direction and discernment that the Spirit gives. The possible applications even of a text that is straightforward are multiple, and we have to make our choice and take our stand. In effect, we have to discern what the will of the Lord is for us. We need guidance in answering questions such as these: How ought we to help our neighbors in Iraq or in North Korea? How shall we understand the finality of Jesus Christ in the sphere of world religions? What is to be done in the defense of freedom? Ought women to be elders in the church? Is Sunday the day to gather for worship? How can we achieve a greater measure of economic justice? What does creation mean in relation to scientific theory? It is urgent that we give answers to questions like these, yet the Bible does not tell us exactly what answers to give.

The Spirit was given precisely to lead us into all truth, that is, to help us see the meaning of what Jesus said in the new contexts that would arise afterward. The Spirit will help us to penetrate the gospel and see it in an ever-new light. What the Spirit gives does not surpass the gospel of Jesus or add to it. As Hans Küng puts it, "The Spirit cannot give a new revelation, but through the preaching of his witnesses he will cause everything that Jesus said and did to be revealed in a new light. The Spirit is not needful because Jesus' teaching was quantitatively not complete, but because Jesus' teaching must qualitatively become a new revelation through the church's preaching."[31] In this way, revelation can constantly present a new challenge in fresh situations.

We see this happening in the New Testament itself, such as in the different ways the gospel is presented to various audiences in the book of Acts and by the great New Testament theologians. We see it in the four different Gospels. We see it in the way the writers employ the Old Testament texts to speak directly to the body of Christ or read them in light of what had happened in Jesus Christ, a greater David and Solomon and Jonah. They read ancient texts not simply for what they once had to say but in a spirit of openness to what God might now be saying through them. It seems clear that Paul combined the text and his spiritual charisma to come up with fresh insights in Romans 11:25–27 and Galatians 3:8, for example. Or consider the way in which Stephen reinterpreted the Old Testament in light of what Jesus had said about the destruction of the temple (Acts 6:14; 7:2–53), or the decision that was reached at the Council of Jerusalem concerning how the Old Testament laws regarding foods were to be applied to the Gentile converts (Acts 15:6–29).[32] These Christians did not limit themselves to the original sense of the passage; they sought the will of the Lord in the reading of the text such that it became the immediate Word of God to them.

Do we not have the same experience ourselves when we find meaning in texts for our own lives that really extends the original meaning in a new direction? Edith Schaeffer has applied to L'Abri in Switzerland an Old Testament prophecy about the nations flowing to the mountain of God (Isa. 2:2–3). She is not wrong to do this. Texts can function as the Word of the Lord with a sense different from that originally intended. This is simply to recognize the reality of the Spirit at work in the church. God is able to apply the Scriptures to us very directly.

Thus, the task of theology today is to find the applications of the Word that are in the will of God. How can we bring the text over the hermeneutical gap of the centuries and have it address our situation? In part, it must be through careful reflection about what the dynamic equivalent of the text would be, and it must also involve the believing

31. Hans Küng, *Church*, 202.
32. On pneumatic exegesis in the New Testament, see E. Earle Ellis, *Prophecy and Hermeneutic in Early Christianity*.

community listening for God's Word in its prayer and worship. The obvious danger of this liberty is that it may be used to sanctify our own causes, although even a legalistic use of the text can do the same thing. It is easy to claim to have a translation of the text in modern terms that is really a transformation of it. For example, it is not appropriate, in our judgment, to claim that Martin Heidegger is saying just what Paul meant, or that Charles Hartshorne captures exactly the dynamic biblical model of the divine action, or that Karl Marx supplies the theory that the Bible's teaching on justice requires us to use.

Despite the dangers of distortion, the liberty to pursue the contemporary significance of the Bible is precious and not to be suppressed. Liberty can always be used "as an opportunity for the flesh," but it does not have to be misused in this way (Gal. 5:13 RSV). As a check against such abuse, we should distinguish the objective authority of the text in its original meaning, which is canonical and universal, and the subjective authority of our own insights into current significance of the text, which are local and timely but not universal. What the text originally meant provides the fixed point of reference for everything else. What we discern in the text for our situation, which may go beyond its initial scope into a fresh insight for today, has the character of a discernment into the will of the Lord for us. As such, even though it was received in connection with the reading of the Bible, it should not be equated with the text as canonical. Rather, it should be held forth as a contemporary conviction of ours into the way God seems to be leading us. Such convictions are, of course, to be evaluated in the light of reason, tradition, and the instincts of the people of God around us.

We are used to thinking about the guidance of the Spirit in the realm of our life decisions, but clearly we ought to be seeking it also in the work of biblical exegesis and application. Guidance is something we know we can expect God to give us, yet we are aware how easy it is to sanctify our own whims as God's leading. Therefore, we must be in an attitude of prayer when we are listening for God's voice (Acts 14:23) and have a hearty respect for the wisdom of our fellow Christians who are prayerfully open in the same way. One is a fool who is not open to the opinions of other saints. As James said, "The wisdom from above is first pure, then peaceable, gentle, willing to yield, full of mercy and good fruits, without a trace of partiality or hypocrisy" (James 3:17). The same belief in the Spirit's guidance applies to other Christians, too, and ought to make us open and receptive to the applications they understand to be approved by God.

In conclusion, we need to keep in mind both the objective and the subjective poles of revelation and of Scripture. The objective pole gives us an anchor of stability and an authority for all seasons. It prevents us from wandering into free-floating subjectivism. The subjective pole, on the other hand, gives us vitality and flexibility and rules out legalistic and insensitive pseudo-orthodoxy, which is so often merely an absolutism of the hermeneutics of one or two centuries ago.[33]

If it is true that the presence of the Spirit is essential for the work of interpretation to be effective, then it follows that the interpreters must be believers filled with the Spirit. They must be people who are personally in touch with the reality of God in our midst. They are those on whom the power has fallen (Luke 24:49), who operate out of radical faith and with the gifts of the Spirit that bear directly on discerning the will of the Lord. Is it not true that biblical interpreters today often seem to lack the ability or willingness to speak confidently of their personal walk with God and in joyful praise of him? Are they not often specialists about religion, engaged with one another in arcane debates about details—members of the academy, preoccupied, introspective, and not the kind of spiritually liberated persons the New Testament says Christians ought to be? Do we not often find ourselves resembling those Ephesians who had not heard that there was a Holy Spirit, and those Samaritans on whom the Spirit was not yet poured out? (Acts 19:2; 8:16). If so, then we need, in addition to our rational training, a liberation of our spirits by the Spirit of God, so that we might be the kind of interpreters that Scripture deserves.[34]

Both religious liberals and conservative evangelicals have managed too often to leave the Spirit out of hermeneutics, and this must come to an end. The liberals have done so because they are afraid to make it too obvious that they believe in God, whereas the conservatives have done it because they are worried about the uncertainty that could be created if we let any amount of experience into the interpretive equation. The New Testament rebukes both and summons us to trust in God for the light that has yet to break forth out of his holy Word. And so we pray

> Come, Holy Ghost, for moved by Thee,
>   Thy prophets wrote and spoke;
> Unlock the truth, Thyself the key,
>   Unseal the sacred book.[35]

33. Tillich, *Systematic Theology*, 1:3.

34. Rodman Williams, *Era of the Spirit*; and idem, *Pentecostal Reality*.

35. From "Come, Holy Ghost Our Hearts Inspire," in *The Book of Praise* (Don Mills, ON: Presbyterian Church in Canada, 1972).

Unfolding Revelation

By their own form and structure, the Scriptures lend themselves to the Spirit and a dynamic interpretation. Our reference is to the internal dynamic in which the biblical traditions develop and change over time, and also to the depth of meaning that belongs to a literary document of this sort. The Bible is more like a wind tunnel than a pile of bricks, more like an orchestra than a solo instrument. It is also an inexhaustible resource for the church because of the development of its themes and the fecundity of possible interpretations. In this way, the Bible makes itself available to the Spirit for fresh and subtle uses (and to human obtuseness for fresh and subtle misuses). It gives room to the Spirit to update the text and apply it in the new situations that never cease to arise. With good reason, then, we read the Bible expectantly, in hope of finding treasures old and new.

The Development of the Biblical Traditions

The Bible does not present a revelation given all at once. The truth it offers was communicated over a long time and by a very dynamic process. The text seems to breathe, to expand and contract, to grow and build toward the full actualization of salvation, the coming of God's kingdom. The truth is given dialectically in a process of conversation and refinement, which makes for a dynamic experience of interpretation. The Bible takes the form, not of a systematic theology, but of a great narrative that presents the grace of God in action for the redemption of the nations. Therefore, the truth it yields is not cut-and-dried, but balanced and nuanced. The truth is given and applied, and then reinterpreted and reapplied. Older material is appealed to again and again and put to new uses. Out of this process of refinement, fresh insights appear.[1]

Liberal scholarship tends to dwell on this freedom to adapt traditions that we see in the text because it fits in with the desire to be free enough to adapt even the gospel itself to changing circumstances. Nevertheless, conservatives should note that respect for what was given obviously did not prevent biblical writers themselves from interpreting the text in new ways for new circumstances. They were concerned both for the meaning of what was given and for the fresh significance it might have for them. It is vital for the work of interpretation today to take note of this. Evangelicals need to give greater recognition to the fact that Scripture itself often cites earlier revelation, not for its own sake but for the sake of what God was saying through it in a new time. Biblical writers were not slaves to the earlier traditions; obviously, they felt free to use them in new and different ways. They did not see God locked in the past. God is free to update his program of salvation and bring new meaning from what had been given before.[2]

As was brought out in chapter 1, God's grace and offer of salvation have been operative from the beginning of history. God has never left himself without a witness. We should not limit our conception of salvation history to the relatively recent biblical stories from Abraham to Jesus but see it as something that encompasses the whole history of the world. Because God is one who desires all to be saved, we can be sure that there always has been some form of divine self-revelation to everyone. Around every soul there swirl the winds of sin and grace. Our concern here is for the way in which the conversation develops within the Bible, where we encounter the definitive word of salvation and the struggle to understand it. In Jesus Christ and the biblical tradition, the saving presence of God makes itself most tangible and accessible and issues the proclamation of the victorious saving plan of God in Jesus.

Starting with the Old Testament itself, we find a text that is oriented to the future of God's salvation. There is the awareness that God has promised to crush the head of the serpent and bless all the nations through Abraham and his offspring. There is also the sense that God is going to do more and reveal more concerning his purpose and plan. We need to learn to look not only at the finished products of revelation but

---

1. Gerhard von Rad (*Old Testament Theology*, 1:119) is particularly concerned to interpret the Old Testament as a process of refocusing the earlier traditions to show their fresh relevance to changing circumstances.

2. This is one of the main points that Paul Achtemeier brings out in *The Inspiration of Scripture*, 76–93.

also at the ways in which the biblical traditions dynamically developed. The Old Testament is, in fact, an ongoing hermeneutic of the fulfillment of the promise of God.[3]

One can read the Old Testament in a way that brings out the concepts that arise from reading the text as a whole, or one can read it more chronologically, observing the successive epochs in the history of revelation and tradition and noting the transitions and changes that were introduced. The content and its unfolding are both important to a full understanding of the Bible. What Stephen does in retelling the Old Testament story of salvation and judgment occurs throughout the Bible.[4] One marvelous way to bring this out is to refer to God's promise and observe how this promise is unfolded and actualized over time in the Bible.[5] It was given in a nutshell to Adam and Eve, then opened up in the specific, although still general, promise to Abraham, and later formalized in the covenant of the Mosaic period. Following this, it went through stages of judges, monarchy, exile, and return, in all of which the direction and meaning of the promise was progressively clarified. What was originally given was expanded and focused in changing circumstances, resulting in an overall picture of rich proportions. "Progressive" may be too simple a term to describe what happened. We cannot exactly say that Haggai was an advance over Isaiah, or Ecclesiastes an improvement of Proverbs. There was, nevertheless, an unfolding and a deepening of the picture that God wants us to have of his character and purposes.

Let us look at two illustrations that pertain to the promise to Abraham. In Genesis 12, God promises to bless Abraham and his seed and to make them a blessing in the earth. Much later, Isaiah picks up this promise and elicits a word of comfort for Israel: God will make the wilderness like Eden and the desert like the garden of God (Isa. 51:1–3). Ezekiel, when he meditates on this promise, takes it in a quite different way. He tells the people that they cannot depend on God blessing them if they persist in disobeying him, and he prophesies judgment upon them (Ezek. 33:23–29). People like that cannot expect to claim promises that implied quite different behavior. In Genesis 15:7, God declares himself as the one who brought Abraham out of Ur, and in Exodus 20:2 God is the one who brought Israel out of Egypt. When Jeremiah reflects on the theme, he says that the phrase will be replaced with one that speaks of God bringing the people out of the north country (Jer. 16:14–15). Clearly,

3. See J. A. Sanders, "Hermeneutics," in *The Interpreter's Dictionary of the Bible*, ed. Keith R. Crim (Nashville: Abingdon, 1976), suppl. vol., 403–7; George W. Coats, *Canon and Authority*.

4. Von Rad, *Old Testament Theology*, 1:115–21.

5. Walter Kaiser, *Toward an Old Testament Theology*.

the promise given can be grasped in fresh ways as the Lord leads in new situations.

There are abundant examples of the interpretation and reinterpretation of earlier material in the prophets. They were spiritually gifted and conscious of the call to update and apply the Word of God. They had the ability and charisma to discern what God was now saying through what had been given. The false prophet Hananiah knew the text about the promise of God to Israel but did not properly discern how to apply it to the Israel facing exile. Jeremiah had to call his interpretation into question and point out the greater severity of the situation (Jer. 28).

In the same way, Amos knew that God had chosen Israel and Judah as his people and vehicle of salvation, but he was convinced that the promise could not be appealed to without reference to the people's conduct in relation to convenantal stipulations. The promise does not make Israel and Judah immune from the judgment of God—in fact, their privileged position puts greater responsibility on their shoulders (Amos 3:2). In an outburst, Amos tells them that God hates their worship and cares as much for Philistines as for them! In this he was clarifying issues about the original promise as well as recalling it. Isaiah also warned them to look twice at the covenant and what it means and not believe the scoffers of Jerusalem who deny that God's work of judgment could ever apply to them (Isa. 28:14–22). Hosea, too, recalls God's tender love in the wilderness, but he warns of God's freedom to turn fierce like a lion if the people continue to be indifferent to him (Hosea 13:4–8). Jeremiah speaks of a coming day when the old covenant and the ark of the Lord would be replaced by God's throne and a new covenant (Jer. 3:16–17; 31:31). Or consider the different reactions to the exile. To some it was an unmitigated disaster. Some hung up their harps. Some blamed God, or their ancestors, or their enemies. It was a crisis of faith for Israel and presents us with the same pattern of richly varying responses.[6]

Because it was written over such a long period of time, the Old Testament is full of good examples of dynamic interpretation. We only have to look at the various books to see the reshaping of earlier traditions. The history of the chronicler is a theological reworking of the same events that are recorded in Samuel and Kings. Legal and cultic material has been brought together in Exodus and Leviticus from various places and times. Books like Job and Ecclesiastes seem to have been written to introduce correctives into the way in which the covenant might be misread. Psalm 139 uses the metaphor of space to illustrate God's continual presence, whereas Amos turns it to warn of inescapable judgment (Amos 9:2–3). The text shows us how an earlier passage or image can be used again in

6. Ralph W. Klein, *Israel in Exile*.

a variety of valid ways. Out of this treasure the scribe can indeed bring things old and new (Matt. 13:52). This is exactly what God intended.

The biblical text is both stable and dynamic. New insight can be brought into contact with the original text, and the Word of the Lord grasped afresh. It is important for us to notice both the continuity and also the discontinuity and revisions wrought in the tradition that leads to Jesus the Christ. We ourselves are the result of a merging of traditions that determine the character of our homes and ourselves. The biblical revelation that lies before us is also a complex text and is able to become the vehicle of revelation for us and for generations to come.[7] It is not necessary to exaggerate the twists and turns of the developing tradition in order to pick up the richness that the Word of God is giving us.

New Covenant and Old

Even more obvious is the way in which the New Testament appears to be a reinterpretation of Old Testament tradition. A new and unprecedented act of God took place in Jesus Christ in fulfillment of Old Testament hopes. All the earlier material is looked at afresh in the light of this event. Promises are seen to have been made good, and correspondences are noted everywhere. The Old Testament makes it possible to understand the New Testament, but the New Testament also penetrates more deeply into what the Old Testament was aiming at. The transition from Old to New was the single most dramatic illustration of dynamic updating in the canon of Scripture. A whole new perspective now influences the field of vision, and everything appears in sharper detail, now oriented to the meaning of the incarnation. Updating and reinterpretation were going on within the Old Testament, but nothing on quite this scale. A covenant of consummation has been struck that fulfills all the covenants that went before.[8] The text is read not as an inflexible code but as a premessianic trajectory, an occasion for the Spirit to testify to Christ, and it is by no means limited to what the Old Testament may originally have intended as the immediate references of its texts.

One would have to admit here that the church, when it took over the Old Testament from the synagogue, did not adopt the Judaic Scripture principle per se. It sounds as if it did when one reads some conservative and traditional authors. In fact, however, Christians used the text as a flexible, messianic promise. Not everything in it is now relevant to Christians. The Old Testament was received gladly as the written Word

7. See James D. Smart, *Past, Present, and Future of Biblical Theology*, 125–29.
8. O. Palmer Robertson, *Christ of the Covenants*.

of God. Because of Jesus, however, it was not considered binding on his disciples in the way it was binding on the Jewish faithful. There was no question of the early Christians totally abandoning the Old Testament (contra Marcion) or fundamentally violating its historic meaning. Rather, the Christians read it as a subordinate standard in light of the New Testament, not as an independent authority.

This becomes obvious when we consider how the New Testament uses the Old Testament. The latter was considered to have been written for Christians and was applied to them. "For whatever was written in former days was written for our instruction" (Rom. 15:4). It was "written down to instruct us, on whom the ends of the ages have come" (1 Cor. 10:11). The Old Testament became a book full of lessons for Christians and full of intimations of the coming Messiah, who was identified as Jesus of Nazareth. Not unlike the Qumran community that, around the same time, read the text in the light of their contemporary situation, the early Christians saw everything in a new and relevant way.[9] The difference, however, is that the Christian "pesher" of the text was christological as well as eschatological. But in each case, the past text was updated and placed in the contemporary setting, even when some textual adapting and modifying was required.

Jesus himself is presented in Old Testament terms. He is the stone that the builders rejected, the one betrayed by his friends, the shepherd of a scattered flock, the one numbered among the transgressors. His birth gave deeper clarity to the promise given to King Ahaz, and he is compared to Adam, Moses, David, Solomon, and Jonah. The text is alive with references to the Old Testament, both direct quotations and allusions. The Old Testament foreshadowed the life and redemptive ministry of Jesus, and the ever-unfolding delight of this realization is constantly on the minds of the New Testament writers.[10]

The Lord himself repeatedly placed new constructions upon old, familiar texts. In the Sermon on the Mount, he pressed Old Testament ethical insights to even greater consistency and rigor (Matt. 5–7). He boldly stated that the essence of the whole law could be summed up in the love for God and one's neighbor (Matt. 22:34–40). He could drop out part of a text, setting himself up as an authority even higher than the Old Testament (Luke 4:18–19). When it came to the laws about ritual purity, he could undermine the whole distinction between clean and unclean foods by speaking about the sins that really defile (Mark 7:15). He felt able to dismiss Moses's permission of divorce because of the higher principle he saw in the creation ordinance (Matt. 19:3–9).

9. Richard N. Longenecker, *Biblical Exegesis in the Apostolic Period*, 38–45.
10. R. T. France, *Jesus and the Old Testament*, chap. 3.

As for the Sabbath, he displayed such freedom of action on that day as to suggest that even this commandment was due for some adjustment (Mark 2:23–28).

Paul's letters afford ample opportunity for us to see the same phenomenon of the adaptation of the Old Testament to the messianic situation. In 2 Corinthians 3, he develops a parallel between Moses's ministry before Christ and his own apostolic calling as minister of a superior new covenant. In Galatians 4, Paul presents an Old Testament story in an allegorical fashion to bring out its meaning for Christians. In 1 Corinthians 9, he finds a lesson pertaining to the financial support of Christian leaders in an obscure pentateuchal regulation. In Romans 10, he refers almost casually to Deuteronomy 30 to put into words what he wants to say. In Galatians 3:16, he finds great meaning in the grammatical singular "seed" and refers it to Christ as the true seed of Abraham. In Ephesians 4, he cites a variant text of Psalm 68:18 to express what he has in mind. As an apostle of Jesus Christ, Paul felt that he had been given special insight into the mystery of God, and one implication of this consciousness was a certain liberty in adapting the Old Testament to the new era. Nowhere was this more dramatically plain than in Galatians, where he contends that the law does not possess the validity it did before Christ came and that circumcision in particular was not to be required of the Gentiles, who had become sons of Abraham by faith.[11]

Within the New Testament, one finds different ways of adapting Old Testament texts. Paul and James quote the same verse from Genesis 15:6 and relate it to the same doctrine, justification, but in very different ways (Gal. 3; James 2), reminiscent of how Isaiah and Ezekiel look back to the same Abrahamic covenant. Whereas Matthew tends to quote the Old Testament to stress fulfillment of prophecy, John refers to it to bring out more of a contrast between eras in salvation history. While Paul sees the Old Testament as a witness to the righteousness of God apart from law, the book of Hebrews declares the old covenant obsolete now that the new has come.

What we see happening here is the earlier text being reinterpreted in the light of the higher stage of revelation that has dawned. The New Testament is not trying to give us an interpretation of the Old Testament only in terms of what it originally meant. Rather, it is proclaiming the gospel, making use of premessianic Scripture to render the new substance of the gospel. The operation is much more creative than what we today would call exegesis. Although we would object to a person setting up a canon within the canon on his or her own authority, the New Testament is, in fact, such a canon in the Bible as a whole. It reinterprets

11. David L. Baker, *Two Testaments, One Bible*, 284–85.

what was given before in the light of itself because divine revelation is progressive and finds its fulfillment in Christ.[12] As Edward Carnell put it, the economy of preparation is interpreted in the light of the economy of fulfillment.[13]

This means that Christians read the New Testament into the Old. The serpent having its head crushed in Genesis 3:15 means a great deal more to us now than it did originally because of the coming of the Savior to destroy the works of the devil. What was only hinted at earlier has become a full-blown understanding. Light has been cast on the protogospel by the gospel itself. Peter linked what Joel said to what happened on the day of Pentecost (Acts 2); James linked what Amos prophesied to the Gentile mission that was getting under way (Acts 15). God's installation of his king in Zion becomes a witness to the enthronement of Christ at God's right hand. The text of Psalm 2:6 has dramatically opened up and become significant to the whole world. What God is saying to us in the gospel sheds light on what he said to Israel in former days.

The New Testament does not care simply about the meaning intended by the original author. It seeks to understand the Old Testament in the light of the climactic revelation in Jesus Christ. Out of the encounter of text and gospel came the Word of God for the church. It is important to remember this in some of the hermeneutical problems we face. How Christians ought to act politically is closely tied to how the Old Testament relates to the New. How we come down on the issue of a "just war" may be reflected in the weight we give to Old versus New Testament texts. How we think of the Sabbath will depend on how much novelty we think the New Testament introduces into the question of holy days. How tolerant we are toward polygamy will hinge on how we construe the ongoing validity of the Old Testament. The Bible we respect is not flat, and how we measure its contours and changes will affect a number of questions we wrestle with.[14]

The Dynamic within the New Testament

In the case of the New Testament, the time span of these writings is too short to demonstrate much development of theology. Even so, there is enough diversity to show, on a smaller scale, the same kind of hermeneutical dynamic that is visible in the Old Testament. The New

---

12. J. I. Packer, "An Evangelical View of Progressive Revelation," in *Evangelical Roots*, ed. Kenneth S. Kantzer, 143–58.

13. Edward J. Carnell, *Case for Orthodox Theology*, 54.

14. Willard M. Swartley (*Slavery, Sabbath, War, and Women*, 139–42, 231–32) is well aware of this factor.

Testament is a complex composition and collection, manifesting surprise and suspense, variety and balance.[15]

One prominent example of hermeneutical diversity is the presence of four Gospels. In each of these books, a portrait of Jesus is presented in which certain features are made to stand out. They are not repeats of one another but individualized remembrances that, by being placed together in the canon, yield great breadth and depth of perception. We are led to believe that the truth about Jesus transcends any one presentation and that several portraits are required to give an adequate sense of the multifaceted importance and significance of Jesus. Alongside the common purpose of telling the story of Jesus, there is a theological and pastoral purpose to present the truth from the angle required by each situation and readership. The result is four portraits or redactions of the life and significance of Jesus Christ. The four Gospels are not snapshots that give us merely the plain facts or pieces of abstract art that relate only remotely to their subject, but portraits that present the Jesus of history from a particular angle relevant to the community that first received these works. The material is not taken as sacrosanct and fixed but as something to be thought through afresh and applied to ever changing situations.[16]

This is easy to illustrate. Matthew shows an unusual interest in Jesus as one who fulfills Old Testament prophecies, using a number of quotations to call attention to this fact. He is also concerned to show how the Christian faith, once confined to Judaism, became a universal message because of the ministry of Christ. Unlike Mark, Matthew balances the emphasis on eschatology with an emphasis on ecclesiology. He is the only evangelist to use the word "church" and wants to show that Jesus originated and provided for it. Mark, on the other hand, wrote a Gospel of action in the style of a drama quickly moving toward the cross. Much less teaching is included, and some of Matthew's Jewish texture is missing. Mark seems to be writing for Gentiles. He presents Jesus as the divine Son of God with tremendous power over nature and demons, and he stresses the suffering that will be the lot of those who follow him.

Luke is especially interested in the universal scope of the gospel. His Gospel and Acts together show his understanding of the momentum of salvation history as it moves inexorably toward the conversion of all nations. He gives special attention to Jesus's attitude to the disadvantaged, such as women, children, and the poor. He likes to write about Jesus's prayer life, the power of the Spirit, and the joy experienced in salvation. John's

---

15. An authoritative book on dating is J. A. T. Robinson, *Redating the New Testament*.
16. Robert A. Guelich, "The Gospels: Portraits of Jesus and His Ministry."

Gospel is even more distinctive than the Synoptics are from one another. John stresses themes such as light, love, truth, and life. He alone plainly states a Christology in terms of the full deity and personal preexistence of Christ. The very term "incarnation" was coined from his remarks (1:14). There is a great deal of the teaching of Jesus, but it differs in content from the blocks of teaching we find in Matthew. This comparison of the Gospels illustrates that the work of interpretation is already in full stride in the New Testament itself. We are confronted with a text that forces us to go deeper as soon as we appreciate the diversity.[17]

Another prominent example of interpretive dynamic is the variety of theological approaches to presenting the Christian faith in the New Testament. Paul, the author of Hebrews, Peter, and Luke all have their own ways of saying what is important and essential. Each employs his own terminology. There is, in effect, a dialogue between them right in the New Testament. If one is going to expound the New Testament according to major themes, it proves necessary to distinguish what the different writers have to say about them in order not to reduce their witness to a lowest common denominator.[18] A study of the Spirit would require noticing the unique nuances brought out by the various biblical authors.[19] A certain amount of diversity is canonized in the New Testament in this way, suggesting that a variety of perspectives in the church today is not surprising, and may not even be a bad thing.[20]

Much of the diversity is because of the circumstantial nature of New Testament teaching. Richard Longenecker calls attention to the "faith of Abraham" theme that occurs in Paul, James, and Hebrews. It is used differently in each case in light of the varying requirements of audience and situation. Paul appeals to Abraham in Romans and Galatians to bring out the patriarch's trust in God as the key to his being accepted by God. It was not obedience to law but faith that led to his being justified. James, on the other hand, saw the need to emphasize the good works that ought to issue from a right relationship with God. He knew how Paul's emphasis could lead to ethical indifference and an abuse of the grace of God. Therefore, he stresses that faith must be much more than bare assent to truth; it must be a vital decision and relationship that transforms the believer's life. Otherwise, faith is worth nothing and leads to nothing. Paul and James are speaking into different situations, and this can account for their decidedly different presentations.

---

17. In addition to the various New Testament introductions, see Jack Kingsbury, *Jesus Christ in Matthew, Mark, and Luke.*

18. Donald Guthrie (*New Testament Theology*) presents the material thematically but observes the distinctives within each topic.

19. As George T. Montague does in *Holy Spirit: Growth of a Biblical Tradition.*

20. James D. G. Dunn, *Unity and Diversity in the New Testament*, chap. 15.

Hebrews, for its part, brings out the forward-looking character of Abraham's faith. He obeyed God when he was called and ventured out on a pilgrimage where nothing was certain except the goal of the city of God. This is what the reading audience members needed to hear, since they were apparently being tempted to go back into Judaism. They needed to see that the significance of Abraham was his going forward without looking back. This focus would help new Jewish Christians to get their own priorities straight. This is a good illustration of the way in which early Christian teachers, like the rabbis themselves, would take the truth handed down and relate it creatively to different circumstances.[21]

Theoretically, it is possible to see differences and developments within an author's own work. Some have suggested that Paul changed his mind on a number of topics, but it is very hard to be sure since the epistles cannot be dated with certainty and the evidence is fairly fragmentary. All we can confidently say is that Paul's focus might have shifted around the time of the writing of Ephesians, for example, and that the different situations he faced would have led him to change his emphasis, approach, and even language from time to time. We think, however, that it is improbable that Paul changed his mind on any important subject during his apostolic career.[22]

In summation, the Bible is a wonderfully complex library. It is like a theology reader in which various viewpoints are presented. In it we hear an orchestra of sound, not merely a single, solo instrument. The Bible gives us multiple approaches to the important themes it treats, making it rich and inexhaustible. The text unfolds before our eyes and flowers like a rose in the morning sun. It draws us into the hermeneutic of the Word of God that was going on long before the canon was fixed. Now that it is closed, the same process of reflection goes on in the community in the form of exegesis, as Christians continue to weigh the significance of what they read. In this process, there is a subtle dialectic to be observed. On the one hand, we must not despise the original sense of the text, which has validity in that God gave it. We have no right to treat the Bible as something to trigger some ideas in our minds that then become the real authority for us. On the other hand, it would be very wrong to ignore the dynamic potential the text has to call attention to fresh applications in our new situations. It can and should be reinterpreted again and again. There ought to be a continual dialogue between the text and the reader's situation.

21. Richard N. Longenecker, "The 'Faith of Abraham' Theme in Paul, James and Hebrews."

22. See D. A. Carson, in *Scripture and Truth*, ed. D. A. Carson and John D. Woodbridge, 84–85.

We want to avoid diminishing the dynamic of the text. The phenomena of Scripture that we have surveyed are the enemies of a flat reading of the Bible. It is not legitimate to pull texts out of their canonical contexts and harmonize their meanings. Although we share the desire to have texts speak beyond their immediate circumstances, we do not have the right to wrench them out of context and flatten them to make every text say more or less the same thing. Luke has the right to make a point about the Spirit without having to make it in Paul's manner. Just because Paul speaks of the Spirit coming into a person's life at the point of faith, Luke should not be prevented from envisioning an infusion of power later on as well.

While it is certainly legitimate for systematic theologians to seek a coherent picture of the whole of biblical teaching on a given topic, they have to be careful not to treat texts as pieces of a flat puzzle and try to force them together, in case there is something to be learned precisely from their not fitting neatly. Our desire for rational, propositional truth must be placed beneath the necessity to allow the text to say what it wants to and in the manner it prefers. Just because the text has been brought into a canon of Scripture does not mean that its historical orientation can be suppressed or that the truth is equally distributed in all parts of the Bible.

Leveling the text dehistoricizes it and is disobedient to the text as given by God. It is wrong to snatch a text from Scripture and pay no attention to the place where it was found or to other texts that bear on the same matter. Reading the Bible as a flat book leads to unbalanced thinking characteristic of fundamentalism. If we only emphasize the future hope, we may leave out the truth about the possession of eternal life here and now. If we focus on justification only in the forensic sense, we may be deficient in our theology of sanctification and community. Each of the circumstantial perspectives of Scripture has a role to play in deepening our own understanding and yielding the full truth. The very diversity helps us to avoid becoming lopsided and unbalanced. It also teaches us to be tolerant of the views of others, once we recognize that God's Word is many-sided and inexhaustible.

On the other side, we need to avoid exaggerating the diversity and dynamic of the Bible. There is a strong tendency in liberal theology to stress the contradictions of the Bible and relocate the meaning of the text in our current situation. Some of the liberation theologians, for example, tend to see the situation as the authority and the text as a resource quite under our control. The Bible itself does not support the notion that it moves from false to true, from discredited earlier insights to later progressive teachings. Nor does it encourage us to look exclusively at the twists and turns in tradition history and not notice the continuity of teaching that is being interpreted. The picture is that of a canon in which the truth unfolds gradually and dialectically and pulls us into the process of grasping the divine self-communication. In the canonical context of the final biblical text, we find the truth and its ongoing reinterpretation, and we are invited to pay attention to them both.

The biblical text is normative over us, but the significance of the text for us needs to be searched out. The canon lays out the area for us to reflect on, while stimulating us to seek the will of the Lord. It constitutes a normative and foundational witness to guide us in our own reflection. Without predetermining all the results of our study, it does provide an anchor and baseline for the church. Like a road map, it lays out the ground and the different ways available for our moving. There is freedom, but not unlimited freedom. The text makes a great deal possible—indeed, more than we have yet realized. But there are limits, too. It does not make just anything possible. Despite all its variety and dynamic, the text is still sufficiently directed and focused to ensure that we will not stray too far.

Surplus of Meaning

How can we explain the richness of the text as a source of instruction apart from the freedom of the Spirit? What is it about the literary nature of texts, and the Bible in particular, that lends it to this dynamic use? What are the sources of this richness? Several features of literary texts permit this to happen. They are not like compact stones but are open and available to almost endless reflection and interpretation.

First, we point to the effect of placing all these biblical texts in a single canonical collection. Books like Luke, Jonah, Ecclesiastes, and Ruth, as well as countless smaller literary units, were originally penned in situationally oriented and independent ways. But they now have been placed in the company of many other compositions that impinge on their subject matter, and vice versa. Whereas earlier they would be read on their own, now they are read in association with other books whose teaching is bound to be linked to theirs. Without thinking about it, the Bible reader places what Isaiah and Jeremiah say alongside one another, creating a fuller effect than could have existed before.

A book like Jonah is now read in relation to the total setting of the Old Testament and, even more important, in relation to Jesus and what he said about the sign of Jonah and his own resurrection (Matt. 12:38–42). It is now impossible to read Jonah, as one once could, in isolation from the sacred collection; it has been grafted onto the canonical vine. Mark and John, Romans and Hebrews, Galatians and James now come together in this collection, and the result is a fuller picture than before. All the originally separate units are part of a combined text, and the possibilities for fresh insight flowing from them are greatly increased. This placing of diverse texts alongside each other affects them all. It gives them not only audiences the writers could not have imagined but also new settings that transcend the original situations. In effect, the text can now say more than it did before. A new world of meaning was opened up by this decision, and the collection has become able to speak to countless persons.

Paul Ricoeur has written about the world of the text that is created when an author commits his or her thoughts to writing. When thoughts become text, they become a world separate from the writer, less under the writer's control than before. Factors like gesture, intonation, and context fall away, and the text takes on some independence. We cannot always be certain what the author meant, and it becomes too late to ask him or her to clarify. All we can do is operate in the world of the text and face its demands. In a sense, the text stands between author and reader. It is free, in that the writer has loosed it and let it go, and the reader has no real choice but to accept it as it comes and not force an agenda upon it. Inescapably, there is a degree of uncertainty and tacitness involved with a written text. We cannot be absolutely sure what was meant and are never in a position to conclude we have drawn all the meaning out. Certainly, the text sets up certain parameters for us, but it does not make interpretation a cut-and-dried procedure. Various interpretive options always exist, forcing the reader to engage in a dialogue with the text and with God.[23]

Imagine meeting a person who is running down the street shouting, "Hurry! The train leaves at two!" The command and the statement are both clear, but many questions are left unanswered. Why should I hurry? What train am I supposed to be catching? What are you talking about? Interpretation has to overcome ambiguity built into speech and text events. We are not saying that we cannot be sure what the Bible teaches, for many things are quite plain and often repeated in several places; but there is a tacit dimension to texts, and there is a freedom in interpretation that cannot be eliminated and should not be denied. This forces the reader to be prayerful and discerning in seeking out the Word of God in the Bible.

Implied in the biblical texts being situated in a canonical collection is the expectation that they will be read as a whole. Each text has internal relations with every other. The meaning is not found in the Old or New Testament alone but in them both together. We read passages

23. Loretta Dornisch, "Paul Ricoeur and Biblical Interpretation."

alongside others and try to grasp the meaning of the whole, the Word of God in the total text. We do this in response to the biblical writers themselves finding Christ in Exodus and making connections between the different parts. The canonical context was bound to influence how each text was read. What Ezekiel said is no longer limited to what the prophet intended (something we cannot entirely recover, in any case). It can now be viewed in numerous new combinations and assume new proportions of meaning. By being placed in the canon, it has not only a past but also a future.

The decision to incorporate texts in a single collection was itself an act of authorship. It meant that originally independent texts would be read together and take on meaning arising from their association with the other texts. The Bible as a whole constitutes the universe of discourse in which God's Word is now sought. We are compelled to look at the Bible as a whole, with all of its tensions and rich conversation. It is important, for example, that Job should exist in the collection with Deuteronomy and Proverbs, because it sounds a critical note that orthodoxy always needs to hear. It calls into question a shallow reading of God's covenant promises and forces one to go deeper. Job's friends had done a super-ficial reading of the covenant, and Job forces them to reconsider their interpretation. The Bible presents us with a rich conversation of various voices designed to challenge us and make us grow. By choosing four Gospels and not only one, the church committed us to hermeneutical variety. It is not our business to isolate one line of interpretation or one insight among many and make it our private canon within the canon. The task of interpretation is to deal with the whole world of the text. Only this will prove fruitful for our own world and all its needs.

A second source of the fertility of meaning for us to examine is the Bible's richness in symbolic and metaphorical language. There has been a tendency for conservatives to think of Scripture as containing only one kind of language, chiefly offering bits of information and propositional truths. Of course, we know better, but this has not prevented us from a narrow orientation dictated by the polemical atmosphere. In fact, the language of the Bible is rich in exhortations and commands, in figures of speech and typology, in poetry and parables, and in symbolism. We are required to do justice to this variety of expression in our interpreta-tion. When Jesus says "I am the door," and when he claims that God's kingdom is like leaven, he is making assertions that transcend the strictly literal and point us in the direction of profound understanding. There is a splendid versatility to such a mode of expression that sets up a range of possible meanings that can scarcely be exhausted. Although the general point is usually plain enough, other possibilities will always exist. What Jesus meant when he said "The kingdom of God is in your midst [or within you]" will never be reduced to a definitive explanation that will allow us to dispense with the text. All language, but especially metaphor and symbol, contains much tacit and implied meaning, and the greatest challenge of interpretation is to bring it out into the open.

The Bible is full of great symbols that bear testimony to mysterious reality that cannot be completely reduced to propositions. It speaks of the fall, the cross, the resurrection, the kingdom, the light, and so forth. To an extent, we can understand what is meant and, to a degree, the Bible itself explains the meaning to us. But these symbols go beyond such explanations and have the power to transform our lives at many levels. It now is hard for a classical Christian to speak of biblical symbol because of what has been done theologically with symbols by liberals like Paul Tillich. He had a way of deliteralizing the content of the Bible and using the evacuated concepts to establish his own Hegelian philosophy.[24] In this way, symbol has been given a bad name. But we cannot allow the term to be stolen from us, because the Bible is deeply symbolic. It is full of rich pictures: exodus, exile, a descending dove, a slain lamb, a thundering mountain, and a wedding feast. The same is the case for the great themes of the Bible, like kingdom, new birth, creation, heaven, and bread of life.

Symbolism is uniquely able to draw us into itself and to have a transforming effect upon us. It opens up to us realms of awareness not easily made accessible by discursive speech. Its meaning cannot easily be nailed down, and its value is in putting us in touch with truth that cannot be captured easily and in giving rise to thought and reflection. In this way, symbols contribute to revelation in the Bible by working on us in a dynamic way. Like the Lord's Supper, they are able to point in so many directions and touch such depths of the personality that they are simply inexhaustible.

Conservatives are certainly right to insist that the core content of the symbols that the Bible provides be kept as the parameters for their possible use. The truth and content of revelation must not be imperiled. In the name of symbol, one can easily float off into realms of feeling and speculation and lose the truth God is communicating to us. The cross, for example, is a symbol whose meaning cannot be exhausted, but it is also the subject of much plain biblical teaching that informs its symbolic use. This teaching does not close off deeper participation in the symbol, but it does anchor it in the system of truth given in the gospel. The propositions cannot substitute for the symbol, but neither can the symbol float free of the content given in the Scriptures. Avery Dulles is

---

24. Leonard F. Wheat (*Paul Tillich's Dialectical Humanism*) was not too hard on Tillich when he saw his work as subtly disguised humanism.

on target when he says: "Christian doctrine sets necessary limits to the kinds of significance that can be found in the Christian symbols. Without doctrines we could hardly find in the cross of Christ the manifestation of divine grace and redemption."[25] Thus, the symbols not only give rise to thought in us but also provide guidelines that ought to shape that thought. Speaking of symbols in the Bible, then, does not rob the images of their clarity of content. Rather, it opens up to us the holistic realm of truth that transcends the merely propositional.

In the same manner, speaking of the symbol of exodus does not mean to deny the factual nature of the deliverance of Israel from Egypt. If this historical deliverance did not happen, we have no right to use the symbol, at least according to biblical thinking. The wider meaning of exodus, such as the new exodus of the gospel or the release of modern peoples from slavery, rests on the proven fact of God's ability to deliver. These mighty acts of God are both facts and symbols—they made a difference to an actual historical experience, and they continue to have impact on our lives in pointing to ongoing divine deliverance. We should utterly reject the notion that symbolic events cannot have both factual and theological significance. It is clear that Luke, for instance, thought he was writing both history and theology at the same time.[26] As Paul said, had the resurrection not happened, it could not serve us as a symbol for faith to grasp (1 Cor. 15:14, 17).

A third instance of this depth of truth is the fullness of meaning that a text can have as a piece of literature. Like a musical score or a painting, the biblical text is available for fresh interpretation without end. As a text, it occupies a position between writer and reader and has a life of its own. That is not to say that the text is autonomous and can mean anything at all, subject to the whims of the readers. It is still anchored in the original situation and still bears the content intended by the writer. To know what a text means, we have to consult the text, not merely the feelings or thoughts it evokes in us.[27] The meaning resides in the words of the text, not in our imagination. Nevertheless, granting these solid parameters of meaning that the text lays down, it is still true that, like a symphony or a sketch, the text cannot be exhausted and can always be seen in new and challenging ways as the angle of vision alters and the Spirit speaks.

Christians find more in Genesis 12:3 than Jews do because they relate the promise to Jesus Christ and its opening up to the Gentiles according to Paul. A text can be seen to possess more significance later than was

---

25. Avery Dulles, *Models of Revelation*, 143.
26. I. Howard Marshall, *Luke: Historian and Theologian*.
27. E. D. Hirsch, *Validity in Interpretation*, chap. 1.

noticed or even intended at first. As God's purpose becomes clearer, we can better see what God was getting at in the earlier situation. Raymond Brown defines this fuller sense as "that additional, deeper meaning, intended by God but not clearly intended by the human author, which is seen to exist in the words of a biblical text when they are studied in the light of further revelation or development in the understanding of revelation."[28]

In a seed lies the potential of a tree that will develop out of it. At first we cannot see the potential, but after the tree has grown we understand the seed better. In the light of the redemption that is in Christ Jesus, we can see in Genesis 2–3 a foreshadowing of the whole history of salvation. From the seed of the woman has come a Savior to destroy the satanic serpent. But this is much clearer to us now than it was to the author of the passage in Genesis. Indeed, much of the Old Testament is opened to us by its fulfillment in Christ. The text can take on deeper meaning when we become more informed of the purpose of God in the world.[29]

Language possesses a dynamic fullness that permits an excess of meaning to emerge over time. Like works of art, literary texts open up a field of interpretive possibilities and allow for ongoing reflection and discovery. Authors are responsible for the words they record, but they cannot exclude, even if they wanted to, the fullness of which we speak. After it is written, the text is not the writer's to control altogether. There is always much more for the reader to find and enjoy than the author might have thought of.[30] As David Tracy points out, the Bible is the church's religious classic and has unlimited power to bring the Word of God to us.[31]

Strange as it may seem, precritical exegesis was far more likely to grasp the rich fullness of the Bible's message than is the technology of modern scholarship. For centuries, Jewish and Christian communities have pored over these texts and listened to them in all sorts of ways not approved by the academic guild today. As a result, they experienced the truth of the Bible in ways closed to the secular reader. The archaeology of the text that modern scholarship attempts to practice with some success is only the beginning of the work of grasping the sense of the Bible. Until we see it as a literary whole, as willed by one Author, we are not likely to get very far or very deep. Our modern exegesis is so scientific that it is impoverished. It discourages readers from putting themselves in the text and therefore misses at least half the point. If it has gained something in focusing more precisely on the original meaning, and it

---

28. Raymond Brown, *Sensus Plenior of Sacred Scripture*, 92.
29. William S. LaSor, "Prophecy, Inspiration, and Sensus Plenior."
30. Bruce Vawter, *Biblical Inspiration*, 113–19.
31. David Tracy, *Analogical Imagination*, chaps. 3–5.

surely has, it has also lost a good deal in closing off other approaches to the text that are also fruitful.

David Steinmetz has shown that precritical exegesis, although it cared about the original meaning a text had in its own situation, also granted the legitimacy of implied meanings that became visible when different questions were posed.[32] As Origen noted long ago, a biblical story may have both a historical sense and some spiritual meaning. Do we not all recognize in the wilderness wanderings of Israel both of these dimensions? Do we not see in the sacrifices of Leviticus both the offerings themselves and the vision of Calvary? Are there not patterns in the history of the Old Testament that foreshadow the ministry of Jesus and the experience of the church? Can we not see in the indignation of the psalmist about Babylon a way to apply his words to the massive social atrocities of our time? It is not a question of giving free rein to the imagination and breaking the link of the text with history. While the literal sense does control what can be done with the text, it does not close off the real possibility of spiritual and theological meanings that go beyond what the writer originally intended. Thus, the songs of David can be our Christian songs as well.

The point is this: the texts of the Bible have a definite meaning in the historical situation in which they were written, and that meaning is the touchstone and anchor of all the interpretations that may be made of it legitimately. Their total meaning is not restricted to what can be discovered in a scholarly way about the original thrust. Texts can carry implied meanings also, and these may be picked up by later readers in different settings. A text cannot simply mean anything we want it to, but it does open up a field of possible meanings, not just one. The idea that a text has only one meaning is a modern, scientific prejudice that does not correspond either to the Bible's own view of itself or to the Christian experience of using Scripture. For an interpretation to be valid, it must fall within the range of possible meanings that the text itself creates, whether or not they were all the direct intention of the writer. Therefore, the meanings of the text are obviously multiple rather than single.

We ought to hold to a middle way. A text consists of both letter and spirit. Because we respect the text, we grant it the right to lay down the parameters of its own meaning. Because we are open to such other meanings as may be implied in it and intended by God, we listen for the rich and fuller meaning it can open up for us. The text sets forth a field of possible meanings, and we are free to seek the Word of the Lord within this abundant set of options. When on mission in every new time and place, the church "needs to be able to understand its message in

32. David C. Steinmetz, "Superiority of Pre-critical Exegesis."

fresh contexts, not in ways that go *beyond* biblical revelation, but in ways
that penetrate the biblical revelation more profoundly. . . . Although the
faith is delivered once and for all time, the church has not grasped its
significance completely—nor will she until the end of time. We are on
an interpretative road, not yet at the end of the journey. . . ."[33]

Some Conclusions

Quite evidently, there is much room for the Spirit to use the text of
Scripture in dynamic ways in the church and in the Christian life. It is
not a collection of timeless oracles given all at one time, like the Qur'an,
but a developing and dialectical text on which endless reflection can be
made. One thing we may conclude from this is the dynamic character of
the divine pedagogy. Why did God give us his truth in such a manner?
After all, a flat text is easier to grasp, and the Bible is open to misinter-
pretation because of its complex character. What advantages does this
mode of disclosure afford?

The only conclusion we can draw is that God must want to force us
to think as mature people. Socrates presented the truth in dialogue and
probing questions to help his disciples think more profoundly themselves. He wanted to convey not only information but the skills of learning that would be usable throughout their lives as they grew into mature
understanding.[34] The Bible, in the form it comes to us, is the kind of
teacher that draws us into the process of learning and helps us to think
theologically and ethically in new situations. God seems to have made
a decision to instruct us in this way in order to bring us to greater maturity. As Paul said to the Galatians, God did not want them to remain
immature children and slaves ordered around by law. Rather, God's
will was that they operate in Christian freedom and learn to respond
to the Spirit (chaps. 4–5). True, there is a risk in giving us humans such
liberty, and disasters occur, partly because of it. Sin itself came into the
world because human beings were created with finite freedom. But the
same risk in freedom can produce the kind of maturity that God has as
a goal for our lives. Hence, the Bible has the shape it does.[35]

It is not our position that the diversity and the dialectic arose merely
from the experience of the people of God over time. If that were so, then

33. Clark H. Pinnock, in *Reading the Bible in Wesleyan Ways*, ed. Barry L. Callen and
Richard P. Thompson, 170.

34. Mortimer J. Adler (*Paideia Proposal*) picked this up and applied it to public
education.

35. On the place of cognitive freedom, see James Richmond, *Theology and Metaphysics*;
and John Hick, *Faith and Knowledge*.

the Bible would deserve very little respect as our teacher. We see this dynamic process as divinely willed. It is the divine pedagogy, giving us both form and freedom, law and liberty. The Bible is God's tether, keeping us connected to the center and giving us abundant room to explore and roam. God gave his truth to humanity gradually and dynamically in order to lead us to maturity, from the stage of drinking milk to eating meat. The rich diet is suited both to nourishing babes in Christ and to satisfying the more mature appetite.

A second conclusion that should be drawn relates to our interpretation of the Bible. Because it is a complex and developmental text, we have to take this dynamic into account and cannot just interpret the text as if it were flat, as orthodoxy often tends to do. We must pay attention to the kind of text it is and the diversity and dialogue in it. Because of the current belief that the text is inspired by God, it is often supposed that the text must be flat and immutable and that each text stands on the same level as every other and speaks with the same absolute authority of God. However sound this deduction may seem, it is not the view the Bible itself invites us to take. It may be characteristic of the Judaic Scripture principle, but it is not true of the Christian Scripture principle. The Pharisees may have seen Scripture as a set of timeless oracles, but Jesus certainly did not.

What is called for is a dynamic reading of the Bible that takes account of the features we have noted and incorporates them into our interpretation of the Bible. This means that the interpretive task will be more like climbing a large mountain than exploring a vast plain. The mountain has valleys and cliffs, meadows and rocky slides, and can always be climbed from a different side and angle. It always stands there inviting us to climb it and never ceases to challenge. It is not right to read the Bible in a flat, static way; that will only lead to false dogmatism and unsound conclusions.[36] Because of the inner dynamics in the text, we must have regard for the canonical wholeness and balance of the Bible and be in agreement with the inner harmony and movement of the total witness. God's Word is most likely to be heard when we take the historical context seriously and when we heed the inner canonical dialogue with the Spirit's guidance. We are likely to miss it when we pick out isolated texts without regard for their setting and look at them all as of equal significance, to be harmonized into some rational system of our own making.

A third conclusion is that we must rule out a pseudo-scientific approach to the text, whether liberal or conservative. The evidence of dy-

36. See Barry L Callen, *Caught between Truths*, for a full discussion of how avoiding flatness and honoring biblical paradoxes is a wise approach to most basic doctrines of Christian faith.

namic features in the Bible means that the sense of Scripture is richer and broader than what can be proven by means of scholarly techniques. There is a place for Spirit-led interpretation that makes use of the inexhaustible possibilities of the text. Because of symbol, dialectic, and the fullness of language, there is always more to discover in the Bible than has yet been found. The writer may have had a single objective meaning, but the text often leaves open more than one. When it comes to applying the text in its significance for us today, the range is rich indeed. The truth for us may be better seen, as Jesus said, by children than by the wise of this world.

Finally, the textual dynamic ought to humble us hermeneutically. It is not so easy to grasp precisely what the Bible is getting at on every occasion. We cannot so readily dismiss other opinions than our own, as we sometimes do. It is hard to be certain one has got the perspective just right. We will have to listen to the Lutherans, the Catholics, the Methodists, the Pentecostals, and so forth, with more of an open mind than has been customary. We will have to grant that the Bible gives license for a considerable degree of hermeneutical variation. Christians do believe and act differently on the basis of the same book. Every position will still have to be shown to be scriptural in the public arena and not just in front of friends and admirers. But we will have to admit that interpretations are not as clear as we used to think and that an open mind is appropriate when it comes to considering the merits of hermeneutical proposals.

God appears to be teaching us through this that it is more important to be fully convinced in one's own mind and to love one another than to all talk and look alike. The Bible, as our authority, gives us much liberty to think and decide about things. This calls for toleration as we seek to grow into the unity of faith and the stature of Christ.

The Act of Interpretation

At long last we come to the goal of the matter. How can readers engage the text so that God can speak to them through it? An answer needs to be given to the one who asks: "How can I [understand], unless someone guides me?" (Acts 8:31). How can we become "a worker who has no need to be ashamed, rightly explaining the word of truth" (2 Tim. 2:15)? There are few questions more crucial to the life, mission, and theology of the church than these. We need to know God's promises if we are to intelligently trust him. We need to learn God's commandments if we are to rightly obey him. We need to become acquainted with God's nature if we are to acceptably worship and praise him.

It cannot be assumed that just because people revere the Bible, they will know how to use it effectively. It may be the reverence of nostalgia that has no practical effect on them. Somehow we must gain the skills that will open the way for Scripture to influence our lives profoundly. The goal is "to bring about an active and meaningful engagement between the interpreter and the text, in such a way that the interpreter's own horizon is reshaped and enlarged."[1] Almost all of our theological and ethical differences ultimately stem from hermeneutical decisions and will need to be resolved with enhanced reference to the Bible text.

The basic key to the art of biblical interpretation is at hand in what has been presented in the book up to now. There are two sides to hermeneutics. First, we listen to the text as God's Word given to us in human language, and second, we open ourselves to God's Spirit to reveal the

1. Anthony C. Thiselton, *Two Horizons*, xix.

particular significance the text has for the present situation. Interpretation is bipolar and moves back and forth between the historical meaning of the Bible and our standing before God. It involves fidelity to the ancient text and creativity in the current context. The first of the two sides provides the objective content and control, and the second opens us up to God's leading and direction. Thus, the interpreter is not autonomous but subject to the text and avoids frozen legalism by being open to God's Spirit.

Our hermeneutical proposal is that we hear the Word of God in the interaction between the Word and the Spirit, not through Scripture or spiritual meditation alone. This makes interpretation more an art and less a science or technique. It is a skill that has to be acquired by a combination of study and prayer. Interpretation cannot be reduced to a strict set of rules.[2]

Points of Clarification

Five points of clarification are offered here for the guidance of the one who sincerely seeks after the meaning of God's Word. These provide a wise path to biblical interpretation.

First, can it be so simple? After all, books about hermeneutics, like books about epistemology, are among the most difficult to understand. Despite this, we believe that interpretation is quite simple in essence. How else could God's Word make wise the simple? How can ordinary believers search the Scriptures properly and meaningfully if the art of interpretation is not within their grasp? Of course, in particular cases a person may struggle to understand a given text or concept, so that help is required. Because of our culture and traditions, our backgrounds and the information available, aspects of the biblical message may pose serious problems for us and need special attention. Even so, the heart of the matter is not exceedingly complicated. We interpret the Bible effectively when we attend to the text in a spirit of openness to God.

Second, what we are presenting can, for the purposes of exposition, be discussed in the form of a two-step operation. In reality, interpretation is a single act that has two concurrent dimensions: we do the reading, and God gives the understanding; we attend to God's Word, and the Spirit gives us discernment as to its significance. The Spirit is active in both steps.

Third, in writing about interpretation, scholars often refer to the two horizons, namely, text and reader. This is an important observation,

2. A. Berkeley Mickelsen, *Interpreting the Bible*, chap. 19.

but it tends to be secular in orientation, as if there were no difference whether it is the Bible or Plato under discussion. Well, there is a difference. We are speaking about an inspired text and a Spirit-filled reader, not just any text and reader. Because we believe in both inspiration and illumination, we expect the living God to honor his Word and cause it to live in our experience. We have no reason to expect the Bible to come alive and prove intelligible where the reader has not been converted and received the Spirit (1 Cor. 2:14).

Fourth, there is an urgency in our proposal. Great damage can result from neglecting either of the two sides of the interpretive act. Valid interpretation in the Christian sense must come as a result of fidelity to the text and openness to the Spirit. Were we to neglect fidelity to the Word and choose the Spirit over the letter, subjectivity would go wild, and all manner of heresies would follow. Were we to neglect openness to the Spirit and choose the text over the Spirit, legalism would confront us and the truth of God would come under human control. Knowing God's Word would become a mental exercise and nothing more. The text would be locked in the vaults of the past and hindered from breaking loose and addressing our situation.

Fifth, we might ask which error would be the more serious, the liberal rebellion against submitting to the dictates of the text, owing to the liberal's own undeniable modernity, or orthodox legalism, in which the mint and the cumin are tithed and the real meaning of the text is passed over? Both errors are strongly denounced in Holy Scripture. Those who twist the text and transform the gospel into a form that suits their own liking are condemned (2 Tim. 4:3–4; 2 Pet. 3:16). But there are no stronger denunciations than those Jesus hurled against the legalists (Matt. 23:1–36). The wise course is for us to attend to the error we ourselves may be guilty of and correct that, hoping others will do the same. It is not right to point out the speck in another's eye when there is a beam in our own.

The key to hermeneutics is to recognize that God has given us the Bible, God's written Word, and enables it to function by giving the Spirit, who brings a comprehension of its truth and a certainty of its divine origin. As Millard Erickson puts it, "The objective Word, the written Scripture, together with the subjective word, the inner illumination and conviction of the Holy Spirit, constitutes authority for the Christian."[3] It is not the text by itself, as in fundamentalism, or the Spirit alone, as in charismatic excesses, but the fruitful combination of the two. The written Word, correctly interpreted, and the illuminating work of the Spirit are the objective and subjective base in the pattern of Christian

3. Millard J. Erickson, *Christian Theology*, 1:251.

authority. The purpose of revelation is encounter and communication. A divine giving and a human receiving are both involved. Because of human estrangement, however, revelation must include a liberation of our cognitive abilities so that we will perceive God's majesty and grasp his will.

The "Word" stands for the giving of revelation, and the "Spirit" represents the possibility of hearing the Word. The Spirit opens our hearts and minds to receive the things freely given to us by God. Objectivistic and subjectivistic approaches are both wrong. The duality of Word and Spirit must be preserved. There is a bi-unity or perfect complementarity in the working of the two. The Word supplies the message of God, while the Spirit inclines us to attend to its truth, so that the Word can become effective and relevant in us.[4]

New Testament Hermeneutics

Abundant confirmation of this two-sided model for interpretation is provided by the New Testament itself. It cares very much about the text God gave and is able to locate fresh significance in it. Granted, we cannot imitate New Testament exegetical methods in every respect. The writers stood on a revelational plateau and could take liberties with the Old Testament because of their privileged position. Even so, it is important not to miss the conviction that underlies New Testament interpretation. There was a vital sense of the Spirit using the text in dynamic ways to guide and instruct us. These writers believed fervently that the Word of God could speak to people in whatever contexts they found themselves. The Word and the Spirit, the text and the situation, exist in a dialectical relationship. God can speak to us in every new situation.

We see this dialectical relationship in the New Testament's use of both the Old Testament and its own traditions. In regard to the use of the Old Testament, it is obvious that the text gets adapted to the New Testament message and interpreted in a Christian way. Paul can detect in the fading glory of Moses's face an analogy to the relation between the old and the new covenants (2 Cor. 3). The rock that Moses struck in the wilderness is a type of Jesus Christ (1 Cor. 10:4). The seed of Abraham in the ancient promise is none other than Christ (Gal. 3:16). The New Testament does not go to the older biblical text just to learn premessianic foundations but to discuss Christian themes in relation to the text.

God had done something wonderful and new in Jesus Christ, and the Old Testament could now be read in the light of it. A subtle example of

---

4. Hendrikus Berkhof, *Christian Faith*, 56–61.

this adaptation would be the use of different text-types and translations to bring out the very point required by Christian teaching. In Romans 1:17, Paul is not so concerned with what Habakkuk may have meant but is very interested in the meaning the words now could have because of the gospel. The same is true in his use of Psalm 68 in Ephesians 4 and Deuteronomy 30 in Romans 10. And what can we say about Matthew 2:23, which quotes a text that seems not to exist? The Old Testament text often is cited not because of its original meaning but because in one form or another it may express what the New Testament writer wishes to say.[5]

Conservative writers like B. B. Warfield tend to pass by the evidence of adaptation and refuse to see its relevance to the doctrine of Scripture. As a result, they give us a rather legalistic view of authority, not unlike the one Jesus encountered in his Jewish opponents. There is a tendency to generalize on divine inspiration and neglect the other side of the coin, divine illumination. The belief that the Spirit is active alongside the text, helping us to see its significance for us even though it was not originally written to us, is an important part of the New Testament doctrine of Scripture. The text is capable of saying fresh things to Spirit-filled readers.

When Luke repeatedly referred to the text as something the Spirit was saying, he had in mind not only an inspiration of the past but also a continuing breath that enables the text to continue speaking prophetically to the Christian community (Acts 1:16; 4:25; 28:25).[6] The text was not viewed as a frozen document that could theoretically be exhausted, but as a flexible utterance that could meet the needs of every changing circumstance. We see no other way to comprehend the neglect of this factor in conservative theology except in reference to the polemical situation, particularly in the late nineteenth and early twentieth centuries. In fear of a liberal extreme, a reactionary extreme has been permitted to exist. Such fear, while understandable, cannot be grounds for denying part of the evidence of what the Bible claims.

In regard to the New Testament's use of its own traditions, we find the conviction that the truth is dynamic and adaptable to changing circumstances. This is not merely a question of different levels of revelation, as in the relationship of Old to New Testament. The flexibility cannot be entirely because of a dispensational change. The dynamic we noted within the Old Testament can be found within the New Testament as well, and it tells us something important about how revelation works through texts.

5. For more data, see E. Earle Ellis, *Paul's Use of the Old Testament*.
6. George T. Montague, *Holy Spirit*, 291.

To grasp this, consider the way Jesus's deeds and words are used by the different Gospel writers, how they are ordered and reordered, phrased and rephrased, how they are expressed to bring out the needed emphasis in the evangelist's community. A text like the one on divorce, for example, can be made to function differently in Mark than in Matthew. In Matthew, the famous "except" clause is added in order to interpret Jesus's meaning to a Jewish-Christian audience (Matt. 19:9). And the words about clean and unclean foods that come out so strongly in Mark 7:14–23 are toned down considerably by Matthew (Matt. 15:10–20). The Markan parenthesis ("Thus he declared all foods clean" [7:19]) is dropped out entirely. The Gospel writers could not have been legalists about the sayings of Jesus when they made adaptations like these. We are forced to ask whether it is right and proper to appeal to these texts legalistically now, if indeed the Spirit is wanting to help us determine their significance in our situation. We ought to be sensitive to the original contexts of the verses and then ask prayerfully what the Lord might be saying to us now. If we did so, it would be difficult to be hard-nosed on such questions as divorce and remarriage today.

In the same way, Paul was no legalist. His stated policy was to be all things to all people (1 Cor. 9:19–23). The truth of the gospel could be adapted to all manner of persons and was not an inflexible mass. Paul could take the truth and work it into different contexts. It was not opportunism but a proper flexibility of approach and elasticity of attitude that made this strategy possible.[7] The truth is not so inflexible that it cannot be resituated again and again. This is how we ought to view the difference between Paul and James on the doctrine of justification. It is not a matter of one being right and the other wrong, but a case of the truth of justification having to be put one way in one context and another way in another. The different formulations were required precisely to maintain the truth. The same word had to be put differently to have the proper impact on the different audiences. Legalistic concern for the letter can be a way to suppress, not maintain, the burning relevance of the truth.

We are required to be liberal and conservative at the same time—liberal in the sense that we are eager to discern the ever-fresh application the Bible may have in the ever-changing situations of life, but conservative in the sense that we respect the text of Scripture as God's written Word. We must be the sort of liberals who respect the inherent authority of the Bible, and the sort of conservatives who seek the direction of the Spirit and are not legalistic. This would no doubt make quite a difference in the area of behavioral standards. What would it mean to heed

---

7. Richard N. Longenecker, *Paul, Apostle of Liberty*, chap. 10.

Peter's word about jewelry and Paul's word about the veil? Surely the particulars in these directions are culturally relative and invite faithful flexibility in considering what they mean for today. It might even help us with a text like 1 Timothy 2:12, where Paul seems to forbid a teaching role for female believers. Susan Foh has noted that, apart from this single verse, the opposition to female elders and teachers cannot be biblically proven.[8] So, if we weigh the situational factors that may have influenced Paul's negative tone in this passage, view his comment in the light of his own (and Jesus's) practice of working along with women in the Christian ministry, and remember what he said about their standing in Christ and their being gifted by the Spirit along with men, this text really is unable to silence the concern in our day to give full recognition to female ministries. It would seem that we have become hung up on this issue because of a tendency to handle the text legalistically, not dynamically as Scripture itself would encourage. How many other issues might be eased were we to stop resisting biblical, as distinct from merely traditional, hermeneutics?

Submission to the Text

The requirement emphasized by conservative theologians is to submit ourselves to the demands of the text. If theology has an obligation to be both faithful and creative, then this textual submission is the fidelity side of the equation. The basis for our submission to the text is the doctrine of Scripture we have already expounded. God gave the text to us as his written Word, and we care about what God says in and through it. This is the most important piece of preunderstanding with which to approach the text.

We come to the Bible believing it to be God's Word in human language, and we are disposed to submit ourselves to its ministries of teaching, exhorting, and shaping us. If it were only a fallible human document, we would feel free to twist, discard, demythologize, decry, or reject part or all of the biblical text. But our belief in the inspiration of Scripture leads us to submit our prejudices to its authority rather than subject Scripture to our biases. God gave the text in all its objectivity and distance, and we care deeply about what it says. If this is what God said to those ancient people, we want to understand what it was. We want to determine, if we can, what the writers were saying in the Bible; this should be our pri-

---

8. Susan T. Foh, *Women and the Word of God*, 238–40. See especially Sharon Clark Pearson, "Women as Bible Readers and Church Leaders," in *Reading the Bible in Wesleyan Ways*, ed. Barry L. Callen and Richard P. Thompson, 188–215.

mary task. What did the writer intend the readers to understand? What was God's Word to them? This question needs to be answered before we inquire about the text's significance for us. To believe in biblical inspiration means to care about what God said to his people in past historical situations so that we might consider what his Word is for us.

Concern for contemporary significance must not lead to the past meaning being covered up and confused. We must not allow a "fusion of horizons" to distort what the Bible is saying and turn it into an instrument of manipulation.[9] Let the text be heard in the exact shade of its sense and meaning as it was first given and not be overwhelmed by the centuries of later interpretation. Let the text be understood faithfully before it is applied creatively. How else can it stand over the church as its norm and judge? Seek ye first the original meaning, and all these relevant applications will be added unto you!

In saying this, we declare ourselves in opposition to trends in interpretation that subjectivize the operation and make the text subservient to the reader. This would render its meaning indeterminate and nullify its truth claims. There would be no way to decide between competing interpretations, leaving the reader in control again. Scripture would be subject to the reader's whims and desires. We must hold to the primacy of the intended sense of the biblical texts. Writers have been stimulated by the Spirit to communicate with us through literature, making it possible for us to receive communication from them. They have encoded a message in the text, and we read it in order to receive the Word. Similarly, we oppose arbitrary presuppositions that would slot the intended meaning of the text into limited channels such as symbolic or existential significance. Granted, there is much in the Bible that addresses the life of the subject and raises issues of ultimate human concern. But there is also much that relates to the way things are in the world and in the kingdom of God that we ought to heed.

As J. I. Packer has noted, before the nineteenth century there was no significant Christian thinker who questioned the right of the Bible to instruct us in historical and doctrinal matters or who declared a moratorium on the truth content of the text in any significant way. It was taken for granted that Scripture was given to teach us in matters of faith and practice, that the categories and arguments employed to tell us about Christ and salvation were God-given and of abiding validity. But in recent times, a basic shift has occurred in which, instead of seeking the divine message in the Bible, people read it as if it were a merely human religious document, opening up for us the dynamics

---

9. Krister Stendahl (*Paul among Jews and Gentiles*, 78–96) worries that this has been done, for example, to Paul and his doctrine of justification.

of experience but not delivering to us the message and truth of God. In this way, we open ourselves to the personalities of ancient writers but not to the beliefs they set forth. This leaves us in complete control of the content of the gospel and its applications in the world. In fact, the only proper way to read the Bible is to seek to learn its truth and to incorporate it into our lives. We have no right to ignore or twist or deny its contents.[10]

If indeed it is crucial to ferret out the meaning of the biblical text, something should be said about the great challenge this presents. We will need to heed Paul's word to Timothy (2 Tim. 2:15) and invest everything we have by way of scholarly ability to arrive at the knowledge of what is given in the text. In ordinary life, the work of understanding goes on all the time without a great deal of consternation and confusion. When a person addresses us, we usually do not need to think about how we understand him or her or to consult a set of hermeneutical rules. Our understanding is spontaneous and comes from belonging to a shared culture and language. But when it comes to the Bible, an ancient book from another culture, complications set in.

There are blocks to our understanding thrown up by the Bible's strangeness. Even when we feel comfortable in our interpretation, we can be quite mistaken about it. So we are forced to think about how understanding occurs. There are obstacles that have to be overcome. We do not find ourselves in the same historical situation as the biblical writers. We view what is written from our perspective. The languages of the Bible are foreign to us, both in vocabulary and expression. There are differences in worldviews that pose difficulties. Because of such things, hermeneutics, the science of understanding, becomes important.

In a general sense, we have never been in a better position to recover what the Bible means than we are today. Although they pose some difficulties (as noted in chapter 6), the biblical critics also provide tools and techniques that are exceedingly helpful in rooting out the original sense. We have at our disposal an imposing array of interpretative resources designed to overcome the obstacles to understanding. No generation of exegetes has ever possessed as fine a set of tools as we do in terms of textual studies; lexicography; linguistics; and social, cultural, and literary history. Even though we are more aware than before of the problem of historical consciousness, we are also heirs to the means of overcoming such difficulties. They can help us hear the Bible speak on its own terms and exercise its authority over us. Readers with their biases come and go, but the text stands from generation to generation. Serious interpreta-

---

10. On evangelical hermeneutics, see J. I. Packer, "Infallible Scripture and the Role of Hermeneutics," in *Scripture and Truth*, ed. Carson and Woodbridge, 325–56.

tion must let the text speak and call the reader into the service of God. Our goal is that the Bible be able to challenge the ideologies brought to it and bring about true conversion.

I. Howard Marshall calls attention to 1 Corinthians 16:22 as an example: "If any man love not the Lord Jesus Christ, let him be Anathema Maran-atha" (KJV). The text had to be partially translated in the first place for the English reader. The word "anathema" is familiar to us because it is a Greek word used in English to mean "accursed." As for the Aramaic phrase "maran-atha," we have to learn that it means "our Lord is coming" or something close to that. We have to ask if it is a declaration of his coming or a hope expressed for the coming to happen soon. In seeking to understand the meaning of this text, we are involved in some scholarly reflections that can assist us to get inside the text. We are forced by the text into linguistic and historical considerations.[11] What this helps to ensure is that the text will be respected in its historical distance from us and be protected from having our ideas read back into it. This is why our study of the Bible must include a careful investigation of its nature and contexts in the ancient world. Divine revelation is historical in nature, and that means we must take account of all the related factors that bear upon understanding it.

We have to learn to listen from within the text in such a way that it generates the meaning and we do the listening. This will mean attending to the text carefully and becoming aware of the literary forms used and the images employed. And we will need to go behind the text, too, and consider the context that cradled the message. We will be concerned to discover the function of a text in the broader canon, as well as within its own setting, and to become informed about the specific historical setting in which the text was written. It will be important to learn of any religious, cultural, economic, or political factors that might have played a significant role in the creation of the text.[12]

Granted, we do not want to deliver the church to a papacy of biblical scholars. Certainly the ordinary reader is capable of grasping the things necessary for salvation without the help of a professional scholar. At the same time, biblical scholarship is one of the gifts of God to the church to help us grow in grace and in the knowledge of God. The scholars have a useful role to play in helping the layperson to overcome the difficulties of interpretation and to become a better steward of the Word of God. Without them, one cannot know the exact meaning of the text as it comes out in the Hebrew or the Greek. They can assist us in catching the exact shade of meaning intended by the biblical writers. At stake here is

11. I. Howard Marshall, *Biblical Inspiration*, 77–93.
12. Willard M. Swartley, *Slavery, Sabbath, War, and Women*, 224–28.

whether we communicate our own ideas cloaked in biblical phraseology, or really deliver what Scripture actually says.[13]

Interpretive Biases

How can one get back to the original thrust of the biblical text when contemporary beliefs and presuppositions seem to block the way and distort all interpretations? How can the text assume such a determining role over us given our own place in history? How practical is it to maintain that the Bible ought to exercise decisive influence over us when distorting assumptions seem impossible to remove?

One thing is certain: Bible readers, including ourselves, encounter the text burdened by all manner of presuppositions. We come to the Bible with an orientation of the early twenty-first century, with current convictions about politics, philosophy, theology, and history. What we hear from the text and what we decide to do about its message are heavily influenced by the baggage we carry. We cannot claim that our interpretation will be purely objective and without presuppositions.

The reader as a neutral observer of biblical data is a myth. There is no such person. Modern consciousness is deeply convinced that we understand everything in relation to what we already know and believe. It is obvious, at least in the case of other people, that interpretation is strongly affected by the historical context. How else could so many German Christians have consented to what Hitler did to the Jews? There is always the temptation to use Scripture for our own purposes rather than to let it be a norm for our beliefs and behavior. If we are honest, we have to admit that this is also the case with our own interpretation. Our historical horizon colors what we see in the Bible. We do not live in a vacuum.

Should we then give up trying to be fair? Shall we stop trying to recover the Bible's original meaning? Of course not. What we need is critical realism. We have to take account of the bias factor when we go about hermeneutics. This does not make us skeptics, thinking that we are trapped in the present and unable to know what the text is saying. It simply requires that we be very careful and self-critical in our interpretation. Getting at the original meaning is harder than we used to think, and it calls for greater effort. We have to work at transcending our historical situation and struggle to hear the Word of God in the text. No one is saying that it is useless to try to understand what Paul was teaching, for example, only that it is harder than we used to suppose and requires a lot

13. See Walter C. Kaiser, *Toward an Exegetical Theology*.

more effort. The goal is to know what the Bible is saying and to subject ourselves to it. If we were satisfied with the contemporary context, we would not need to consult the Bible in the first place. The key to success in this endeavor is to see the work of interpretation as a spiral motion. We do not reach the goal of the original sense in a single move but through repeated approaches and by spiraling in on the target.

The whole point of the doctrine of inspiration is that the text of the Bible rule over rather than be ruled by the assumptions of the reader. It is our rule and norm, not the reverse. The text was given precisely to prevent us from following the devices and desires of our own minds and to put us in touch with the mind of God in matters of faith and practice. Therefore, we must handle this problem of assumption and bias with care and respect. We must not allow it to be a screen for Scripture twisting and denial.

It should be noted at the outset that not all assumptions are negative and prevent good exegesis. Some of them can help us identify with what the text is saying and sensitize us to it. As Paul Tillich pointed out, the situation contributes to theology by setting a useful correlation between the Word of God and the hearers of the Word. The church's encounter with revelation takes place in a particular historical situation, and God's Word becomes effective in new ways. Of course, the biblical message sets the norm, but the historical situation is the medium in which it is interpreted and seen to be relevant. True, the message judges the fallen, distorted character of that medium, but only in this medium does the norm become effective.[14] Thus, for example, the awful fact of the Holocaust caused Christians to examine afresh the place of Israel in the economy of God according to the New Testament. Modern science has forced us to consider much more carefully what we believe about the beginning of creation. Social developments in the West are requiring a closer consideration of what the Bible says about gender roles. John Calvin's belief that social structures could be changed helped him see in a new way Christ as the transformer of culture. The Pentecostals have helped us see what Luke was getting at, whereas the Catholics help us understand passages oriented to the church as institution. The more international the church becomes in the coming years, the more we will have to read the Bible with new questions in mind, and the more we will discover there to instruct us. Modern assumptions send us back to the text with all sorts of questions and put us in a position to grow in our understanding.

A problem arises when these assumptions find themselves opposed by Scripture, when there is a collision between the authority of the text and

14. Paul Tillich, *Systematic Theology*, vol. 1, introduction.

the authority of contemporary opinion. When that happens, according to the doctrine of Scripture being developed here, Scripture must rule. The really serious problems we face today are from the negative assumptions deliberately held, self-consciously in opposition to Scripture. Since the rise of religious liberalism, it has been common to find people holding certain presuppositions that they will not permit Scripture to correct and with which, in fact, they even critique the Bible. They maintain that certain modern beliefs of theirs are so authoritative that they warrant criticizing biblical teachings. In this case we face a spirit of rebellion, a deliberate twisting of Scripture, a malignancy in theology that really constitutes a crisis.

This is undoubtedly an area in which it is necessary to walk very cautiously. Jesus said that we were not to judge other people. He seems to have been warning against the harsh and negative kinds of judgments we humans so often engage in (Matt. 7:1–6). It requires us to be careful not to confuse an honest difference of opinion in interpretation with a deliberate decision to deny Scripture. Nevertheless, rebellion is what we often face today. It not only constitutes a threat to the church, which lives out of the truth of the Bible, but hastens that loss of clarity and impact that is currently undermining Christian civilization and world evangelization.

With the rise of religious liberalism, theology passed over a critical threshold. Before that time, Christians had taken for granted that one should consider what the Bible taught and then try to put it into effect. But now, for many people, the modern experience constitutes a second source of authority that entitles them to critique the biblical source where it seems irrelevant. Our modern standpoint has become "an intrinsic and determinative element for understanding God's revelation," as Edward Schillebeeckx puts it.[15] Unless we find the Bible helpful and supportive in relation to what we already believe to be true, it will not be taken very seriously. We face today a critical theology that does not submit itself to the Scripture principle. This means, in practice, that the text is brought under the judgment of modern people and edited according to their will.[16]

William Hordern has classified theologians as transformers and translators. The translators keep the content of the Bible but try to explain it in the most intelligible way they can. Transformers, on the other hand, make major changes in the content of Scripture in order to bring it into line with modern beliefs. Transformers deny the Scripture principle by

15. Edward Schillebeeckx, *Interim Report on the Books Jesus and Christ*, 3.
16. Helmut Thielicke (*Evangelical Faith*, vol. 1) seems to be getting at this crisis in contemporary theology when he speaks of Cartesian and non-Cartesian approaches.

holding that people in the modern world cannot believe what the Bible teaches unless it is deliteralized or demythologized. The only option we really have, they insist, is to modernize Christian belief.[17] By construing Scripture as the precipitate of faith experience, Friedrich Schleiermacher was trying to make it unnecessary to critique or suppress the biases of modernity. By putting the emphasis on the existential value of the New Testament, Rudolf Bultmann could boldly announce that modern Christians do not have to believe those doctrinal and factual claims in the text that offend their up-to-date opinions. By stressing symbol, Paul Tillich could ease away from the literal content of the Bible and promote his own ontology under the guise of biblical terms.

The liberal transformers, old and new, are in rebellion against the content of the Bible and are determined to adapt it to the itching ears of the present. A clear case of this was the "death-of-God," or secular theology of the 1960s, but we should not suppose that it was a fanatical and atypical phenomenon. As we know, people like John Robinson and Thomas Altizer proposed that belief in God be dropped, at least in the traditional and biblical sense, simply because modern people find it difficult to believe. Humanity was said to have come of age, and it is necessary for theology to tailor the message to modern requirements. Modern thought is taken to be the standard of truth, and nothing that is not reasonable under its standards should be retained in Christian theology.

According to this mentality, it is obvious that belief in a miracle of the magnitude of the incarnation, for example, cannot stand in a truly modern theology. Therefore, something has to be done. There are three options currently being tested. First, there is the frank denial preferred by the modernists, which is the easiest to deal with from a conservative point of view. The modernists simply declare that they cannot live with the traditional biblical belief and draw up a new Christology they can accept. It is not crucial that it be biblically defended, although, if this can be done to some extent, so much the better. Second, there is biblical reconstruction. No doubt the New Testament as it stands witnesses to a Christ both truly human and mysteriously divine. But what if we could show the historical Jesus and the original kerygma to be not as clear-cut and definite? What if we could uncover a Jesus who called for existential decision and little else? Could he not be the real canon within the New Testament, enabling us to avoid the orthodox conclusions that otherwise seem justified?

Third, there is hermeneutical ventriloquism, which is difficult but has great promise for appealing to Christians who have an instinct for want-

17. See Erickson, *Christian Theology*, 1:112–25.

ing to believe the Bible rather than the critic. Maybe we could show by fresh exegesis that belief in the incarnation is limited to a small sector of the New Testament, or not even present at all. Granted, this is not easy to do, but J. A. T. Robinson, at least, tried to do it.[18] In this way one could simultaneously deny the incarnation in the traditional sense and seem to defend the real meaning of the Bible. This is, of course, historically the preferred way for theological aberrations. A heresy will have the most effect on the church if it is presented in the guise of an overlooked scriptural truth—even if it is only the false teacher's personal opinion. In all such cases, the church ought to practice a sympathetic investigation of the debated point before concluding, as it might be forced to do, that theological deception is being practiced.

The problem of opposition to Scripture is widespread and has begun to affect how people approach the Bible. It has become commonplace to hear human opinion and sentiment boldly exalted over God's Word. Let us list a number of familiar examples. How can we call God "father" in an age of women's rights? How can we believe Jesus is the absolute Savior in a pluralistic world? How can we consider the Jews in need of Christ after Auschwitz? How can we consent to the notion of divine judgment when we reject retribution? How can one say gay lifestyles are wrong when some psychologists now tell us they are normal? How can we believe, in an age of secular economics, that countries may be rich or poor according to their response to the law of God? The fall of Adam is out of the question as far as history is concerned. Atonement through a vicarious sacrifice is meaningless, or worse. God may exist, but only in terms of a process metaphysic. The New Testament is true, but only in an existential way. The Bible is socially relevant so long as it is interpreted along socialist lines. Women can affirm Scripture in the feminist parts but reject the texts that suggest patriarchalism. The list could go on. Everywhere, the Bible is being questioned; we need a Martin Luther to rise up again and make his stand for the Scripture principle.

No one is free from the temptation to substitute what he or she believes for what Scripture says. At point after point, even conservatives pass over what they do not want to hear. We may not want those troublesome charismatic gifts. We may not want to face the Bible's call for involvement in issues of peace and justice. But at least we acknowledge the written Word of God as binding on us and might just come to repentance. The challenge today is to know what to do about self-conscious rebellion against Scripture as people deliberately allow nonbiblical assumptions to corrupt the Word of God. In response, we must insist on the binding authority of the Bible and on its right to set limits on the epistemological

18. J. A. T. Robinson, *Truth Is Two-Eyed*, chap. 5.

and ethical "rights" of modern human beings. The Bible, not modernity, is normative, and our thoughts are to be shaped by its teaching, not the reverse. Only by acknowledging this can we prevent revelation from being buried under the debris of human culture and opinion and from disappearing as a liberating Word from outside the human situation. A stance of determined faithfulness to Scripture is what our day calls for.

Openness to God

Having looked at the need to be humble and obedient in the presence of an authoritative text, let us go on to consider the second requirement, the importance of being open to the Spirit in hearing the Bible as a Word to us today. This is a valid concern that religious liberals are much involved with and that conservatives need to pay closer attention to. It points to the fact that theology can be creative as well as faithful.

Underlying our hermeneutics is a belief in the reality of the Spirit of God, who helps us to recognize God's Word for what it is, aids us in grasping the point, and assists us in applying it to our circumstances so that the Bible speaks as a living Word within our horizon. It ought to be part of our daily experience to feed on God's Word in God's presence and have God speak to us personally. Such is the sacramental nature and potential of Scripture in the Christian life. We pray with Samuel, "Speak, Lord, for thy servant heareth." Donald Bloesch has written:

> Evangelical theology holds that what Christ says today does not contradict what his witnesses say in Scripture, but may go beyond it as the Spirit of Christ clarifies and makes explicit what may be only implicit in the text. Against an orthodoxy that is content to live in the past and does not seek a fresh word from God in Scripture, evangelical theology shares the confidence of the Puritan divine John Robinson that "The Lord has more light and truth yet to break forth out of his holy Word."[19]

Centuries ago Martin Luther found truth in Romans and Galatians with which to reform the church's theology of salvation by grace through faith. But he did not just read Paul in a detached and objective way. He adapted the text to conditions in the sixteenth-century church and drove the point home. One would read Luther not in order to find the best commentary on what Paul originally meant but to see how God's Word can, by the power of God, come to life in the encounter of text and situation. If we approve of this Reformation, surely we must approve also of reading the Bible with a view to discerning its true significance for

19. Donald Bloesch, *Future of Evangelical Christianity*, 17.

our day. The Spirit gives the text a dynamic pointedness so that the text can be resituated and become fresh revelation for us. Beginning with the inscripturated Word out of the past, the Spirit leads us to the Word for us in the present. Making use of the sources of flexibility noted in chapter 8, the Spirit goes on to apply the Word to our needs, so that it becomes sharp and powerful within our situation.

On this point we may note a discrepancy between evangelical theory and practice. In practice, we know very well that God's Word is heard in an interaction between the text and our walk with God. We listen to God speaking to us from the pages of the Bible. We place ourselves in front of the text and try to be open to God's creative Word, which can free us to live the new life in Christ. We put ourselves in the biblical contexts and gaze upon our image as in a mirror. We strive to respond to what the text is calling us to do. We meditate on the Word and expect God to address us in our situation. Bible study is not only a scholarly science but also a spiritual discipline of prayerful expectancy. We refuse to trust the interpreters who do not pray. God leads us through verses not originally addressed to us at all. Do we not constantly take the promises and warnings of the Bible as directed to ourselves? Is not God saying these very things to us today? These are not simple, pious thoughts that the educated Christian should get away from; they are the highest wisdom and the key to the Bible as a living authority.

Our theory, however, is often quite different. It sounds as though there were no Holy Spirit, as if one need only recover the original biblical meaning and nothing more, as though the interpretive operation were best performed by a trained technician. We fear that this imbalance between practice and theory is due to the polemical atmosphere. Faced with the kind of blatant Bible denial just reviewed, classical Christians are frightened of anything that might seem to deviate from an essentially legalistic authority. Seeing some people stray from the text causes others to stick to it very closely and even to minimize the work of the Spirit for fear that it would introduce unpredictability into hermeneutics. But this is overreaction. At first, Protestants tended to deny church tradition for fear that Roman Catholics would use it to obscure the message of the Bible; now we are minimizing the Spirit for fear that, in the name of the Spirit, people will wander far from the text. In neither case are these fears wholly unjustified. Even so, fears must not be allowed to shape our theology. They must not lure us into an orientation toward Scripture that sees it only academically as a frozen text. Upholding the authority of the Bible is going too far if it minimizes the spiritual dimension of interpretation or largely disregards the relevance of the history of interpretation.

Far from being something we should fear, the dynamic character of the Scriptures through the Spirit is the glory of our doctrine of the Scripture principle. We can count on the activity of the Spirit to help us bring the text into the twenty-first century. The Bible is up-to-date, not so much because of our wise efforts at theological translation, but because the Spirit takes these time-transcending themes and makes them live. What seems impossible from an intellectual standpoint is made gloriously and effectively possible by the Spirit of God. Evangelicals should retain great confidence in the Spirit's ability to bridge the gap of the centuries.

Validity in Interpretation

There is an obvious danger in all of this. What constitutes a valid interpretation if we loosen the link between text and meaning by emphasis on the fresh work of the Spirit? How is the Scripture our authority if its meaning for us is different from what the text actually says? What is to prevent this kind of two-sided hermeneutics from becoming a cloak for Scripture twisting and subversion? Have we not landed ourselves in the liberal camp by a circuitous route? Is it not fatal to give up total continuity between what the text says and what it means for us? Is not the door wide open to private revelations in interpretative guise?

In response to these questions, we admit that looking to the Spirit does introduce a certain elusiveness and mystery into the hermeneutical operation. It is not such a cut-and-dried activity as it is in legalistic usage. God can indeed surprise us when we listen for his Word in the Bible. There is no set of tests that can absolutely determine validity in interpretation. Openness to the Spirit makes inflexible legalism impossible for us, even though it is as attractive to us today as it was to the Judaizers in New Testament times. Attractive or not, we have no right to quench God's Spirit, whose ministry alongside the Word is crucial. We have to be more open when we evaluate claims about the meaning of the Bible coming from readers different from ourselves. It will not be as easy as it once was to distinguish a faithful from an unfaithful rendering. If spiritual involvement with the text is important, we will have to be less quick on the draw when it comes to shooting down what may be false doctrines. Even so, we are not left with chaos.

There are some highly effective safeguards and controls that fend off radical subjectivity. The most important of these is the text itself. Any claim to interpretation has to appear credible in light of the text and must be a legitimate and possible use of it. One can claim that process theism or Calvinist soteriology or revolutionary politics are what the Bible signifies for us today, but one must be able to go on and substantiate such hypotheses. Does the text, fairly interpreted, support any or all of these proposals? The Bible is not a defenseless, waxen nose that can be twisted at will. It has a backbone. Over time, it has a way of resisting false claims made about its meaning. The text sets up parameters that discipline honest interpreters. We must not exaggerate the novelty that is possible when one opens oneself to the Spirit. There are definite limits to the range of fresh interpretation. A large part of what is involved is simply the Spirit causing the content of the text to live for us and become experientially vital. The Spirit can help us to apply the text creatively to our lives and circumstances. After all, the text leaves open what directions should be followed within our contemporary horizon in order to apply the Word faithfully.

There is also the safeguard of past hermeneutical wisdom—what we call tradition. We are not the first Christians to read the Bible. The Spirit has already been active in people's lives for centuries. Seeking the insight that was achieved in tradition is an act of respect for all our fathers and mothers in the faith. We should not so emphasize the authority of the Bible that we fail to see the positive significance of tradition. Indeed, Scripture itself came out of the life of the early faith community and has been proclaimed and preserved by it ever since. Slogans aside, the Bible is not "sola" among the factors that influence us. No one can leap over twenty centuries and grasp the text uninfluenced by the understanding of previous generations. Radical biblicism is a delusion and often a cloak for absolutizing the theology of a sentimentalized and relatively recent past.

Tradition is the embodied and distilled wisdom of the ages. In particular, it guards against Scripture twisting. It is a common joke that any pious fraud can cite Scripture to support his or her case, however weird it may be. Tradition is a defense in the church against rank individualism in interpretation. It is needed in order to protect God's people from private misinterpretations of the Bible. The church would be foolish to turn its back on tradition. As John Macquarrie puts it, "To deny fundamental doctrines, like that of the Trinity; to reject the creeds; to set aside the beliefs of the early councils of the still undivided church—these may be actions to which individuals are impelled by their own thinking on these matters, but they cannot take place in Christian theology, for they amount to a rejection of the history and therefore of the continuing identity of the community within which Christian theologizing takes place."[20] Tradition plays a stabilizing role in hermeneutics. It places a fence around the Torah, as it were, to protect the text from heretical pillaging. It makes us raise our eyebrows when we encounter a novel proposal and requires such a proposal to be very well supported. There is little chance that a theory that John does not teach incarnation or that Paul really supports

20. John Macquarrie, *Principles of Christian Theology*, 12.

gay lifestyles will ever be widely accepted. Tradition cannot and should not prevent new insight from edifying the church, but it can and should have a cautioning voice in evaluating its reliability.

The authority of tradition is one of counsel, not of command. It is fallible, not infallible. There can be uncritical and excessive regard for what it teaches. It can become merely dead tradition that impedes the legitimate development of interpretive insight. We may well need to ask if the ban on female ministry or the bias in favor of infant baptism or even the pattern of Sunday observance—all of which are strong in the tradition but unclear in the Bible—are truly in keeping with Scripture. But that does not change the fact that tradition in general represents a life-giving complement to Scripture and cannot be set aside without harming the identity of the faith community.

Another safeguard is the living community of believers who collectively hear the Word and assess the interpretation. Richard Thompson explains well a wise reading of Scripture by means of the "community of conversation."[21] This collaborative approach was illustrated at Corinth. Paul says that when prophets speak, "Let the others weigh what is said" (1 Cor. 14:29). Even as authoritative an utterance as an inspired prophecy should not go unchecked by the spiritual instinct resident in the community as a whole. Similarly, the Bible is the book of the church, not of individuals only. Therefore, the community has the right and responsibility to evaluate the interpretation it hears. God has given gifts to the body that should be adequate to assess the quality of interpretation. Proposals have to be tested, not only or primarily in front of academic colleagues, but also before other believers. In our denominational pluralism, this means sharing the insights of one community with others in order to test for cross-community validation. Needless to say, this presupposes a congregation that is alive in the Spirit, well informed, and ecumenically active. It may be necessary to seek out a live, joyful, prayerful church to experience this.

Hermeneutics as Translation

Earlier, we questioned the practice of theological transformers, who force the Bible to fit modern beliefs, and we commended the work of translators, who genuinely try to convey the message of the Bible in a fresh and intelligible way to the modern audience. If it is necessary to render the Greek of the New Testament into modern tongues, surely it

21. Richard P. Thompson, in *Reading the Bible in Wesleyan Ways*, ed. Callen and Thompson, chap. 9.

is right also to render the ancient categories of thought into new forms that would bring out the same meaning for the twenty-first century. Theological translation is what we ought to be doing to help people grasp the message of the Bible. As theologian Gabriel Fackre says, "The crucial task of translation is to find ways in each generation and location to bring the basic convictions of the Christian faith into the thought world of its hearers."[22] Other terms will be brought into service to convey the meaning of the Christian story. In Fackre's case, the image of liberation is judged one that can make the biblical message live for people today.

On the surface, this suggestion sounds fine. It takes the content of the Bible seriously and tries to express it faithfully in modern times. No classical Christian could object to translation, if that is what really happens. However, we would be naive if we did not notice that something very different usually goes on. Transformation of the biblical message is often done in the name of translation. Both Paul Tillich and Rudolf Bultmann thought of their work as translation. They claimed to be taking the biblical categories and expressing them in modern terms, while in fact they were doing much more. They were substituting for biblical content twentieth-century philosophical ideas. As David Kelsey observes, what these theologians offer as translation bears very little resemblance to what the New Testament had in mind. They are simply stretching the term to make it coincide with transformation. They may have reasons for the substitution, but they have no right to pretend that they are only translating.[23] Translation implies true conceptual continuity between what the Bible teaches and what our theology says. It can be used only by those who believe that the task of theology is to explicate the content of the Bible by translating it into contemporary idiom, not by those who have a much larger intention.

Translation of the content of the Bible into contemporary idiom is what we ought to be doing. In this operation exegesis is properly basic. Normativity is located in the expressed mind of the biblical writers as far as we can determine it through careful study. Explanation of the text precedes and underlies any translation of its meaning. Application of the text to the contemporary setting builds on the exegeted content and does not supply its own. In application we ask the question, If God said thus and so in those circumstances, what can we suppose that God is saying to us now? We take the Scriptures to be providing us with trajectories of perennial significance and paradigms always relevant to discerning how God deals with us humans. In the Bible, our human minds come into contact with the revealed mind of God shedding light upon our path. Scripture gives us divine instruction, and our duty is to apply it faithfully and creatively.

22. Gabriel Fackre, *Christian Story*, 17.
23. David H. Kelsey, *Uses of Scripture in Recent Theology*, 185–92.

The key words are "dynamic equivalence." We certainly are free to go beyond merely explaining the content of the Bible to trying to render it meaningfully in images native to our culture. But the result must be truly equivalent and not a crude substitution. Experience in cross-cultural communication is what interpreters need because their work involves taking a text that was intelligible in one ancient culture and situating it in another, remaining sensitive to the perceptual factors that help or hinder good understanding. We start with the original communication and determine what was being said; then we attempt to encode that message in the modern hearer's frame of reference such that both the communication and the response are dynamically equivalent to those of the original situation. Because translation will always be culture-specific, we must be open to unfamiliar ways of doing the translation in contexts other than our own.[24]

Translating the Bible involves both distancing and fusion. On the one hand, we have to distance ourselves and allow the text to say what it means to. On the other hand, we want to bring the text into our own situation and have it address us. First, we want to understand what Paul meant, and then we want to be grasped by it and made new. Allowing distance ensures that the text is truly heard in its own right, and seeking fusion helps us to become engaged with the text. In reading a parable like the Good Samaritan, we need to listen to the original story in terms of what was really going on between these individuals in the ancient context, and then consider how the same kind of impact could be achieved within the modern world. There needs to be faithfulness to the Word as first given and creativity in placing it in the contemporary context.

What did "shepherd" mean to the Hebrews? What associations surrounded the figure of Satan for them? How can we render the truth of an atoning sacrifice? What would the Jews have taken a resurrection to mean? How does the nearness of the return of the Lord function in biblical language? First of all, we want to understand the teaching of the Bible itself as accurately as possible so that we will not be guilty of reading our own prejudices into it, and then we want to consider how to express that in modern terms. What did Paul mean by his instruction to slaves, and what does this mean now in our Western world where there are no longer slaves?

The goal is that our translation be both dynamic and equivalent. Heretical proposals are usually dynamic but not equivalent, and ineffective exegesis is often equivalent but unrelated to life today. We are called to be both faithful and creative. Our creative imagination should be placed in the service of the Word of God. We have no right to invent new doctrine, but we do have the responsibility of rendering the meaning of the text

24. Charles Kraft, *Christianity in Culture*, chaps. 13–15.

in a currently understandable way. Amos listened to the story of bondage in Egypt and noticed that some people in his day were treating the poor much as the pharaoh had treated the Israelite slaves long ago. The meaning of the text was not entirely welcome, but it was right on target. Similarly, when we read Jesus's harsh words about certain Pharisees, we should consider where this kind of perversion of religion is occurring today and not simply take it as the indictment of a past group.

There are both past and future meanings of biblical texts. While making careful and appreciative use of literary and historical scholarship, we nonetheless "are not prisoners of a textual past but are privileged for the opportunity and accountable for listening for the Word of the Lord and watching for the fulfillment of God's promises that are still outstanding. . . . We want to avoid being like the scribes of Jesus' day who studied the text carefully, but were blind to ways in which its message was being worked out in their own generation."[25]

Conclusion

Good interpretation is a skill, like swimming or horseback riding. It cannot be achieved merely by applying a set of rules. It requires both scholarly diligence and a readiness to hear and obey the Lord. Paul gave Timothy good advice when he said, "Think over what I say, for the Lord will give you understanding in all things" (2 Tim. 2:7). He was to ponder carefully what Paul actually said and think it over himself in openness to God. We are not alone in this effort. We can benefit from generations of interpreters before us as well as from the body of Christ now living. The interpreter is not a solo virtuoso but the member of an interpreting team and fellowship that collectively seeks to know the mind of God for the whole of life.

Our two-sided proposal indicates how we ought to proceed. It will help us avoid the disobedience of religious liberalism with regard to the givenness of the text and the inflexible legalism of some conservatives that overreacts to the liberals' misuse of Christian freedom. It may be able to help us get back on track and heal some of our divisions and misunderstandings. It describes the playing field on which the game of hermeneutics ought to be played. The game itself is what matters now. And as we get into specific cases in our study of the Bible, there is no way to predict what joyful discoveries, as well as painful struggles, we will experience. This is the way of our whole life with God. It is a journey with the Spirit.

25. Clark H. Pinnock, in *Reading the Bible in Wesleyan Ways*, ed. Callen and Thompson, 159.

The Central Conclusions

We have argued that the Scripture principle belongs to the essence of Christianity and constitutes a crucial component in its pattern of authority and revelation. Our aim has been to present a systematic treatment of the concept in the context of a crisis of the Scripture principle and a struggle to maintain it in light of some difficult questions. God gave the Bible to the church to bear an authoritative witness to Jesus Christ and the gospel. It is something to be treasured and defended. Salvation, of course, rests on sincere faith in God the Redeemer, while the well-being of the church and its mission to the world depends on keeping this conviction clear, strong, and relevant by the wisdom of the Spirit. One thing evangelicals are called to do in contemporary theology and church life is to add their voice to the weight of tradition on behalf of the Scripture principle and to offer a sturdy defense and an intelligent exposition of it. This we have sought to do here.

Ludwig Wittgenstein has emphasized the importance of having a good model when one tries to make sense of reality. Confusion results from having a false or inadequate paradigm. Our approach has been to supply a general orientation to the Scripture principle that would open up our understanding in fruitful ways and lead us away from traps and pitfalls. It is important to call attention to the three most crucial dimensions of the subject. (1) If we do not embrace the divine inspiration of Scripture, we risk losing our apostolic norm and truth standard. (2) If we neglect the human character of the Bible, we will not be able to grasp what it is saying and will give it misplaced respect. (3) If we forget about the Spirit, we risk falling into legalism and losing the freshness and relevance

247

of scriptural piety. It would be a wise policy to orient ourselves to these three guiding lights. We can say with Paul, in line with the three crucial dimensions, that (1) we have a divine treasure, (2) in human vessels, (3) empowered by God (2 Cor. 4:7).

In the course of working this out, we have interacted with other Christian thinkers. Some we found it necessary to oppose, quite strongly at times, because of the denial of biblical authority that we see in religious liberalism. A great deal is at stake here, and strong emotions are to be expected. For this reason, it has not been easy to be fair and charitable and to place the best interpretation on the work of some. We recall with regret how difficult it was for Luther and Rome to understand each other and how their discussion deteriorated into bitter polemics and schism. We see how important it is to heed the words of Ignatius of Loyola:

> In order that the one who gives these exercises and he who makes them may be of more assistance and profit to each other, they should begin with the presupposition that every good Christian ought to be more willing to give a good interpretation to the statement of another than to condemn it as false. If he cannot give a good interpretation to this statement, he should ask the other how he understands it, and if he is in error, he should correct him with charity. If this is not sufficient, he should seek every suitable means of correcting his understanding so that he may be saved from error.[1]

It gives us no pleasure to say that we think some are wandering from the truth of the Scripture principle. Yet, a great divide does seem to dominate the scene, not so much between Catholics and Protestants, but between classical Christians of every kind and liberals who seem bent on shifting the church from her scriptural foundations. If this is not so, we will be the first to rejoice; if it is, we are in for another long and hard struggle.

There is a danger of our being too much affected by the polemical atmosphere caused by our reaction to religious liberalism. Overreaction pushes us in directions we should not go. Obviously, it makes us defensive and uptight, even nervous with respect to the Bible. We can become afraid to see what is there and feel we have to force the text to meet requirements we establish out of our concern to preserve a high doctrine of inspiration. Clearly, this is not right and goes against our own view of the Bible's self-determining authority. Worst of all, it throws us out of focus. Deep in our hearts, we know that the central purpose of Scripture is to bring people to know and love God, and that it achieves

---

1. *The Spiritual Exercises of Saint Ignatius*, trans. Anthony Mottola (Garden City, NY: Doubleday, 1964), 47.

its purpose even though the existing Bible has unresolved problems. Its truth and power are not nullified by this fact. Even though it is not perfect by contemporary literary and scientific standards, the Bible is wonderfully able to make us wise unto salvation and to teach us all things needful. Even though the Bible is not "inerrant" at this present moment, it can accomplish exactly what it claims for itself. The difficulties do not obscure the good news or prevent the Spirit from using the text in human lives. Can we not stand back from the battle and see this? In its present condition, the Bible is proving reliable, nourishing, and precious.

Part of the problem is that we have been pushed into defending the Bible in the wrong way. The liberals, fresh from the modern Enlightenment, look at the Bible from a human and academic point of view. They raise difficult academic questions, and we try to answer them. But, in the process, we are maneuvered into an alien defense formation. We agree, in effect, to discuss the issue on the basis of scholarly considerations divorced from the context of life in the church and in the Spirit. This, in turn, requires us to tighten up the intellectual side and neglect the spiritual side of this question. It becomes essential to argue with all sorts of scholarly apparatus for a Bible more perfect than the one that exists, and it becomes an embarrassment to admit that Christians have always found the existing Bible, with its difficulties, quite sufficient in authority and truth. It has even caused some evangelicals to turn against others, with unfortunate results.

Our suggestion for avoiding this unpleasant and ill-conceived dispute among evangelicals is to recover the Christ-centered and nontechnical approach that the Bible itself seems to take. There is something terribly wrong when we argue about the Bible more and benefit from it less. God gave us his Word to make us wise, to instruct our minds, to revive our spirits, to guide our feet in his ways. We stand together with all those who are of this disposition. This is what the Bible itself claims, and this is what really matters.[2]

We struggle over whether it would be wise for us to continue to speak favorably of "biblical inerrancy" as language adequate to convey the Scripture principle in our time. Although the term is not ideal by any means, it does at least possess the proper strength of conviction concerning the truthfulness of the Bible. We recognize that the Bible does not make any technical inerrancy claim for itself (in its original or present versions) or go into the kind of detail usually associated with this term in the contemporary discussion. We see a solid basis for trusting the Scriptures in a more general sense, with reference to all that they teach

---

2. We think this is what Jack Rogers, Don McKim, Bernard Ramm, and now I. Howard Marshall have been trying to tell their fellow evangelicals.

and affirm, and a real danger in giving the impression that the Bible errs in significant ways—it does not. Even so, we do need a metaphor for conveying the determination to trust God's Word completely.

Inerrancy certainly is a difficult metaphor to accept for the need at hand since it is used by some to deny the human dimension of the text or is applied only to the nonexistent autographs. We do appreciate the more responsible definitions of the term that seek to bridge this awkward circumstance. Note, for instance, the *Chicago Statement* of 1977 and the many commentaries from within that circle.[3] The burden is to preserve the Scripture principle, affirming that the Bible can be trusted in what it teaches and relied on as the infallible norm of the church. All classical Christians should support this concern and be cautious about the language being used at present to represent it.[4]

For historical reasons, inerrancy language has come to symbolize the full confidence that Christians have always had in the Scriptures. Unfortunately, it also has been hardened into meanings indefensible in the face of the humanness of the biblical text itself. Therefore, the wisest course now is either to abandon this term altogether or to alter its common meaning to better fit the purpose of the Bible and the actual phenomena that its text displays. Many thoughtful Christians naturally fear that attempts to nuance the common meaning of "inerrancy" will cause the term to die the death of a thousand qualifications.

Whatever one finally does with the language, the bottom line is that commitment to the Scripture principle has to take into account the literary genre and vocabulary being displayed in any given passage. Truth has to be evaluated in context. The ancient text must be allowed to remain pliable in the hands of the ministering Spirit of God so that what was once said by God can gain fresh relevance for us and our times. Through the process of biblical interpretation, at a minimum we must maintain an unquestioned stance of affirming the inherent trustworthiness of the biblical text.[5] We are comfortable with this summative statement by Donald Bloesch: "I affirm that the message of Scripture is infallible and that the Spirit infallibly interprets this message to people of faith. But

3. See, for example, Roger Nicole, "The Nature of Inerrancy," in *Inerrancy and Common Sense*, ed. Nicole and Michaels; and Paul D. Feinberg, "The Meaning of Inerrancy," in *Inerrancy*, ed. Norman L. Geisler (Grand Rapids: Zondervan, 1979). The *Chicago Statement* reads in part: "We affirm that the Scriptures, as the infallible Word of God, are the basis of authority in the church. . . . We affirm that the Bible is to be interpreted in keeping with the best insights of historical and literary study, under the guidance of the Holy Spirit, with respect for the historic understanding of the church."

4. James I. Packer (*Beyond the Battle for the Bible*) has always upheld the importance of inerrancy while espousing a flexible understanding of how to apply it.

5. Millard Erickson (*Christian Theology*, vol. 1, chap. 10) shows himself very wise in his treatment of the inerrancy issue.

the perfect accuracy of the letter or text of Scripture is not an integral part of Christian faith. Because the term *inerrancy* is so often associated with the latter position . . . it is not the preferable word to use in theological discussion today, even though it should not be abandoned, for it preserves the nuance of truthfulness that is necessary for a high view of Holy Scripture."[6]

We need to believe and carefully convey faithful confidence that the Bible tells the truth when it speaks. If we are unable to affirm this, the whole biblical faith is in peril. Even though rejecting the term "inerrancy" is understandable because of the narrowness of its typical definition and the crudity of polemics that have accompanied its use, we still need language that makes unmistakably clear our strong conviction about biblical authority. The Bible can be trusted to teach the truth in all that it affirms.[7] In closing, then, we offer this little prayer:

> Blessed Lord, who caused Scripture to be written for our learning,
> Grant that we may read, hear, and inwardly digest these sacred texts,
> That we may embrace and ever hold fast the blessed hope of everlasting life,
> Which Thou hast given to us in our Savior, Jesus Christ the Lord. Amen.

6. Donald G. Bloesch, *Holy Scripture*, 116.

7. This ought to clarify the issue raised by Rex A. Koivisto, "Clark Pinnock and Inerrancy: A Change in Truth Theory?"

The Inspiration and Authority of the Bible: Thoughts since 1984

The Scripture Principle was originally published in 1984. Now, with the appearance of a revised edition in 2006, we want to share related thoughts on the subject of biblical inspiration and authority since the 1980s, based in part on recent evangelical scholarship.[1]

Word and Spirit

How have the central concerns of this book been handled in evangelical scholarship since the book's original edition was published? How is the Scripture principle doing? This certainly has been an active arena of study, one with various dimensions that we see as highly compatible with our broad perspective. One prominent publication in recent years is the extensive historical study *Canon and Criterion in Christian Theology* by William J. Abraham. He revisits the evolution of a canon of Scripture in the earliest church, shows how its key orientation was "systematically dismantled in the Western Church before, during, and after the Protestant Reformation," and attempts to rescue Christian theology "from the epistemological captivity to which it has been subject since it lost

1. My personal reflections (Pinnock) are indebted in part to the work of Barry L. Callen, who authored my intellectual biography, *Clark H. Pinnock: Journey toward Renewal* (2000), and also has written helpfully about my work elsewhere.

253

its moorings in the canonical heritage of the early Church."[2] Abraham wants to relocate the idea of canon within the "means of grace," removing it from the rationalistic arena that distorts its essential nature and purpose. We concur. We view the current need among evangelicals as a better balancing of Word and Spirit.

There has been constant talk in recent years about the meaning of the supposed demise of modernism and the possible triumph of the newer postmodernism. There has been emphasis by some on the continuance of a strict theory of inerrancy and a sharply contrasting emphasis by numerous others on the considerable problems of any rationalist propositionalism. For the latter group, a theory of how God must have inspired the Bible—based on rationalist presuppositions—is seen as being imposed on the Bible rather than allowing the actual phenomena of Scripture itself to guide our understanding of how God apparently did inspire the writers, the text, and now the readers. We agree with the judgment of Alister McGrath: "There is a growing realization within evangelicalism that the Princeton position is ultimately dependent upon extra-biblical assumptions and norms [the ideas and outlooks of Enlightenment rationalism]. The commitment to biblical authority remains; it is merely the mode of its articulation which is changing."[3]

There is no question that at the heart of evangelical theology is the authoritative Bible. Being proper hearers of God's word in Scripture, however, is not an easy and automatic accomplishment for a contemporary reader. Stanley Grenz makes a telling observation:

> In the modern era, a misunderstanding of Luther's principle of *sola scriptura* led many theologians to trade the ongoing reading of the text for their own systematic delineation of the doctrinal deposit that was supposedly encoded in its pages centuries ago. Thereby, the Bible was all too readily transformed from a living text into the object of the scholar's exegetical and systematizing prowess. The postmodern situation has laid bare the foundationalist presuppositions lying behind this modernist program.[4]

If, indeed, we now live in a postfoundationalist context, the challenge is to discover how best to understand the Bible as the instrumentality of the Spirit as the Spirit seeks to appropriate the sacred text so that it speaks relevantly to us today.

2. William J. Abraham, *Canon and Criterion in Christian Theology*, 21.
3. Alister McGrath, *Passion for Truth*, 117.
4. Stanley J. Grenz, "Articulating the Christian Belief-Mosaic," in *Evangelical Futures: A Conversation on Theological Method*, ed. J. G. Stackhouse Jr. (Grand Rapids: Baker, 2000), 124.

Rather than a heavy rational and even isolated individual-reader approach, it has become obvious to many that the need is for a fresh Word-Spirit theology. Donald G. Bloesch moves in this direction,[5] as does Steven J. Land, who sees heavy stress on infallibility and verbal inerrancy as a reduction of "a much fuller doctrine of the Word of God" involving its dynamic interaction with the Holy Spirit.[6] Similarly, Grenz calls for a "reorientation of the doctrine of Scripture under the doctrine of the Holy Spirit . . . thereby considering the Bible as the book of the Spirit."[7] We readily affirm this call.

Journey of Conscience (Clark H. Pinnock)

For most Christians, especially conservative Protestants, the Bible is an authoritative starting point for identifying the orthodox substance of the faith. The question is not whether Scripture is our primary authority but what kind of authority it is. Today some evangelicals promote the Bible as a stern rule of authority, while others appeal to it as a source of life and renewal. Some focus on the miraculous origin of the Bible that makes it a rational guarantee of the truth; others treasure the message of Scripture and encounter Jesus Christ. Some put the Bible forth in the mode of a deadening authoritarianism, while others experience it as a liberating word.

In my own pilgrimage, I (Pinnock) have moved in the direction of seeing the Bible as a witness to the life-giving message of our Lord Jesus Christ rather than as a kind of rationalistic axiom. In my career of theological research, I have experienced changes with regard to this subject, changes that I hope may help others in their thinking. I have moved from defending the Bible in a scholastic manner to understanding it in a more pietistic way. With this new edition of *The Scripture Principle*, I join Barry Callen in having the opportunity to address some of the issues again.[8]

Between the books *A Defense of Biblical Infallibility* in 1967 and *The Scripture Principle* in 1984, I had been on a journey in regard to my understanding of the precise nature of revealed truth. Both early and later

5. Donald G. Bloesch, *Holy Scripture*.

6. Steven J. Land, *Pentecostal Spirituality: A Passion for the Kingdom* (Sheffield, UK: Sheffield Academic Press, 1993), 74.

7. Stanley J. Grenz, *Revisioning Evangelical Theology*, 114–15.

8. I am indebted to Barry L. Callen for help in tracing my pilgrimage. See his essay in *Reading the Bible in Wesleyan Ways*, ed. Callen and Thompson, chap. 7. See also Ray C. W. Roennfeldt, *Clark H. Pinnock on Biblical Authority: An Evolving Position* (Berrien Springs, MI: Andrews University Press, 1993).

on this journey, I cared deeply and spoke convictionally about the reality of biblical revelation as a central principle on which the Christian faith rests. I did, however, make significant adjustments to my own thought along the way, adjustments I found warranted and important, ones that some of my evangelical colleagues have judged questionable and even unacceptable. I have always thought of myself as a committed and loyal evangelical. Finally, I emerged as a self-styled peacemaker on the controversial issues of the nature of biblical authority and interpretation.[9] My journey on this subject sheds light on contemporary evangelicalism and the constructive role that pietist ways of Bible reading might play.

Of particular concern to me has been "the skeptical attitude toward the unique authority and relevance of Holy Scripture."[10] Into this area of concern I boldly stepped, ready to defend the presumed technical, foundationalist, and revelational integrity of the Bible against all comers. Later I found myself reviewing critically some aspects of the nature of my own vigorous defense and the motivations for its intensity. The influential periodical *Christianity Today* helped make inerrancy the badge of evangelical authenticity, even as Francis Schaeffer insisted that it was the watershed of evangelical fidelity. This periodical once lauded my stalwart fidelity, saying that my "bareknuckles" challenge of current leading theological ideas "will be cheered by people who possess but cannot adequately articulate a disdain for the irrational abstractions sweeping through the ecclesiastical intelligentsia."[11] Later this same magazine would take a much more cautious approach to the value of my contributions, seeming to judge the revised Pinnock in a way similar to the 1986 conclusion of Henry Holloman. In the *Journal of the Evangelical Theological Society,* Holloman commended me for capably criticizing the "liberal theological revision" with its "flat denial of the Scripture principle in the classical sense," and yet he insisted that "unfortunately Pinnock's proposed Scripture principle, with its very lenient view of inerrancy, does not offer evangelicals a Biblically sound and logically consistent position to stabilize Christian faith and to withstand the onslaughts of destructive Biblical criticism."[12]

9. Trent Butler, in reviewing *The Scripture Principle* for the *Journal of Biblical Literature* (105, no. 4 [December 1986]: 700–701), highlights my obvious awareness of excess on all sides of the debate about biblical inspiration and interpretation and the expressed hope of supplying a model that might help transcend the impasse. For an extensive exploration of my intellectual journey and thought in general, see Barry L. Callen, *Clark H. Pinnock: Journey toward Renewal.*

10. Clark Pinnock, "Evangelicals and Inerrancy: The Current Debate," *Theology Today* 35 (April 1978): 65–66.

11. *Christianity Today,* endorsement on the cover of my book *Set Forth Your Case* (Nutley, NJ: Craig, 1967).

12. Henry Holloman, review of *The Scripture Principle* in the *Journal of the Evangelical Theological Society* 29, no. 1 (March 1986): 96–97.

My journey toward renewal in the evangelical understanding of biblical authority led me from a "philosophical biblicism" to a "simple biblicism." This postmodern-like shift had begun with an earlier preoccupation with verifiable revelational data that could speak with rational certainty to the world. I championed the assumption of divinely given propositional truths that could save humankind from relativism. The journey later moved me to a focus that I always had in an incipient way, but one that became dominant for me and now lacked the foundationalist overlay. By the resulting "simple biblicism" I mean

> the delight evangelicals experience from meditating on Scripture and submitting to it. They feel immense gratitude for this means of grace that the Spirit has bestowed on the church to equip it. Scripture is a gift of the Spirit, and evangelicals want to be open to all that God says in this text. Scripture for them is the tangible sacrament of the Word of God nourishing them like milk and honey. Not a theory about the Bible, simple biblicism is the basic instinct that the Bible is supremely profitable and transforming, alive with God's breath. Without being free of every difficulty, the Bible nevertheless bears effective witness to Jesus Christ. . . . Although wanting a reasonable faith, simple biblicism is not overly anxious about erecting rational foundations in the modern sense. It reflects a postmodern lack of anxiety about such foundations and is content with soft rather than hard rational supports.[13]

To begin with, in the 1960s I was primarily a vigilant doorkeeper of "assured biblical truth." Soon I journeyed to the place where most of my energy was being expended in ways other than withstanding the onslaughts of destructive biblical criticism. I had begun listening to the Bible, learning all I could, not defensively, but openly and expectantly. Like the Wesleyan/Pietist tradition, I opened myself to both the historic and the contemporary work of God's Spirit in inspiration and illumination.

Regardless of my commitment to revealed truth, which I have tied directly to biblical authority and still define intentionally by use of the word "inerrancy," I have remained in motion on the subject. By the early 1970s, I had become better able to reign in my enthusiastic crusading and make any needed confrontation increasingly constructive. Then came three years of teaching at Regent College in Vancouver, Canada (1974–77), where I experienced a freedom to quest and do creative work. In this context, I was impacted by Stephen Davis's book *The Debate about the Bible: Inerrancy versus Infallibility*, which openly challenged certain

---

13. Clark Pinnock, "New Dimensions in Theological Method," in *New Dimensions in Evangelical Thought*, ed. David Dockery (Downers Grove, IL: InterVarsity, 1998), 200.

assumptions about biblical inerrancy that I then held. I began to review carefully and revise cautiously my views of inerrancy.[14] Increasingly I was questioning openly certain traditional defenses and expressions of inerrancy treasured by conservatives.[15]

In my early period of fundamentalism, I had leaned on 2 Timothy 3:16–17, the only place in Scripture where the term "inspired" (*theopneustos*) occurs. But now, as a neo-evangelical, I was looking beyond the inspiration issue to appreciate also Paul's emphasis on practical spirituality. What is inspired is "useful for teaching, for reproof, for correction, and for training in righteousness, so that everyone who belongs to God may be proficient, equipped for every good work."[16] That is, God's Spirit breathes through the text to transform believers into maturing and obedient disciples. The focus should be less on textual technicalities of the past (the original text no longer wholly available) and more on faithful and transformative relevance in the present.

It was obvious that reforming a cherished element of fundamentalism like biblical inerrancy would be slow and painful. I quickly found myself being criticized by traditionalists, including Harold Lindsell, who earlier had counted me as a valuable ally in the "battle for the Bible." I was beginning what would become a familiar experience of walking a tightrope, explaining to the liberals why so few revisions were being made and to the fundamentalists why there were so many.[17] Recalling my two early mentors, F. F. Bruce and Francis Schaeffer, I characterized my shift in the 1970s as a move from Schaeffer's militant rationalism to Bruce's more bottom-up irenic scholarship. My move bore similarity to another key figure, C. S. Lewis. This Englishman represented for me a reasonable, commonsense approach to Christian belief that is enriched with wonderful visions and the ability to live with ambiguity.

What intervened to alter my view? I came to realize that I had "inflated the biblical claims for inspiration in the interests of a rationalist

14. See my "Three Views of the Bible in Contemporary Theology," in *Biblical Authority*, ed. Jack Rogers (Waco, TX: Word, 1977), 45–73; and "Evangelicals and Inerrancy," 65–69.

15. Later I would see the degree to which the foundationalism of modernity had been reflected in my own early work. "It did so in a covert way," I reported, "since I was not tuned into these subtleties. Because religion appeals to the need for security in life, it is easy to fall into foundationalism as a way of attaining it. It has a particularly seductive appeal for fundamentalists with their passion for certainty" (in an unpublished paper delivered to an evangelical-process dialogue convened at Claremont School of Theology, 1997).

16. My 1963 doctoral dissertation at the University of Manchester in England was titled "The Concept of the Spirit in the Epistles of Paul."

17. For example, *The Scripture Principle* was reviewed critically by James Barr (he judged it unacceptable from the left—I did not go far enough) and by Roger Nicole (he judged it unacceptable from the right—I went too far).

paradigm. . . . I had been engaged in making the Bible say more than it wanted to say in the interests of my system."[18] In fact, for me the rationalism of a scholastic theological system was slowly crumbling in light of an enhanced appreciation for the dynamic work of the Spirit in relation to the biblical authors/editors and my own thought and life (and potentially the thoughts and lives of other contemporary Bible readers). Such divine work came to have a substantive impact on my view of biblical revelation and interpretation.

I now affirm a progressiveness of revelation and the need for the interpreter to give heed to the letter, spirit, and direction of the principles of a text. Thus, with the Spirit's help, one "may need to go beyond Scripture in carrying out its intentions."[19] I had come to recognize that Jesus and the apostles, while holding a high view of biblical inspiration and authority, used the text in more practical and flexible ways than inerrantists typically have allowed. I am now open to a more inductive approach to the text that avoids the tendency to strained exegesis forced by a presuppositional theory. I have been helped by scholars like Edward Farley and James Barr to realize without embarrassment that God has given the Scriptures in human forms and languages.

The Bible, so it increasingly has appeared to me, should be allowed to teach God's will and way out of its distinctive diversity rather than out of a forced uniformity. Robert Johnston reflects as follows on the reasons for my broadening use of the term "inerrancy": "The perfect errorlessness of non-extant autographs was an abstraction that had died the death of a thousand qualifications. More importantly, it failed to prove the dynamic authority of the present text."[20] After all, it is the Spirit who causes the reader to be receptive to a text's "surplus of meaning," and, I would observe, "whatever the reason, stress on the Spirit is noticeably lacking in the literature of inerrancy."[21]

The force that can liberate the message of Jesus for the needs of life today is the Bible, read in the wisdom and power of the Spirit. Focusing inordinately on the presumed necessary accuracy of all textual detail, however marginal, can easily become dysfunctional. There was a growing realization that for many believers strict adherence to the inerrancy

18. In Roennfeldt, *Clark H. Pinnock on Biblical Authority*, xix. I attribute much of my new viewpoint to the writings of I. Howard Marshall, F. F. Bruce, James D. G. Dunn, and James Barr.

19. Clark Pinnock, "An Evangelical Theology of Human Liberation," *Sojourners* 5 (February 1976): 30. This article was originally a 1975 address to a workshop sponsored by Evangelicals for Social Action.

20. Robert Johnston, "Clark H. Pinnock," in *Handbook of Evangelical Theologians*, ed. Walter Elwell (Grand Rapids: Baker, 1993), 434.

21. Clark Pinnock, *The Scripture Principle* (San Francisco: Harper & Row, 1984), 154.

doctrine endangers rather than protects evangelical faith.[22] Accordingly, I commended the 1977 anti-inerrancy polemic of Stephen Davis for its "pastoral service" to those who are troubled with marginal difficulties in the Bible but who, nonetheless, are deeply committed to a biblically based evangelical faith. The theory of errorlessness sometimes leaves such persons stranded "if a single point, however minute, stands in any doubt."[23] The intent of divine revelation surely is human transformation. People are to be changed, not stranded by their rational engagement with the biblical text.

From a new academic post at McMaster Divinity College, in 1977 I began to convey my maturing thought to the wider Christian public and explore the range of possible implications. Regarding biblical inspiration and authority in the modern world, I now identified three general positions within evangelicalism. The first, my own personal heritage, centers in a militant advocacy of a virtually unqualified biblical inerrancy, an errorless Bible presumed to be the essential anchor of true Christianity. The second position actively opposes such strict inerrancy. Although a minority of evangelicals, there were prominent names here, including my own revered teacher F. F. Bruce of the University of Manchester in England. These thinkers questioned the assumption of scientific precision and accuracy usually connoted by inerrancy, arguing that such an inerrancy mentality is a modernistic approach not appropriate to the biblical text and not evidenced in how the Bible treats its own material or in what it claims for itself. They saw inspiration as "a much less formal and more practical affair," a divine action on behalf of the sufficiency of Scripture meant to "nourish and instruct the church for its faith and life, and not to [guarantee] an abstract perfection" in regard to the technicalities of its text or its incidental references to matters outside its central concern.[24]

The third position, which by 1978 had become my own, involved a preference for the term "inerrancy," but only after modifying its definition so as to take into account certain biblical phenomena not compatible with any absolute view of an errorless text (like the presence of a Semitic cosmology, variants of parallel material appearing in the Synoptic Gospels, etc.). My book *Biblical Revelation* (1971) was representative of

22. This judgment, of course, was hardly universal in the world of evangelical theologians. For example, Roger Nicole's review in *Christianity Today* of my 1984 book *The Scripture Principle* was provocatively titled "Clark Pinnock's Precarious Balance between Openmindedness and Doctrinal Instability." Nicole's inference was that there is an establishment evangelical theology that should not be threatened by a methodology that is dynamic enough to be open to any significant theological alterations.

23. Clark Pinnock, foreword to *The Debate about the Bible*, by Stephen Davis.

24. Pinnock, "Evangelicals and Inerrancy," 67.

this third position, as soon would be my softer *Reason Enough* (1980) and then my major work *The Scripture Principle* (1984).[25] In the latter, I rethought biblical authority in light of its witness to itself, including both its divine and human character and its spiritual dynamic. My style of argument was less rationalistic than my earlier apologetic works and my stance a less strict and more nuanced form of inerrancy. On the one hand, I was acknowledging the need to deal with the biblical text as it is, not with the abstraction of an ideal text (the autographs) that God did not choose to give the church across the centuries. Reverently pursuing critical scholarship has its place, I judged, as does a Spirit-led dynamic reading of the biblical text. On the other hand, such scholarship and hermeneutical focus do not lessen the fact that Scripture is genuinely authoritative in what it intends to teach. There is an objective content to biblical revelation that should caution both against skeptical and subjective biblical criticism and any Spirit focus that disassociates itself from the control of the revealed biblical text. The word "inerrancy" can be retained legitimately, I concluded, when defined as "a metaphor for the determination to trust God's Word completely."[26]

I was now championing a potentially awkward and certainly controversial middle position criticized by advocates of the other two positions. I assessed the resulting awkwardness this way: "The militant advocates suspect them [and me] of watering down the inerrancy conviction close to meaninglessness, and left wing Protestants like James Barr ridicule the effort to be critically honest and still retain biblical inerrancy in any form."[27] Regardless of criticisms from representatives of both alternatives and my increasing willingness to qualify carefully the exact meaning of my own inerrancy stance, I continued to maintain: "The Bible, not modernity, is normative, and our thoughts are to be shaped by its teaching, not the reverse. Only by acknowledging this can we prevent

25. A portion of the material in this 1984 book was first presented at Fuller Theological Seminary as the 1982 Payton Lectures. The title of my lectures was "Holy Scripture: Divine Treasure in Earthen Vessels," drawn from 2 Cor. 4:7.

26. Pinnock, *Scripture Principle*, 225. The review of *The Scripture Principle* by Randy Maddox affirms the book as "the most nuanced and critically aware exposition of biblical inerrancy available." Even so, Maddox was perplexed by the argument for retaining the term "inerrancy" after defining it basically as the belief that Scripture never leads one astray in regard to what it intentionally teaches. Retaining it when it is thus defined appeared to him to be essentially a political move, "using the approved password to placate a constituency," a move that will not be accepted by others who use the term and retain its traditional meaning (*Wesleyan Theological Journal* 21, nos. 1–2 [Spring–Fall 1986]: 206). For evidence that Maddox was correct, see Nicole, review of *The Scripture Principle*. Nicole quotes Carl F. H. Henry (68): Pinnock "retains inerrancy as a concept, but seems to thin it out almost to the breaking point."

27. Pinnock, "Evangelicals and Inerrancy," 66–67.

revelation from being buried under the debris of human culture and opinion and from disappearing as a liberating Word from outside the human situation."[28]

By 1984, I was speaking in terms of "the Scriptural principle," taken from Ed Farley, by which I meant that the Bible is to be viewed as God's written Word. God "has communicated authoritatively to us on those subjects about which Scripture teaches and we believers willingly subject ourselves to this rule of faith." The Bible is "a content-full language deposit" that addresses us with God's authority, a deposit that should not be "reduced to a mere expression of human experience and tradition."[29]

Delwin Brown rightly observed that the 1984 book *The Scripture Principle* "is as much an internal self-criticism of conservatism as it is an external critique of liberalism."[30] Inerrancy had come to mean that the Bible can be trusted in what it teaches and intentionally affirms. A key passage like 2 Timothy 3:15–16 authorizes sturdy belief in the instructional significance of the Bible in matters relating to human salvation, but not necessarily in marginal matters unrelated to the need for, basis of, and practice of new life in Jesus Christ. All Scripture is to be regarded as authoritative, but the character of the authority is relative to the actual content and form of any given text. Those portions of the Bible that plainly intend to teach the will of God constitute the core of authoritative Scripture. The Christian should accept the Bible as teacher in a way consistent with the diversity that the Bible contains. For instance, the way the New Testament uses the Hebrew Scriptures ("Old" Testament) makes plain that a text can possess "a surplus of meaning potential that transcends the meaning it originally had." The original meaning is to be the anchor of interpretation, but under the guidance of the Holy Spirit "the significance of the text for us needs to be searched out. . . . The picture is that of a canon in which the truth unfolds gradually and dialectically."[31] The Bible remains the norm of belief and must rule in opposition to the liberal reformers who "are in rebellion against the content of the Bible and are determined to adapt it to the 'itching ears' of the present."[32]

28. Pinnock, *Scripture Principle*, 213.

29. Ibid., 62.

30. Delwin Brown, "Rethinking Authority from the Right," *Christian Scholar's Review* 19, no. 1 (1989–90): 67.

31. Pinnock, *Scripture Principle*, 45, 186. I say further: "The Bible in the form it comes to us is the kind of teacher that draws us into the process of learning and helps us learn to think theologically and ethically ourselves in new situations" (194).

32. Ibid., 208, 211. Some conservatives, of course, now insist that I myself have become a liberal reformer still trying to wear inerrancy clothes. Norman Geisler, for instance, judges: "Strangely, some neotheists such as Clark Pinnock claim to believe in the infallibility and inerrancy of the Bible. However, this is clearly inconsistent" (*Creating God in the Image of Man?* [Minneapolis: Bethany, 1997], 131).

Innovative and on a journey I surely was; rebellious and antibiblical I certainly was not. It had become crucial for me that one both affirm biblical authority in principle and define it with care. I was seeking to claim middle ground in a crucial and complex issue.

Freedom from Rational Epistemology

It has remained my firm assumption that true Christianity depends on a truth deposit once delivered to the saints, a deposit that must be maintained and accepted by faith. This is why I hold staunchly to the text horizon of the faith in the face of the obvious role always played by the reader horizon. The problem I now see, however, is that evangelicals, for whom the Word of God is of utmost importance, "have spent a great deal of energy defending the authority or inerrancy of the Bible and [have] given little attention to the equally important matter of its interpretation." They have, in fact, often evidenced a "naiveté in hermeneutics" that threatens "to drag the meaning of the text into the range of what we want it to say." The text is not there to do human bidding, and it does not mean whatever readers want it to mean. But interpretation is no easy process, in part because "the Bible is not a flat text but a symphony of voices and emphases."[33] I thus place myself today in an "inerrancy of purpose" category that allows room both to significantly nuance the specific textual meanings of inerrancy[34] and to continue to sign the statement of the Evangelical Theological Society, which affirms that "the Bible alone, and the Bible in its entirety, is the Word of God written, and is therefore inerrant in the autographs." I actually prefer the wording of the Lausanne Covenant, which says that the Bible is "inerrant in all it affirms," or that of the *Chicago Statement of Biblical Inerrancy*, which says: "We deny that it is proper to evaluate Scripture

33. Clark Pinnock, "Catholic, Protestant, and Anabaptist: Principles of Biblical Interpretation in Selected Communities," *Brethren in Christ History and Life* 9 (December 1986): 268, 275.

34. Note, for instance, my "Climbing out of a Swamp: The Evangelical Struggle to Understand the Creation Texts," *Interpretation* 43 (April 1989): 143–55. I am concerned that evangelicals be true to their own premise of "letting Scripture speak definitively above the noise of human opinions" (153). I am also concerned, however, that near the surface of evangelical interpretation is a docetic tendency, "an unconscious wish not to have God's Word enter into the creaturely realm" (153). I concluded: "Evangelicals are understandably nervous about existential hermeneutics, but that is no reason to overreact and make the Bible a victim" (154). Modern scientific perspectives and calls for "factual" information may be quite other than the biblical intent in the Genesis texts (and elsewhere). To honor biblical authority is to affirm claims to assured truth only within the context of the intent of biblical teaching (which relates to salvation and not science, for instance).

according to standards of truth and error that are alien to its usage or purpose." In other words, the Bible may contain errors of incidental kinds, but it teaches none.[35]

Clearly, by the 1980s I had opened myself to biblical scholarship to a degree I had previously rejected. In 1968 I had warned Southern Baptists about new teachers then in their ranks who "had found it expedient to jettison the historic high view of Scripture and accept a scaled down version. . . . Scholarship is the gift of God. But scholars have erred time and time again, while Scripture has never erred!"[36] The next year I had joined the faculty of Trinity Evangelical Divinity School and affirmed its statement of belief, point one of which was: "We believe . . . the Scriptures, both Old and New Testaments, to be the inspired Word of God, without error in the original writings, the complete revelation of His will for the salvation of men, and the Divine and final authority for all Christian faith and life." But by the 1980s, I had qualified the precise meaning of appropriately affirming an inerrant Bible, insisting that "qualify" and "scale down" differ in meaning. For me, the Bible's authority and reliability had not thereby been diminished.

Both early and late in my personal journey, I have believed the Bible to be inerrant in all that it intentionally affirms. What changed in my view is the identification of exactly what the Bible affirms. Identifying this is a central and ongoing challenge for contemporary Christians. The task of interpretation would be much easier, of course, if the actual words of the Bible were identical with divine revelation. But it may be said that human words are to divine revelation as form is to content. Therefore, there is danger in any rote application of Augustine's classic statement: "What the Bible says, God says." When such a statement is applied mechanically to the biblical text, there is the tendency to dehistoricize the vehicle of revelation and make each text an immutable and inerrant proposition. In fact, tradition, experience, and reason (key elements of the Wesleyan quadrilateral) all are needed to assist the community of faith in understanding and applying the Word of God. *Sola Scriptura* may have been a distinguishing slogan of the Protestant

35. Note this from Bloesch (*Holy Scripture*, 116): "I affirm that the message of Scripture is infallible and that the Spirit infallibly interprets this message to people of faith. But the perfect accuracy of the letter or text of Scripture is not an integral part of Christian faith. Because the term *inerrancy* is so often associated with the latter position, I agree with Clark Pinnock that it is not the preferable word to use in theological discussion today, even though it should not be abandoned, for it preserves the nuance of truthfulness that is necessary for a high view of Holy Scripture." Bloesch refers to this statement of mine (*Scripture Principle* [San Francisco: Harper & Row, 1984], 225): "I wish to retain the word *inerrancy* because it 'has come to symbolize in our day that full confidence that Christians have always had in the Scriptures.'"

36. Clark Pinnock, *A New Reformation* (Tigerville, SC: Jewel, 1968), 7, 10.

Reformation, but it was never literally practiced. Probing the sacred text is always done within some reading tradition that relies, at least in part, on a given pattern of logic and experience. Even so, it remains the case for me that the Bible—with all its humanness—extends beyond being merely a crucial cultural heritage for believers to being the normative rule of faith that should define belief and practice.

I came to affirm this revised inerrancy position because it is justified by the facts, textual and contextual, historical and hermeneutical, and it is able to provide a viable position to mediate the authority struggle in the evangelical community.[37] In 1965 I had seen the Southern Baptist Convention, into which I then was entering as a new professor, in danger of serious infiltration by a Bible-evading and doctrine-eroding liberalism. This I fought. By 1987, however, I saw the primary danger to the SBC having shifted from the external assault of liberalism to a dangerous division within the Convention itself, nearly a holy war among the parties of its nonliberals (ranging from moderates to fundamentalists). A primary dividing line was between competing theories of biblical inspiration. The truly frightening prospect now was that, in a time of unprecedented worldwide mission potential, "the possible fragmentation of believers could have disastrous consequences for world evangelization," even causing Baptists to "snatch defeat from the jaws of victory."[38] I announced to a large gathering of Baptist scholars that there was the option of peace without compromise, saying that "the key issue is to maintain the right amount of form and freedom." I supported this perspective with my own experience: "I did not see my colleague at L'Abri, the strict inerrantist Francis Schaeffer, spending his time seeking to drive out my doctoral mentor, the moderate F. F. Bruce, from the evangelical coalition just because of a difference of opinion over a theological theory and not the gospel."[39]

I spoke in 1987 to a large body of mostly Southern Baptist scholars gathered for the Conference on Biblical Inerrancy at Ridgecrest, North Carolina. In the midst of presentations by persons ranging from strict inerrantists to significant revisionists, my inclination was to be a peacemaker. I supported the 1978 *Chicago Statement* of the International

---

37. Carl F. H. Henry was a stalwart evangelical defender of the distinctiveness and propositional nature of divine revelation, the one thing, he argued, on which evangelicals can confidently construct a substantial, coherent, and trustworthy theological system. I countered that it is impossible to set forth an infallible Scripture as the foundational axiom of Christian theology. I wrote: "The problem in a nutshell: If reason is given its head, will it reliably lead to orthodox conclusions? Progressives certainly do not believe that it will" (*Tracking the Maze*, 46–47).

38. Clark Pinnock, *The Proceedings of the Conference on Biblical Inerrancy, 1987* (Nashville: Broadman, 1987), 73.

39. Ibid., 74.

Council on Biblical Inerrancy, which declared in its famous article 13 that textual phenomena like chronological order, loose quotations, and disagreeing numbers should not be considered errors. I argued that Bible believers over the centuries have come to no consensus on the precise meaning of inerrancy, that the *Chicago Statement* made room for nearly every well-intentioned Baptist, and that "old-fashioned love and understanding" was the real need of the hour. On the one hand, there should be correction of any "unbalanced over-belief that overlooks the human and historical dimension of the Bible." On the other hand, I warned, "let us never fail to express our unsurpassed confidence in the divine treasure which the Bible surely is."[40]

What is the bottom line? It should be mission, I said to that 1987 gathering, not fruitless and debilitating internal combat over technicalities largely of human devising. What I saw happening was that the liberals already had lost the day, while conservatives, properly but not very gracefully, were now "trying to get the wrinkles out of their sounder view of inspiration."[41] My own approach was to adopt "a simpler, more spontaneous biblicism" that trusts the Bible without reservation, but at the same time does not "burden the Bible reader with too much human theory lest he or she miss what God is saying in the text."[42]

This more simple and spontaneous biblicism approach was similar to that of fellow Baptist theologian Bernard Ramm who, toward the end of his career, "was able to experience freedom from the methodological fixation."[43] Ramm had wearied of evangelicals fighting over inerrancy and longed for them to rejoice in the Bible's solid testimony to Jesus Christ in the power of the Holy Spirit. I had come to the place at which Ramm also had arrived. For us, the Bible seldom addresses its authority and says nothing about its inerrancy. The rationalistic (Western) model of biblical authority that I had learned early from B. B. Warfield and others had exaggerated these concepts to fit a theological system that had been adopted in advance. I was learning "not to force the Bible onto a Procrustean bed of extra-scriptural assumptions about authority and perfection."[44] Wesleyan scholar Timothy Smith was right: "Those of us who come from Wesleyan, Lutheran or Calvinist backgrounds draw upon the writings of the Reform-

---

40. Afterword, in *The Unfettered Word: Southern Baptists Confront the Authority-Inerrancy Question,* ed. Robison B. James (Waco, TX: Word, 1987), 186–87.

41. Ibid.

42. Pinnock, *Proceedings of the Conference on Biblical Inerrancy,* 75. For an excellent overview of the apparent strengths and weaknesses of this "later" position of mine, see Roennfeldt, *Clark H. Pinnock on Biblical Authority,* 321–41.

43. Clark Pinnock, "Bernard Ramm: Postfundamentalist Coming to Terms with Modernity," in *Perspectives on Theology in the Contemporary World: Essays in Honor of Bernard Ramm,* ed. Stanley Grenz (Macon, GA: Mercer University Press, 1990), 26.

44. Pinnock, "New Dimensions in Theological Method," 204.

ers themselves to affirm our conviction that the *meanings*, not the *words*, of biblical passages are authoritative, and that understanding these meanings requires close and critical study of the texts, rather than incantation of supposedly inerrant words."[45]

Gary Dorrien offers a good perspective. In midcareer I had realized that evangelicalism was needlessly struggling and dividing over an assertion of total biblical inerrancy, an assertion that cannot be sustained by the biblical text itself. So I "redrew the line at infallible-teaching inerrancy and invested the same passion he [I] had earlier shown for strict inerrancy in defending this fallback position against theological relativism."[46] I now knew that Karl Barth had good reason for rejecting the concept of revelation as primarily information (which turns revelation into an object that is available for human control); but I also remained troubled about how this "neo-orthodox rejection had led so much of modern theology to retreat from the belief that revelation yields necessary content, leaving theologians free to pursue enticing doctrines of their own making and preference."[47] There must be forged a middle ground where revelation is real and meaningful without being prejudged and restricted to a human system of thought that is brought to the biblical text more than found in it.

I had found a relative freedom from an epistemology that is mechanical and rationally restrictive. Biblical texts are not free of the issues of cultural relativism. Biblical revelation is progressive in character, requiring attention to where a text lies in the living organism of Scripture. What something meant originally and what it means authoritatively now may differ, at least at the levels of language and culture. Even so, the Scripture principle holds. The necessary nuancing of the inerrancy concept had not violated the heart of what evangelicals had taught all along. Scripture can be trusted to be truthful in all that it intentionally affirms, especially on matters pertaining to salvation. Rather than the hard rationalist approach to biblical authority and interpretation, I had come to appreciate the story and mystery of Scripture, the key role of the Spirit's ministry in original inspiration and current illumination, and the need to listen as well as to reason.

My core conviction had become one of certainty of truth arising more from the work of the Spirit through the biblical text than from a tight rationalism rooted in the supposed human theory of biblical errorlessness of the text per se. I nonetheless saw retaining the word "inerrancy" as a possible path of wisdom given circumstances in the evangelical

45. Timothy L. Smith, "Determining Biblical Authority's Base," *Christian Century* 94 (March 2, 1977): 198.
46. Gary Dorrien, *The Remaking of Evangelical Theology*, 140.
47. Pinnock, *Scripture Principle*, 26.

community (admittedly more a political than a theological stance). I also saw the need to carefully nuance the implications of this word given the circumstances of the biblical text itself. I recalled that Paul in 1 Corinthians 2:4 speaks about a certainty that results not from the wisdom of human words but from the Spirit's witness to human hearts. Finally, then, for adequate biblical interpretation, attention must be given to the key place of authentic piety or Spirit reality in Christian life.

Coordinating the Roles of Mind and Heart

My (Pinnock) agenda in the early years was centered on a concern to enable conversion to Jesus Christ. As changes came in some of my views, I did not retreat from that central evangelistic concern, and I did not rebel and generally reject evangelical Christianity once I had examined it critically. Some others did bolt from their evangelical upbringings and become some of today's liberal theologians. Why not me? It might have been my temperament, maybe my ability to make changes without throwing out the baby with the bathwater. Perhaps it was "the depth of my own conversion which would not be denied, or the fact that I was raised in liberal Christianity and knew how little it has to offer. . . . Not having been a fundamentalist culturally was a definite advantage."[48] Whatever the reasons, I was on a journey of renewal that later would bring me "from the scholastic to the pietistic approach" to Christian believing and living. In fact, I would see postmodern developments in the late twentieth century, with their emphasis on the particular and experiential, as favoring an "evangelical pietism."[49]

Previously, I had expressed suspicion about any evangelical focus on charismatic renewal that was not thoroughly checked by biblical definitions and restrictions. Back then, I tended to denigrate subjective religious experiences as indistinguishable from a case of indigestion unless there was an inerrant Bible to separate the true from the false.[50] There was worry that Baptists, mixing noncreedalism with revivalism, tend to locate truth in the saving encounter with Christ—maybe a key reason

48. Pinnock, in Roennfeldt, *Clark H. Pinnock on Biblical Authority*, xvii.
49. Clark Pinnock, "Evangelical Theologians Facing the Future: Ancient and Future Paradigms," *Wesleyan Theological Journal* 33, no. 2 (Fall 1998): 11. Note the similar thesis of colleague Stanley Grenz (*Theology for the Community of God* [Nashville: Broadman, 1994], x): "I discovered anew the importance of the pietist heritage in which I had been spiritually nurtured. Since 1988, I have been seeking to integrate the rationalistic and pietistic dimensions of the Christian faith. . . . Thus, while theology may be an intellectual search for truth, this search must always be attached to the foundational, identity-producing encounter with God in Christ. And it must issue forth in Christian living."
50. Pinnock, *Set Forth Your Case*, 73.

why many were "ravaged by liberal and later neo-orthodox theology" and thus became vulnerable to theological compromise. This tendency, I judged, "is even more true of the world-wide Pentecostal movement whose emphasis on religious subjectivity is even more complete."[51]

During the 1970s, however, I came to soften my negative critique of Pentecostalism, but without granting to spiritual experience a position of equal partnership with biblical authority in defining Christian truth. Soon I would freely endorse a more overtly charismatic spirituality like John Wesley, who did not separate spiritual experience from the defining roles of the Bible and church tradition but granted enough significance to religious experience to be accused of being an "enthusiast." Robert Rakestraw concludes about me: "For a Southern Baptist leader in the conservative South in the 1960s, this was a remarkable occurrence, indicating in him a thirst for God and His truth wherever that may lead and regardless of whose theological system it may violate."[52] I would later report a divine healing in one of my eyes, commenting: "I know from personal experience that one such incident can be worth a bookshelf of academic apologetics for Christianity (including my own books)."[53]

I had published pace-setting articles in *Christianity Today* with the provocative titles "A Truce Proposal for the Tongues Controversy" (October 8, 1971), "The New Pentecostalism: Reflections by a Well-Wisher" (September 14, 1973), and "Opening the Church to the Charismatic Dimension" (June 12, 1981). I argued that Bible-believing evangelicals would have to find a way to get over their rationalism and inordinate fear of emotional excess in order to avoid a quenching of the Spirit. I had no personal case to make for any divisive spiritual elitism or for anyone insisting that a divine gift like speaking in tongues is for every believer as a necessary sign of the reception of the Spirit. It was just that I appreciated charismatics as evangelicals with a little more spiritual voltage. I was one with them, at least in their newly claiming the "heart dimension" of the faith—what to me was like returning to the best of the older and less scholastically bound evangelicalism (such as I had experienced in the early honeymoon years of my faith).

Since then I have written about the coordinate roles of mind and heart (for instance, *Flame of Love*, 1996), so much so that Pentecostal scholar Terry Cross offered this generous judgment in 1998:

51. Clark Pinnock, "Baptists and Biblical Authority," *Journal of the Evangelical Theological Society* 17 (1974): 203.

52. Robert Rakestraw, "Clark Pinnock," in *Baptist Theologians*, ed. Timothy George and David Dockery (Nashville: Broadman, 1990), 662.

53. Clark Pinnock, "A Revolutionary Promise," review of *Power Evangelism*, by John Wimber and Kevin Springer, *Christianity Today* 30 (August 8, 1986): 19.

Because of its method and message, *Flame of Love* is a vital theological treatise for Pentecostals and charismatics. It is the most needful and yet most provocative book I have read in a decade. It is needful for the church at large since the doctrine of the Spirit is visibly absent and the urge to consider the work of the Spirit in our lives is also missing; it is needful for the renewal movement since we are lacking good systematic theological reflection on the whole.[54]

Regarding biblical inspiration and authority, I think I have retained a sturdy grip on the significance of real divine revelation dependably made available in the biblical text for serious seekers. Nonetheless, I have been on a spiritual journey, too, and, as Millard Erickson has observed, "It is apparent that his [my] aim is not to propound a Barthian view of revelation but to revitalize the evangelical doctrine of illumination of Scripture by the Holy Spirit."[55] Clearly, I have come to value function as much as form in the area of biblical authority and meaning, looking with disfavor at any excessive intellectualism and abstraction that detracts from concrete Christian discipleship and mission. The important question for me has come to be: How can Scripture be a lamp to our feet and a light to our path, the vital function of Scripture that "has little to do with the perfect errorlessness of non-existent autographs and a great deal to do with the continuing authority of a (slightly) imperfect document"?[56] The Christian agenda should be preoccupied less with a theory of precise inerrancy and much more with a healthy concern for a spiritual power enabled by the Spirit of God, who both speaks through ancient Scripture and illumines the contemporary reader for real life and mission.[57]

What about Robert Price's judgment that my theology is now profoundly experience-centered, even experience-generated, making me more of a liberal than I recognize—a fear at the heart of any proposed change among evangelicals? Without question, I have been on a spiritual journey that I refuse to separate from my theological work. My persistent intent has been to retain a good balance between revealed and experienced truth. On the one hand, I have openly and repeatedly rejected the theism of most process theologians, in part because I have

54. Terry L. Cross, "A Critical Review of Clark Pinnock's *Flame of Love: A Theology of the Holy Spirit*," *Journal of Pentecostal Theology* 13 (1998): 4.

55. Millard Erickson, *The Evangelical Left*, 79.

56. Pinnock, "Evangelicals and Inerrancy," 68.

57. Clark Pinnock, "The Past and Future Meaning of Texts," in *Reading the Bible in Wesleyan Ways*, ed. Callen and Thompson, chap. 8. Also Stanley J. Grenz, "Nurturing the Soul, Informing the Mind," in *Evangelicals and Scripture: Tradition, Authority and Hermeneutics*, ed. Vincent E. Bacote, Laura C. Miguelez, and Dennis L. Okholm (Downers Grove, IL: InterVarsity, 2004), chap. 1.

judged their concept of God inadequate in the face of Scripture, evangelical experience, and the religious needs of fallen humans.[58] On the other hand, I have also rejected the suggestion of Price that, like Schleiermacher, I have been extrapolating theology from the consciousness of piety. I have written: "Just because a person sees more importance in experience than he used to does not make him/her a liberal!"[59] Regarding Schleiermacher's use of religious experience as a critical criterion for assessing the teachings of Christian faith, I argue:

> The use of an outside criterion by which to understand the kerygma appears to allow the Gospel itself to come under alien control. Instead of Scripture being the norm, theology is governed by the 19th or 20th century cultural ego instead. . . . We are often attracted by the novel theology which comes up with a brilliant fusion between the Bible and something contemporary. But this is not what God is after. He desires us to be faithful stewards of his Word, who do not seek glory in this age, and do not value what man thinks above what God has said, but open ourselves to his Spirit, walk by faith and not by sight, and proclaim the Gospel with fearlessness and undiminished power.[60]

Conclusion

There are a variety of opinions among evangelicals concerning the inspiration of the Bible. None of them are necessarily denying its trustworthiness in all matters of faith and practice; they are arguing chiefly about the extent of its perfections. Is it the case that inspiration is verbal and all-controlling with respect to the human component, or is it a more dynamic category? We are more attracted to the latter view because we believe it can do greater justice to the genuine humanity of the text. We also find it helpful, along with Donald Bloesch, to think of Scripture as sacramental and life giving. The Bible can be a dead book in some hands, but it can also come alive given the agency of the Spirit.[61]

58. See, e.g., Clark Pinnock, "Between Classical and Process Theism," in *Process Theology*, ed. Ronald Nash (Grand Rapids: Baker, 1987), 313–25.

59. Clark Pinnock, letter to Diane De Smidt, Bethel Theological Seminary, November 11, 1988. Also, see my book *Tracking the Maze*, 99–102, for more of my views about the theological method of Schleiermacher.

60. Clark Pinnock, *Three Keys to Spiritual Renewal* (Minneapolis: Bethany, 1985), 95, 100.

61. Roger E. Olson, *The Mosaic of Christian Belief: Twenty Centuries of Unity and Diversity* (Downers Grove, IL: InterVarsity, 2002), 101–9. The shift to a more dynamic understanding of biblical inspiration is undoubtedly part of a larger paradigm shift from theological determinism to free-will theism (noted by Roennfeldt, *Clark H. Pinnock on Biblical Authority*, 349–61).

Now, concerning the hot button issue, biblical inerrancy, the item for which some battle most vociferously, it is not our preferred term for rendering the concept of biblical trustworthiness. Why? One reason is that inerrancy begs clear definition (which is why, ironically, we can continue to use it), and more importantly because it suggests a degree of technical accuracy that is foreign to Scripture. It places, in effect, a modern standard of accuracy upon the text and is then forced to explain away the phenomena of scores of minor flaws. The Bible does not use the term "inerrancy" but places emphasis upon its own saving and sanctifying power as witness to Jesus.

What really disturbs us with regard to the term "inerrancy" is the harm that it does. It almost makes one afraid to open the Bible lest some flaw in the text might overthrow confidence in God. It places the church at a perilous and unnecessary risk. It is surely suicidal, as Orr pointed out in reply to Warfield, to claim that Christianity would be false if a single statement of the Bible on a matter of science, history, or geography might turn out to be inaccurate in some way. We think it better to use a term like "trustworthiness" or "infallibility," which speak of Scripture as reliable and never failing in its intended purpose. Is it not true that in the Bible we hear the Master's voice in spite of scratches of the needle on the record? The issue is not whether the Bible is totally accurate as we define accuracy, but whether it leads us to the truth of God as all evangelicals believe.

It is not our intent to disturb the theological peace of evangelicalism. We have just tried to explain what we have learned. In brief, whereas I (Pinnock) used to hype the perfection of Scripture for apologetic reasons, to secure its place as the foundation stone of a dogmatic belief system, now we have a better cornerstone, Jesus Christ, who is more than adequately witnessed to by this sacred text (1 Cor. 3:11). One could say that we have become disenchanted with the rationalistic view of the Bible and have found the pietist orientation more convincing and agreeable. Donald Dayton writes, "Would it not be ironic if it should turn out that the despised and suppressed traditions of pietism and its successors turned out to provide the clues which one needs to escape the impasses of the orthodox doctrine of Scripture and find a better way to a more adequate doctrine of Scripture?"[62] Yes, it would be ironic, and it would be more adequate and would bring to the surface the pietist roots of modern evangelicalism that often remain unrecognized.

---

62. See Donald W. Dayton, "The Pietist Theological Critique of Biblical Inerrancy," in *Evangelicals and Scripture*, ed. Bacote, Miguelez, and Okholm, chap. 4.

Works Cited

Abraham, William J. *Canon and Criterion in Christian Theology: From the Fathers to Feminism*. Oxford: Clarendon, 1998.

———. *The Divine Inspiration of Holy Scripture*. Oxford: Oxford University Press, 1981.

———. *Divine Revelation and the Limits of Historical Criticism*. Oxford: Oxford University Press, 1982.

Achtemeier, Paul J. *The Inspiration of Scripture: Problems and Proposals*. Philadelphia: Westminster, 1980.

Adler, Mortimer J. *The Angels and Us*. New York: Macmillan, 1982.

———. *The Paideia Proposal: An Educational Manifesto*. New York: Macmillan, 1982.

Archer, Gleason L. *Encyclopedia of Bible Difficulties*. Grand Rapids: Zondervan, 1982.

Baillie, John. *The Idea of Revelation in Recent Thought*. New York: Columbia University Press, 1956.

Baker, David L. *Two Testaments, One Bible*. Downers Grove, IL: InterVarsity, 1976.

Barr, James. *The Bible in the Modern World*. London: SCM, 1973.

———. *Fundamentalism*. London: SCM, 1977.

———. *Holy Scripture: Canon, Authority, Criticism*. Philadelphia: Westminster, 1983.

Barth, Karl. *Church Dogmatics*. 4 vols. Edinburgh: T&T Clark, 1936–69.

Bauer, Walter. *Orthodoxy and Heresy in Earliest Christianity*. Philadelphia: Fortress, 1971.

Berkhof, Hendrikus. *Christian Faith: An Introduction to the Study of the Faith*. Grand Rapids: Eerdmans, 1979.

Berkouwer, G. C. *Holy Scripture*. Grand Rapids: Eerdmans, 1975.

Bloesch, Donald G. *Essentials of Evangelical Theology*. Vols. 1–2. San Francisco: Harper & Row, 1978–79.

———. *The Future of Evangelical Christianity*. Garden City, NY: Doubleday, 1983.

———. *Holy Scripture: Revelation, Inspiration, and Interpretation*. Downers Grove, IL: InterVarsity, 1994.

Brown, Raymond E. *The Critical Meaning of the Bible*. New York: Paulist Press, 1981.

———. *The Sensus Plenior of Sacred Scripture*. Baltimore: St. Mary's University Press, 1955.

Browning, Don S. *The Moral Context of Pastoral Care*. Philadelphia: Westminster, 1976.

Bruce, F. F. *Tradition: Old and New*. Exeter, UK: Paternoster, 1970.

Bultmann, Rudolf. *Existence and Faith*. New York: World, 1960.

———. *Jesus Christ and Mythology*. London: SCM, 1958.

———. *Kerygma and Myth: A Theological Debate*. Vol. 1. Edited by H. W. Bartsch. New York: Harper & Row, 1961.

Caird, George B. *The Language and Imagery of the Bible*. London: Duckworth, 1980.

Callen, Barry L. *Authentic Spirituality: Moving beyond Mere Religion*. Grand Rapids: Baker, 2001. Reprint, Lexington, KY: Emeth, 2006.

———. *Caught between Truths*. Anderson, IN: Warner, 2006.

———. *Clark H. Pinnock: Journey toward Renewal*. Nappanee, IN: Evangel, 2000.

———. *Discerning the Divine: God in Christian Theology*. Louisville: Westminster John Knox, 2004.

Callen, Barry L., and Richard P. Thompson, eds. *Reading the Bible in Wesleyan Ways: Some Constructive Proposals*. Kansas City, MO: Beacon Hill, 2004.

Carnell, Edward J. *The Case for Orthodox Theology*. Philadelphia: Westminster, 1959.

Carson, D. A. *Divine Sovereignty and Human Responsibility: Biblical Perspectives in Tension*. Atlanta: John Knox, 1981.

Carson, D. A., and John D. Woodbridge, eds. *Scripture and Truth*. Grand Rapids: Zondervan, 1983.

Childs, Brevard S. *Biblical Theology in Crisis*. Philadelphia: Westminster, 1970.

———. *Introduction to the Old Testament as Scripture*. Philadelphia: Fortress, 1979.

Coats, George W. *Canon and Authority*. Philadelphia: Fortress, 1977.

Coleman, Richard J. *Issues of Theological Conflict: Evangelicals and Liberals*. Rev. ed. Grand Rapids: Eerdmans, 1980.

Cullmann, Oscar. *The Early Church*. London: SCM, 1956.

Davis, Stephen T. *The Debate about the Bible: Inerrancy versus Infallibility*. Philadelphia: Westminster, 1977.

———. *Logic and the Nature of God*. Grand Rapids: Eerdmans, 1983.

Demarest, Bruce A. *General Revelation: Historical Views and Contemporary Issues*. Grand Rapids: Zondervan, 1982.

De Moor, J. C. *Towards a Biblically Theological Method*. Kampen: Kok, 1980.

DeWolf, Harold L. *The Case for Theology in Liberal Perspective*. Philadelphia: Westminster, 1959.

Donner, Theo. "Some Thoughts on the History of the New Testament Canon." *Themelios* 7, no. 3 (1982): 23–27.

Dornisch, Loretta. "Paul Ricoeur and Biblical Interpretation: A Selected Bibliography." *Semeia* 4 (1975): 23–26.

Dorrien, Gary. *The Remaking of Evangelical Theology*. Louisville: Westminster John Knox, 1998.

Downing, F. Gerald. *Has Christianity a Revelation?* Philadelphia: Westminster, 1964.

Dulles, Avery. *Models of Revelation*. Garden City, NY: Doubleday, 1983.

———. *Revelation and the Quest for Unity*. Washington, DC: Corpus, 1968.

———. *Revelation Theology: A History*. New York: Herder & Herder, 1969.

Dunn, James D. G. "The Authority of Scripture according to Scripture." *The Churchman* 96, no. 2–3 (1982): 104–22, 201–25.

———. *Christology in the Making*. Philadelphia: Westminster, 1980.

———. *Jesus and the Spirit*. London: SCM, 1975.

———. *Unity and Diversity in the New Testament*. London: SCM, 1977.

Ebeling, Gerhard. *Word and Faith*. London: SCM, 1963.

Ellis, E. Earle. *Eschatology in Luke*. Philadelphia: Fortress, 1972.

———. *Paul's Use of the Old Testament*. Grand Rapids: Eerdmans, 1957.

———. *Prophecy and Hermeneutic in Early Christianity*. Grand Rapids: Eerdmans, 1978.

Erickson, Millard J. *Christian Theology*. 3 vols. Grand Rapids: Baker, 1983–85.

————. *The Evangelical Left: Encountering Postconservative Evangelical Theology*. Grand Rapids: Baker, 1997.

————. *Postmodernizing the Faith: Evangelical Responses to the Challenge of Postmodernism*. Grand Rapids: Baker, 1998.

Evans, C. F. *Is "Holy Scripture" Christian?* London: SCM, 1971.

Fackre, Gabriel. *The Christian Story: A Narrative Interpretation of Basic Christian Doctrine*. Grand Rapids: Eerdmans, 1978.

Farley, Edward. *Ecclesial Reflection: An Anatomy of Theological Method*. Philadelphia: Fortress, 1982.

Flesseman-van Leer, Ellen. *The Bible: Its Authority and Interpretation in the Ecumenical Movement*. Geneva, Switzerland: World Council of Churches, 1980.

Foh, Susan T. *Women and the Word of God*. Phillipsburg, NJ: Presbyterian & Reformed, 1979.

Fosdick, Harry E. *A Guide to Understanding the Bible*. New York: Harper & Brothers, 1938.

France, R. T. *Jesus and the Old Testament: His Application of Old Testament Passages to Himself and His Mission*. London: Tyndale, 1971.

Frei, Hans W. *The Eclipse of Biblical Narrative: A Study in Eighteenth and Nineteenth Century Hermeneutics*. New Haven: Yale University Press, 1974.

Frye, Northrop. *The Great Code: The Bible and Literature*. New York: Harcourt Brace Jovanovich, 1982.

Geffré, Claude. *A New Age in Theology*. New York: Paulist Press, 1972.

Geisler, Norman L. *Decide for Yourself: How History Views the Bible*. Grand Rapids: Zondervan, 1982.

Gilkey, Langdon L. *Message and Existence: An Introduction to Christian Theology*. New York: Seabury, 1979.

Glaser, Ida. "Towards a Mutual Understanding of Christian and Islamic Concepts of Revelation." *Themelios* 7, no. 3 (1982): 16–22.

Goldingay, John. *Approaches to Old Testament Interpretation*. Downers Grove, IL: InterVarsity, 1981.

Goodrick, Edward W. "Let's Put 2 Timothy 3:16 Back in the Bible." *Journal of the Evangelical Theological Society* 25 (1982): 479–87.

Gottwald, Norman K. *The Tribes of Yahweh: A Sociology of the Religion of Liberated Israel*. Maryknoll, NY: Orbis, 1979.

Green, Joel B. "Is There a Contemporary Wesleyan Hermeneutic?" In *Reading the Bible in Wesleyan Ways: Some Constructive Proposals*, ed. Barry L. Callen and Richard P. Thompson, 123–34. Kansas City, MO: Beacon Hill, 2004.

Grenz, Stanley J. *Renewing the Center: Evangelical Theology in a Post-theological Era*. Grand Rapids: Baker, 2000.

————. *Revisioning Evangelical Theology: A Fresh Agenda for the 21st Century*. Downers Grove, IL: InterVarsity, 1993.

Gruenler, Royce G. *The Inexhaustible God: Biblical Faith and the Challenge of Process Theism*. Grand Rapids: Baker, 1983.

————. *New Approaches to Jesus and the Gospels: A Phenomenological and Exegetical Study of Synoptic Christology*. Grand Rapids: Baker, 1982.

Guelich, Robert A. "The Gospels: Portraits of Jesus and His Ministry." *Journal of the Evangelical Theological Society* 24 (1981): 117–25.

Gundry, Robert H. *Matthew: A Commentary on His Literary and Theological Art*. Grand Rapids: Eerdmans, 1982.

Guthrie, Donald. *New Testament Introduction*. London: Tyndale, 1970.

————. *New Testament Theology*. Leicester, UK: Inter-Varsity, 1981.

Habermas, Gary R. *The Resurrection of Jesus: An Apologetic*. Grand Rapids: Baker, 1980.

Hamilton, Kenneth. *Revolt against Heaven*. Grand Rapids: Eerdmans, 1965.

Hanson, Paul D. *The Diversity of Scripture: A Theological Interpretation*. Philadelphia: Fortress, 1982.

———. *Dynamic Transcendence: The Correlation of Confessional Heritage and Contemporary Experience in a Biblical Model of Divine Activity*. Philadelphia: Fortress, 1978.

Harrison, R. K. *Introduction to the Old Testament*. Grand Rapids: Eerdmans, 1969.

Harvey, Van A. *The Historian and the Believer*. New York: Macmillan, 1966.

Hasel, Gerhard. *New Testament Theology: Basic Issues in the Current Debate*. Grand Rapids: Eerdmans, 1978.

———. *Old Testament Theology: Basic Issues in the Current Debate*. Grand Rapids: Eerdmans, 1972.

Hatch, Nathan O., and Mark A. Noll, eds. *The Bible in America: Essays in Cultural History*. New York: Oxford University Press, 1982.

Helm, Paul. *The Divine Revelation*. Westchester, IL: Crossway, 1982.

Hengel, Martin. *Acts and the History of Earliest Christianity*. London: SCM, 1979.

Henry, Carl F. H. *God, Revelation, and Authority*. 6 vols. Waco, TX: Word, 1976–83.

———, ed. *Revelation and the Bible*. Grand Rapids: Baker, 1958.

Hick, John. *Faith and Knowledge*. Ithaca, NY: Cornell University Press, 1957.

Hirsch, E. D. *Validity in Interpretation*. New Haven: Yale University Press, 1967.

Hitchcock, James. *What Is Secular Humanism?* Ann Arbor, MI: Servant, 1982.

Hodgson, Peter C., and Robert H. King, eds. *Christian Theology: An Introduction to Its Traditions and Tasks*. Philadelphia: Fortress, 1982.

Jeremias, Joachim. *New Testament Theology: The Proclamation of Jesus*. New York: Scribner's Sons, 1971.

Jewett, Paul K. *Man as Male and Female*. Grand Rapids: Eerdmans, 1974.

Kaiser, Christopher B. *The Doctrine of God: An Historical Survey*. Westchester, IL: Crossway, 1982.

Kaiser, Walter C. *Toward an Exegetical Theology: Biblical Exegesis for Preaching and Teaching*. Grand Rapids: Baker, 1981.

———. *Toward an Old Testament Theology*. Grand Rapids: Zondervan, 1978.

Kantzer, Kenneth S., ed. *Evangelical Roots*. New York: Nelson, 1978.

Käsemann, Ernst. *New Testament Questions of Today*. London: SCM, 1969.

Kaufman, Gordon D. *Theological Imagination: Constructing the Concept of God*. Philadelphia: Westminster, 1981.

Kaye, Bruce. *The Supernatural in the New Testament*. London: Lutterworth, 1977.

Kelsey, David H. *The Uses of Scripture in Recent Theology*. Philadelphia: Fortress, 1975.

Kingsbury, Jack. *Jesus Christ in Matthew, Mark, and Luke*. Philadelphia: Fortress, 1981.

Klein, Ralph W. *Israel in Exile: A Theological Interpretation*. Philadelphia: Fortress, 1979.

Kline, Meredith G. *The Structure of Biblical Authority*. Grand Rapids: Eerdmans, 1972.

———. *Treaty of the Great King*. Grand Rapids: Eerdmans, 1963.

Knight, Henry H., III. *A Future for Truth: Evangelical Theology in a Postmodern World*. Nashville: Abingdon, 1997.

Koivisto, Rex A. "Clark Pinnock and Inerrancy: A Change in Truth Theory?" *Journal of the Evangelical Theological Society* 24 (1981): 139–51.

Kraft, Charles H. *Christianity in Culture: A Study in Dynamic Biblical Theologizing in Cross-cultural Perspective*. Maryknoll, NY: Orbis, 1979.

Krentz, Edgar. *The Historical-Critical Method*. Philadelphia: Fortress, 1975.

Kümmel, W. G. *The New Testament: The History of the Investigation of Its Problems*. Nashville: Abingdon, 1972.

Küng, Hans. *The Church*. New York: Sheed and Ward, 1967.

———. *Infallible? An Inquiry*. Garden City, NY: Doubleday, 1971.

———. *Signposts for the Future*. Garden City, NY: Doubleday, 1979.

Ladd, George E. *The New Testament and Criticism*. Grand Rapids: Eerdmans, 1967.

Lane, William L. *Commentary on the Gospel of Mark*. Grand Rapids: Eerdmans, 1974.

LaSor, William S. "Prophecy, Inspiration, and Sensus Plenior." *Tyndale Bulletin* 29 (1978): 49–60.

LaSor, William S., David A. Hubbard, and Frederic W. Bush. *Old Testament Survey: The Message, Form, and Background of the Old Testament*. Grand Rapids: Eerdmans, 1982.

Lewis, C. S. *Reflections on the Psalms*. London: Bles, 1958.

Lindsell, Harold. *Battle for the Bible*. Grand Rapids: Zondervan, 1976.

Loewen, Howard J. "Karl Barth and the Church Doctrine of Inspiration." Ph.D. diss., Fuller Theological Seminary, 1976.

Lonergan, Bernard. *Method in Theology*. New York: Herder & Herder, 1972.

Longenecker, Richard N. *Biblical Exegesis in the Apostolic Period*. Grand Rapids: Eerdmans, 1975.

———. "Can We Reproduce the Exegesis of the New Testament?" *Tyndale Bulletin* 21 (1970): 3–38.

———. "The 'Faith of Abraham' Theme in Paul, James and Hebrews: A Study in the Circumstantial Nature of New Testament Theology." *Journal of the Evangelical Theological Society* 20 (1977): 203–12.

———. *Paul, Apostle of Liberty*. New York: Harper & Row, 1964.

Lovelace, Richard F. *Dynamics of Spiritual Life: An Evangelical Theology of Renewal*. Downers Grove, IL: InterVarsity, 1979.

Macquarrie, John. *Principles of Christian Theology*. 2nd ed. New York: Scribner's Sons, 1977.

Marshall, I. Howard. *Biblical Inspiration*. Grand Rapids: Eerdmans, 1982.

———. *Luke: Historian and Theologian*. Grand Rapids: Zondervan, 1970.

Martin, Brice L. "Some Reflections on the Unity of the New Testament." *Studies in Religion* 8 (1979): 143–52.

McGrath, Alister. *A Passion for Truth: The Intellectual Coherence of Evangelicalism*. Downers Grove, IL: InterVarsity, 1996.

Mickelsen, A. Berkeley. *Interpreting the Bible*. Grand Rapids: Eerdmans, 1963.

Miller, Donald E. *The Case for Liberal Christianity*. San Francisco: Harper & Row, 1979.

Montague, George T. *The Holy Spirit: Growth of a Biblical Tradition*. New York: Paulist Press, 1976.

Montgomery, John W. *The Suicide of Christian Theology*. Minneapolis: Bethany Fellowship, 1970.

Morris, Leon. *I Believe in Revelation*. Grand Rapids: Eerdmans, 1976.

Nash, Ronald H. *The Word of God and the Mind of Man*. Grand Rapids: Zondervan, 1982.

Nicole, Roger R., and J. Ramsey Michaels, eds. *Inerrancy and Common Sense*. Grand Rapids: Baker, 1980.

Novak, Michael. *Confessions of a Catholic*. San Francisco: Harper & Row, 1983.

Ogden, Schubert M. *Christ without Myth*. New York: Harper & Row, 1961.

———. *The Point of Christology*. San Francisco: Harper & Row, 1982.

Orr, James. *Revelation and Inspiration*. Grand Rapids: Eerdmans, 1952.

Owen, H. P. *The Christian Knowledge of God*. London: Athlone, 1969.

Packer, James I. *Beyond the Battle for the Bible*. Westchester, IL: Cornerstone, 1980.

———. "Upholding the Unity of Scripture Today." *Journal of the Evangelical Theological Society* 25 (1982): 409–14.

Pannenberg, Wolfhart. *Basic Questions in Theology*. Vol. 1. Philadelphia: Fortress, 1970.

Pearson, Sharon Clark. "Women as Bible Readers and Church Leaders." In *Reading the Bible in Wesleyan Ways: Some Constructive Proposals, ed. Barry L. Callen and Richard P. Thompson, 188–215. Kansas City, MO: Beacon Hill, 2004.

Pelikan, Jaroslav. The Christian Tradition: A History of the Development of Doctrine. Vol. 1. Chicago: University of Chicago Press, 1971.

Pinnock, Clark H. Biblical Revelation. Chicago: Moody, 1971.

———. Flame of Love: A Theology of the Holy Spirit. Downers Grove, IL: InterVarsity, 1996.

———. Most Moved Mover: A Theology of God's Openness. Grand Rapids: Baker, 2001.

———. "The Past and Future Meanings of Biblical Texts." In Reading the Bible in Wesleyan Ways: Some Constructive Proposals, ed. Barry L. Callen and Richard P. Thompson, 157–71. Kansas City, MO: Beacon Hill, 2004.

———. Reason Enough. Downers Grove, IL: InterVarsity, 1980.

———. Tracking the Maze: Finding Our Way through Modern Theology from an Evangelical Perspective. San Francisco: Harper & Row, 1990.

Pinnock, Clark H., et al. The Openness of God: A Biblical Challenge to the Traditional Understanding of God. Downers Grove, IL: InterVarsity, 1994.

Price, Robert M. "The Crisis of Biblical Authority: The Setting and Range of the Current Evangelical Crisis." Ph.D. diss., Drew University, 1981.

Rad, Gerhard von. Old Testament Theology. 2 vols. New York: Harper & Row, 1962, 1965.

Rahner, Karl. Foundations of Christian Faith: An Introduction to the Idea of Christianity. New York: Seabury, 1978.

———. Inspiration in the Bible. New York: Herder & Herder, 1966.

Ramm, Bernard. After Fundamentalism: The Future of Evangelical Theology. San Francisco: Harper & Row, 1983.

———. The Christian View of Science and Scripture. London: Paternoster, 1955.

———. The Pattern of Authority. Grand Rapids: Eerdmans, 1957.

———. Special Revelation and the Word of God. Grand Rapids: Eerdmans, 1961.

———. The Witness of the Spirit. Grand Rapids: Eerdmans, 1959.

Reardon, Bernard M. G. Religious Thought in the Reformation. London: Longman, 1981.

Richardson, Peter. "'I Say, Not the Lord': Personal Opinion, Apostolic Authority and the Development of Early Christian Halakah." Tyndale Bulletin 31 (1980): 65–86.

Richmond, James. Theology and Metaphysics. New York: Schocken, 1971.

Ridderbos, Herman. Studies in Scripture and Its Authority. Grand Rapids: Eerdmans, 1978.

Roberts, Robert C. Rudolf Bultmann's Theology: A Critical Interpretation. Grand Rapids: Eerdmans, 1976.

Robertson, O. Palmer. The Christ of the Covenants. Grand Rapids: Baker, 1980.

Robinson, J. A. T. Can We Trust the New Testament? Grand Rapids: Eerdmans, 1977.

———. "Did Jesus Have a Distinctive Use of Scripture?" In Christological Perspectives, ed. Robert F. Berkey and Sarah A. Edwards, 49–57. New York: Pilgrim, 1982.

———. Redating the New Testament. Philadelphia: Westminster, 1976.

———. Truth Is Two-Eyed. Philadelphia: Westminster, 1979.

Rogers, Jack B., and Donald K. McKim. The Authority and Interpretation of the Bible: An Historical Approach. San Francisco: Harper & Row, 1979.

Ruether, Rosemary R. The Church against Itself. New York: Herder & Herder, 1967.

———. To Change the World: Christology and Cultural Criticism. New York: Crossroad, 1981.

Runia, Klaas. Karl Barth's Doctrine of Holy Scripture. Grand Rapids: Eerdmans, 1962.

Rushdoony, Rousas J. *The Institutes of Biblical Law*. Phillipsburg, NJ: Craig, 1973.

Sabatier, Auguste. *Religions of Authority and Religions of the Spirit*. New York: McClure, Phillips, 1904.

Schaff, Philip. *The Creeds of Christendom*. 3 vols. Reprint, Grand Rapids: Baker, 1966.

Schillebeeckx, Edward. *Interim Report on the Books Jesus and Christ*. New York: Crossroad, 1982.

Schleiermacher, Friedrich. *The Christian Faith*. Edinburgh: T&T Clark, 1928.

Schmithals, Walter. *An Introduction to the Theology of Rudolf Bultmann*. Minneapolis: Augsburg, 1968.

Smart, James D. *The Past, Present, and Future of Biblical Theology*. Philadelphia: Westminster, 1979.

———. *The Strange Silence of the Bible in the Church*. Philadelphia: Westminster, 1970.

Smith, Barry. "Rudolf Bultmann's Hermeneutical Theory." M.Div. diss., McMaster Divinity College, 1983.

Steinmetz, David C. "The Superiority of Pre-critical Exegesis." *Theology Today* 37 (1980): 27–38.

Stendahl, Krister. *Paul among Jews and Gentiles*. London: SCM, 1977.

Stott, John R. W. *God's Book for God's People*. Downers Grove, IL: InterVarsity, 1982.

Swartley, Willard M. *Slavery, Sabbath, War, and Women: Case Issues in Biblical Interpretation*. Scottdale, PA: Herald, 1983.

Temple, William. *Nature, Man and God*. London: Macmillan, 1934.

Tenney, Merrill C., ed. *The Bible: The Living Word of Revelation*. Grand Rapids: Zondervan, 1968.

Thielicke, Helmut. *The Evangelical Faith*. 3 vols. Grand Rapids: Eerdmans, 1974–82.

Thiselton, Anthony C. "Truth." In *The New International Dictionary of New Testament Theology*, ed. Colin Brown, 3:874–902. Grand Rapids: Zondervan, 1978.

———. *The Two Horizons*. Exeter, UK: Paternoster, 1980.

———. "Understanding God's Word Today." In *Obeying Christ in a Changing World*, ed. John R. W. Stott, 154–82. Glasgow: Collins, 1977.

Thompson, Richard P. "Community in Conversation: Multiple Readings of Scripture and a Wesleyan Understanding of the Church." In *Reading the Bible in Wesleyan Ways: Some Constructive Proposals*, ed. Barry L. Callen and Richard P. Thompson, 173–86. Kansas City, MO: Beacon Hill, 2004.

Tillich, Paul. *Systematic Theology*. 3 vols. Chicago: University of Chicago Press, 1951–63.

Tracy, David. *The Analogical Imagination: Christian Theology and the Culture of Pluralism*. New York: Crossroad, 1981.

———. *Blessed Rage for Order: The New Pluralism in Theology*. New York: Seabury, 1975.

Turner, H. E. W. *The Pattern of Christian Truth*. London: Mowbray, 1954.

Vawter, Bruce. *Biblical Inspiration*. Philadelphia: Westminster, 1972.

Wainwright, Geoffrey. *Doxology: The Praise of God in Worship, Doctrine, and Life*. New York: Oxford University Press, 1980.

Walgrave, Jan. *Unfolding Revelation*. Philadelphia: Westminster, 1972.

Warfield, Benjamin B. *The Inspiration and Authority of the Bible*. Philadelphia: Presbyterian & Reformed, 1948.

Wells, David F., and John D. Woodbridge. *The Evangelicals: What They Believe, Who They Are, Where They Are Changing*. Nashville: Abingdon, 1975.

Wells, Paul R. *James Barr and the Bible: Critique of a New Liberalism*. Phillipsburg, NJ: Presbyterian & Reformed, 1980.

Wenham, David. "Jesus and the Law: An Exegesis on Matthew 5:17–20." *Themelios* 4, no. 3 (1979): 92–96.

Wenham, John W. *Christ and the Bible*. London: Tyndale, 1972.

———. *The Goodness of God*. Downers Grove, IL: InterVarsity, 1974.

Westcott, B. F. *The Bible in the Church*. New York: Macmillan, 1964.

———. *The Gospel according to St. John*. London: Murray, 1881.

Wheat, Leonard F. *Paul Tillich's Dialectical Humanism: Unmasking the God above God*. Baltimore: Johns Hopkins University Press, 1970.

Wiles, Maurice. *The Remaking of Christian Doctrine*. Philadelphia: Westminster, 1978.

Williams, Rodman. *The Era of the Spirit*. Plainfield, NJ: Logos, 1971.

———. *The Pentecostal Reality*. Plainfield, NJ: Logos, 1972.

Wilson, Marvin R. *Our Father Abraham: Jewish Roots of the Christian Faith*. Grand Rapids: Eerdmans, 1989.

Wink, Walter. *The Bible in Human Transformation*. Philadelphia: Fortress, 1973.

Woodbridge, John D. *Biblical Authority: A Critique of the Rogers/McKim Proposal*. Grand Rapids: Zondervan, 1982.

Yocum, Bruce. *Prophecy: Exercising the Prophetic Gifts of the Spirit in the Church Today*. Ann Arbor, MI: Word of Life, 1976.

Subject Index

accessibility, biblical, 22–23
accommodation, 122–27, 137–42
actualism, Barth's, 185
apostles, the, 66, 68–69, 74–76
application, scriptural, 197–200
authority, apostolic, 75–76. *See also* apostles, the
authority, biblical
  biblical witness to, 80–86
  church and, 104–7
  humanity and, 117–22
  inerrancy and, 20–21, 95–104
  interpretation and, 229–38
  revelation and, 40–45, 94–95
  Scripture principle and, 11–24, 87–89
authorship, scriptural, 127–32. *See also* humanity, scriptural; revelation, divine
autonomy, human, 49–51, 129–30. *See also* humanity, scriptural

Barth, Karl, 184–85
biases, interpretive, 233–38. *See also* interpretation, scriptural
biblicism, simple, 257
bipolarity, revelatory, 29, 181–82, 223–26
Bultmann, Rudolf, 47–48, 50, 185

canon, biblical, 79–80, 213–15. *See also* authority, biblical; New Testament; Old Testament; revelation, divine
Christ, Jesus the. *See* Son, God the
church, the, 73, 104–7, 241–42
coherence, scriptural, 95–101. *See also* inerrancy, doctrine of

conservatism, theological. *See* evangelicalism, theological
content, biblical, 39, 43–44, 45–53, 240–41. *See also* inerrancy, doctrine of
context, Scripture and, 82–83
covenant, new. *See* New Testament
covenant, old. *See* Old Testament
Creation, the, 29–32
criticism, biblical. *See also* interpretation, scriptural
  biblical authority and, 17, 91–92, 157–60
  faith and, 160–64
  negative, 171–76
  positive, 115–17, 164–71
culture, relativity of, 117–22, 135–37. *See also* humanity, scriptural

deism, 46
dictation, scriptural, 127–29. *See also* authorship, scriptural
diversity, revelatory, 29–32
diversity, scriptural. *See* coherence, scriptural
Dulles, Avery, 48–49
dynamic, interpretive. *See* progressive revelation

equivalence, dynamic, 244. *See also* translators, theological
eschatology, 73
evangelicalism, theological, 14–15, 21
evangelism, 18–19. *See also* salvation
evidence, belief and, 192–94
exegesis. *See* interpretation, scriptural

Scripture Index